THE
EMPIRE OF INDIA

THE
EMPIRE OF INDIA.

BY

SIR BAMPFYLDE FULLER

GYAN

Published by

GYAN

Gyan Publishing House
5, Ansari Road
Daryaganj, New Delhi-110002
Phone: 011-47034999, 9811692060
E-mail: books@gyanbooks.com

Distribution Network
gyanbooks.com
India, USA, Canada, UK, Australia

ISBN: 978-93-6433-869-1 (HB)
First Published, 1913

2nd Impression 2024

Printed at: Gyan Press, Delhi.

THE EMPIRE OF INDIA
Author: BAMPFYLDE FULLER

THE ALL RED SERIES

THE EMPIRE OF INDIA

Hoffmann, Calcutta

STREET SCENE, DELHI, WITH VIEW OF THE GREAT MOSQUE

THE EMPIRE OF INDIA

BY

SIR BAMPFYLDE FULLER

K.C.S.I., C.I.E.

OF THE INDIAN CIVIL SERVICE (*retired*)

BOSTON

LITTLE, BROWN, AND COMPANY

1913

TABLE OF CONTENTS

PART I—THE COUNTRY

CHAPTER I

PHYSICAL ASPECTS

CHAPTER II

NATURAL HISTORY

CHAPTER III

AGRICULTURE

CHAPTER IV

FAMINE AND IRRIGATION

CHAPTER V

MANUFACTURES

CHAPTER VI

COMMERCE

PART II—THE PEOPLE

CHAPTER VII

POPULATION, RACES, AND CASTES

CHAPTER VIII

MANNER OF LIFE

CHAPTER IX

RELIGIOUS BELIEFS AND OBSERVANCES

CHAPTER X

EDUCATION AND ITS EFFECTS

CHAPTER XI

EUROPEANS IN INDIA

PART III—THE GOVERNMENT

CHAPTER XII

HISTORICAL SKETCH OF INDIAN GOVERNMENTS

CHAPTER XIII

BRITISH PROVINCES AND NATIVE STATES

CHAPTER XIV

THE EXECUTIVE GOVERNMENT

CHAPTER XV

LEGISLATION AND LAW COURTS

CHAPTER XVI

THE ARMY AND THE POLICE

CHAPTER XVII

TECHNICAL DEPARTMENTS OF GOVERNMENT

CHAPTER XVIII

TAXATION (INCLUDING LAND REVENUE), FINANCE, AND CURRENCY

PART IV—FUTURE PROSPECTS

CHAPTER XIX

SOCIAL AND ECONOMIC PROGRESS

CHAPTER XX

POLITICAL CONDITIONS

LIST OF ILLUSTRATIONS

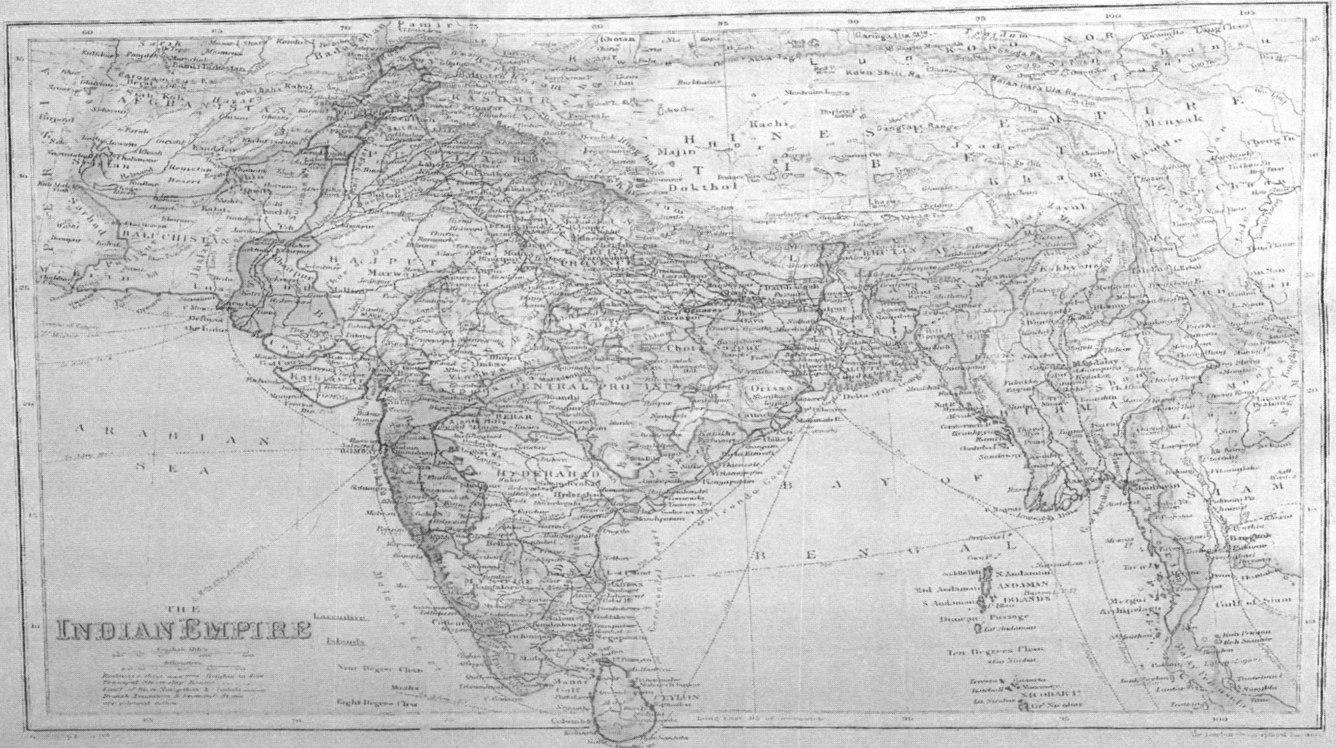

SIR ISAAC PITMAN & SONS, LTD., LONDON & BATH.

THE EMPIRE OF INDIA

PART I
THE COUNTRY

CHAPTER I

PHYSICAL ASPECTS

INDIA is the midmost of three peninsulas which the continent of Asia throws off into the southern seas. On the one side is the Malayan peninsula, a portion of which —Burma—has been incorporated in the Indian Empire. On the other side is Arabia. The southern configuration of the continent of Europe is not dissimilar,—on a miniature scale; but Europe faces to the south the great land expanse of Africa, while Asia looks upon an ocean which flows without a break between her and the giant island of the Antarctic circle. There was a time, in the Mesozoic period of geological chronology, when Asia also fronted a continent that stretched across from India to Madagascar, and occupied a large portion of what is now the Indian Ocean. The peninsula of India is a relic of this lost continent. It was divided from the mainland of Asia by a broad and deep sea channel, at least as extensive as the Mediterranean. Part of this channel has been filled up by river deposits, and now forms the flat expanse of the Indo-Gangetic plain, in which the cities of Lahore, Allahabad and Calcutta are situated. Part of it is now occupied by the southern ranges of the Himalayas, which were thrust up by an upheaval of comparatively recent date, and owe their vastness to the fact that water has not had time to wear down their summits.

The Indian Empire then falls into four well-marked regions. There is the peninsula of India, embracing the country that lies south of a line stretching from Karachi to Delhi, and from Delhi to Calcutta, and including an area of 784,000 square miles and a population of 132 millions. There is the Indo-Gangetic plain, lying between the peninsula and the Himalayas, which, with its easternmost extension, forms an expanse of about 300,000 square miles, with a population of 162 millions. There is the Himalayan range which overlooks this plain. And to the east there is Burma, which forms part of a different peninsula, and differs from India proper in its conditions very markedly indeed. Its area may be estimated at 237,000 square miles, and its population at 12 millions. This classification, it should be explained, is so far incomplete that it does not take into account extensions of the Empire across the mountain ranges which, running southwards from the Himalayas, form the natural western and eastern boundaries of the Indo-Gangetic plain. In both cases the boundary has been carried outwards in order to repress marauding by the hill-men. On the western frontier some advance has also been dictated by strategical reasons, which have led to the inclusion of the large excrescence of British Baluchistan.

The Peninsula

The peninsula of India may be described as an elevated plateau, diamond-shaped, with two long sides running southwards and washed by the sea, and two short sides running northwards and abutting on the flat expanse of the Indo-Gangetic plain. Delhi is at its northern extremity. Along its northern boundaries a line of low hills and scarps marks it off from the plain that stretches between it and the Himalayas. Its southern margins are raised and buttressed by coast ranges which overlook the sea from a height varying from a few hundred to many thousands of feet. These coast ranges are known as the Western and Eastern Ghâts. The western range is much the more considerable. It increases in altitude as it runs southwards, rising from an elevation of 3,000 feet above Bombay to 8,000 feet as it approaches the extremity of the peninsula. It forms a gigantic and continuous sea-wall, pierced by no valleys of any size, and unbroken save for a very curious gap, 200 miles from its southern extremity. The eastern range is much less distinctive, and consists of broken and comparatively low hills, interrupted by broad valleys which lead the drainage of the peninsula into the Bay of Bengal. South of Madras this eastern coast range is but faintly marked, and the configuration of the peninsula is determined and guarded by hill masses which run eastwards from the western coast range, and are in fact a part of it.

Across the upper portion of the plateau, along a line between Bombay and Calcutta, there runs a mountain-range—the Satpuras—which attains in some places an altitude of 4,000 feet. North of this line the drainage of the peninsula flows, as might be expected, from the centre to the sea on either side of it ; south of this line the rivers all flow eastward into the Bay of Bengal. The country is curiously tilted, its surface lying highest along its western border, close above the Arabian Sea, so that its great rivers, the Godávari, the Kistna, and the Tungabhadra, take their rise almost within sight of one ocean, but flow across the peninsula into the other. The plateau may in fact be compared to a gabled roof of which one slope is missing. Its backbone, so to speak, lies along its western margin ; and this bears out the belief, supported by more substantial facts, that its area formerly extended far to the west, and that it represents only a portion of an ancient continent.

From the geological point of view the peninsula offers some remarkable features. The sedimentary rocks of which it is composed lie, speaking generally, in horizontal *strata*, and exhibit very little of the curving and twisting which in most other countries demonstrate the force of volcanic upheavals. And, away from the coast line, they contain no marine fossils whatever,—nothing to show that any portion of the land has ever been submerged below the sea. The peninsula has stood above the ocean since the very commencement of geological time. The rocks of its foundations—generally crystalline in the south, sandstone in the north—are of the most ancient that are known to us. Above them there occurs a series of fossiliferous rocks, containing coal beds, known as the *Gondwána*. But these are fresh-water, not marine deposits. They correspond, roughly speaking, with the coal measures of Europe, and their fossils exhibit a similar preponderance of ferns amongst vegetable, and of reptiles amongst animal life, in forms so closely connected with fossils occurring in South Africa, and indeed in Australia and South America, as to encourage a surmise that these rock beds are the remains of a huge continent, or of a continent and a chain of islands, that stretched across the southern hemisphere and filled part of the domain of the Indian Ocean and the South Atlantic. The disappearance of this continent was followed, or accompanied, by an extraordinary outpouring of molten rock over the northern part of the peninsula. It welled up from below and spread over the country, levelling its surface, like a gigantic deluge. Over an area of 200,000 square miles it covers the older rocks with horizontal layers of black basalt which are in some places 6,000 feet thick. There were several periods of flow, with intervening periods of rest, sufficient to allow of the formation of fresh-water lakes, which were overwhelmed by fresh outpourings, but can be traced in beds of mud and gravel, containing fresh-water shells, that run through the mass of basalt, at considerable depths below its surface. The levelling effect of this lava-flow has left its mark in the existing scenery of the upper portion of the peninsula. The hills are generally flat-topped, bounding the view by successions of terraces. And where the basalt has been much denuded, as along the western coast above Bombay, there remain, as monuments of a more ancient level, flat-topped pinnacles, often of grotesque appearance, which stand above the country like tall fortresses, and in the disturbed days of Indian history have been convenient strongholds for marauding or insurgent forces.

The surface of the peninsula is generally uneven and rocky. Although the plough has been urged up to the extreme margin of fertility, not more than a third of the total area is under cultivation. The range of Satpura hills which crosses its northern part has already been mentioned. From a distance they appear to be entirely covered with jungle, and although, on ascending their slopes one comes across open cultivated plateaux of considerable extent, they may generally be described as wild and forest-clad. They have provided an asylum for the tribes which have been swept aside by the immigration of more energetic and enterprising races from the north. Throughout the peninsula, hill peaks and ranges are seldom absent from the landscape. As a rule they are forest-clad, but not very thickly, and their vegetation has little in common with the dense impassable jungle generally known as tropical. Forest growth is commonly thickest towards the east under the influence of moist winds from the Bay of Bengal; and as one progresses westwards trees give way to scrub, except at high levels, until on reaching the west coast the hills are almost as bare as those of a desert country. But these remarks do not apply to the Malabar coast—on the south-western shore of the peninsula—where humidity from the sea, condensed by overhanging mountains, produces the climate of a palm-house and a tropical vegetation of great luxuriance. These mountains are the Nilgiris, an extension of the west coast range reaching an altitude of 8,000 feet. They introduce the traveller from Madras to scenery and a climate that is more European than Indian. Broad grassy downs, with closely coppiced hollows, swept by sea mists during the rainy season of summer, and whitened by hoar frost in winter, are supported by steep scarps that command magnificent prospects of the low country around. Scarp and plateau are indeed the typical features of the peninsula hill scenery. But here and there the straight lines of the landscape are broken by the protrusion of irregular masses of crystalline rock, the best known of which is the rock of Trichinopoly.

The village scenery of the peninsula is exceedingly varied. In the east the low hills look down upon stretches of rice land; to the west, as the land rises, and the rainfall lightens, rice gives place to millets and cotton, grown on broad treeless plateaux, which when the crops are off the ground present a most desolate appearance. Towards the north expanses of wheat make, during the cold winter months, a brilliant contrast with the dark foliage of the surrounding forest. The village houses are gable-roofed, collected together and not scattered over the fields. To each is attached a fruit or vegetable garden; and these gardens lend a note of picturesqueness which can relieve even the depressing monotony of the hot weather months.

At the present day India is typified to Europe by the great northern plain, and the visions its name evokes are those of Delhi, Agra and Benares. But in the times of classical Rome, and down to the fifteenth century, it was the peninsula that was the India of geography and commerce. It is true that in still earlier days the Greek armies of Alexander had lifted India's veil from the north, and that on the north-western border Indo-Greek kingdoms were founded which maintained for over a century connections between Northern India and the Levant. But these kingdoms fell, and from the second century before Christ Northern India hid itself again behind its mountain barriers. It was with the peninsula that the Romans traded in the days of Pliny ; it was from the peninsula that the Arabs introduced cotton and the sugar-cane into Europe, and it was the spices and calicoes of the peninsula which lured first the Portuguese and then the other nations of Europe to perilous adventures round the Cape of Good Hope.

The Indo-Gangetic Plain

The Indo-Gangetic plain, which lies to the north of the peninsula and between it and the Himalayas, is the most extensive sheet of level cultivation in the world. Excluding the valleys of the Indus and the Brahmaputra at its western and eastern extremities, it has a length of 1,500 and an average breadth of 200 miles. Over this vast tract of country not a stone of any kind—not a pebble—is to be found. The land is entirely composed of river sand and silt, and, since borings have shown that this deposit extends to a depth of at least 1,000 feet below the present sea-level, it is obvious that we stand here upon the site of an ancient sea which has gradually been filled up by the denudation of the mountains that overlooked it. The influence of this sea still persists in the salts which, in the drier parts of the plain, effloresce during the hot season, and sterilize in irregular patches many hundreds of square miles of its surface. The rivers which now traverse the plain tend in two directions. The five western rivers (from which the Punjab takes its name)—the Indus, Jhelum, Chenáb, Rávi and Sutlej—flow down the lower reaches of the Indus into the Arabian Sea. Seven other large rivers to the east—the best known of which are the Ganges and the Jumna—similarly unite in the Ganges to reach the Bay of Bengal. Approaching the sea through a network of wandering channels, their waters are mingled with those of an eighth large river—the Brahmaputra—which flows from the east down the valley of Assam. The silt brought down by these rivers is gradually enlarging an extensive delta—at the head of the Bay of Bengal—which is perhaps the most characteristic portion of the province of Bengal. Upon it is situated the city of Calcutta. The Indus at the extreme west, and the Brahmaputra at the extreme east, have their sources in Tibet, behind the snow peaks of the Himalayas, at no great distance apart; and, curving round, in opposite directions, include in their embrace practically the whole of the Himalayan mountain chain. The sources of the other rivers are less remote. But their upper valleys all end in snowfields, and they begin to rise from the melting of the snow before they are replenished by the summer rains.

The plains are, as already stated, the creation of the rivers which flow through them. But in their higher reaches these rivers are now destructive not creative forces, since, owing to a rise in the surface slope of the country, their currents are too rapid to deposit the silt with which their water is charged. They drop the heavier sand, but carry the silt down to their lower reaches or out into the sea beyond their mouths. It seems that a slope of 6 inches to the mile is the steepest that will permit of the deposition of fine silt by river water. The slope of Bengal, which the Ganges traverses during the lower third of its course, is within this limit. But further west the slope of the country increases rapidly and is three times as steep as this along the upper third of the river channel. The dividing line between the rivers that flow on one side towards the Arabian Sea, and on the other side towards the Bay of Bengal, is about 800 feet above sea-level. This exceeds by at least 300 feet the height to which we should be carried by a slope of 6 inches

Hoffmann, Calcutta

VILLAGE SCENE IN EASTERN BENGAL

to the mile, and this increase in altitude must be ascribed to a gradual upheaval of the surface. In present circumstances the river system of the plains between Patna on the east and Multan on the west adds nothing to their fertility, must, indeed, be constantly diminishing it by the surface drainage which is drawn to the river beds. At the time the rains break, the country is bare and unprotected by vegetation, and down the channels which drain its surface surge muddy torrents that carry off into the rivers the fine particles of which they have robbed the soil.

The delta of Bengal presents most of the features of a tropical country. The land is carpeted with a sheet of rice, broken here and there with fields of tall jute. The cottages of the peasants—high-gabled constructions of bamboo and grass—nestle half-concealed in clumps of bamboo and palms. They are dispersed about the fields, not massed together connectedly as is the case up-country. As one travels west the aspect of the country reflects more and more distinctly the increasing differentiation between the seasons of the year. Palms and bamboos give place to trees which are not dissimilar in general appearance to those of Europe ; during the cold season temperate crops, such as wheat, barley and peas, come into cultivation ; since the rainfall is still heavy in its season, roofs are still gabled, but tiles take the place of thatch, and mud walls are substituted for a bamboo framework. Further west again, with a lighter rainfall, rice becomes a subordinate crop. During the season of summer rain the fields stand high with maize and millets which occupy about half the area ; the remaining half is devoted during the cold weather to wheat and barley, which in some places covers such wide expanses as to call to mind the prairies of Canada. During the dry months of the hot weather the fields are bare and the country is swept by a wind as burning as the blast from a furnace mouth. The houses are flat-roofed, constructed of sun-dried mud, and collected together—

originally no doubt for purposes of defence—so as to make of each village a miniature town. There are no house gardens, such as elsewhere in India enliven the surroundings of the peasant's home, and these Northern Indian villages have an air of sun-baked squalor, especially during the dry months of the hot weather when life is a listless struggle with the unnerving effects of scorching heat.

Hard though these conditions of life may appear, it is to these plains of Northern India that we owe the treasures of Sanskrit literature and philosophy. They are *par excellence* the home of Hinduism. Into them, perhaps 4,000 years ago, descended from Central Asia the race, in blood akin to ourselves, the infusion of which energised the people of Northern India with talent that is ranked by some alongside the genius of Greece. This country, in turn saturated by warm rain, chilled by light frost, and scorched by desert winds, produced one of the richest and most elaborate languages of antiquity, four schools of philosophy alike distinguished for depth of thought and audacity of speculation, studies in mathematics to which we owe the first conception of algebra and perhaps our system of notation, poetry, epic and dramatic, which in dignity and in fecundity, if not in grace, may at least be compared with the classics of Mediterranean civilisation, and a system of civil order which, however disappointing in results, indicates a careful appreciation of eugenic theories. In these plains, at no great distance from the city of Patna, was the home of Buddha—the Illumined Master—who, at the time when in Greece Herodotus was introducing the study of secular history, insisted upon the importance of the mystical side of life, and founded a religion which in the East still moves the hearts of millions of mankind, and in the West can please minds that find Christianity disappointing. Nor did the Indian genius of those days flower only in the domains of philosophy and literature. It developed the highest martial virtues, and the history of Rajputána—where the immigrant blood was not over-diluted by inter-marriage with the daughters of the soil—is a record of courage, of courtesy and of self-sacrifice such as the annals of classical or mediæval Europe would find it difficult to equal.

Large areas of the plains remained under scrub jungle till a century ago. But at present very little that is culturable escapes cultivation, and from two-thirds to three-fourths of the total area is broken by the plough. The population is extraordinarily dense; over wide expanses of country it reaches an average of one person to the acre of total area, and this in localities where there are no large towns. If we take into consideration only the area actually cultivated there are large districts in which each acre supports two persons. Only a tenth of the population can be classed as urban, and yet its density, over thousands of square miles is as high as that of Belgium. In no large country of the world, not even excepting China, does the land directly support so large a population.

THE HIMALAYAS

The great plains of India are overlooked by the highest mountains of the world. Some of the peaks of the Himalayas soar to nearly 30,000 feet above sea-level—nearly twice the elevation of Mont Blanc. But the lines of snow crests stand seventy or eighty miles back from the foot hills, and it is only on exceptionally clear days that they appear, like clouds on the horizon, to the people of the lowlands. We speak of the Himalayas as a mountain chain. But they are really a series of enormous buttresses that support the tableland of Tibet. On the further side of their passes there is no great descent, and the traveller finds himself in a desert of gloomy rocks and barren valleys swept by the piercing wind of a plateau that ranges between 10,000 and 15,000 feet above sea-level. The Himalayas were thrust upwards in, geologically speaking, recent times and at a period when the Indian peninsula had for ages been standing upon its present foundations. Marine deposits are to be found at a height of 20,000 feet, containing fossils (nummulites) which indicate that they formed a sea-bed during the Tertiary period.

At the eastern end of the Himalayas the lower slopes are densely forest-clad ; at the western end, with a lighter rainfall, they are bare, or scarcely covered by ragged pine forest and scrub. As one ascends, the air grows cooler : the character of the landscape rapidly changes : oaks and magnolias, firs and deodars throw dark shadows on the hillsides. Above them grassy peaks stand out from which one may obtain a first sight of the snowy range. But the snows are still eight or ten days distant, and, by the time they are approached, vegetation has almost disappeared. The valleys which lead up to the glaciers are bare and stony ; ice and snow shed their brilliancy upon desolation, and there is no such contrast as in the Alps is afforded by the near proximity of forests and the abodes of men.

Towards the western extremity of the range a drive of 200 miles through the mountains conducts us into the Vale of Kashmir, where the deposits of the river Jhelum, dammed by a rocky barrier, have filled a broad valley with rich soil. Carpeted with crops and flowers, adorned with noble trees, brightened by lakes, and circled round by snow mountains it presents a vision of Paradise to the traveller from the plains. In the days of the Moghal empire Kashmir was a favourite summer resort of the emperor and his court. To the British a cool retreat from the scorched plains was still more attractive ; and they have established, along the crest of the outer Himalayas, a chain of hill stations, the best known of which are Simla, Naini Tal, and Darjeeling.

Up to a height of at least 8,000 feet the Himalayas are inhabited by as large a population as they can support.

Hoffmann, Calcutta

KINCHINJUNGA, IN THE HIMALAYAS, FROM DARJILING

Little can be grown without irrigation. Rivers are carefully led over their valley beds, and not a stream falls from the hillside but a village lies beside it, conducting its waters down the fields that are terraced on the slopes. West of Nepál the hill people are mostly Hindus, with regular features, and complexions lighter than one notices in the plains. The women are often exceedingly attractive. In Nepál the character of the population changes. Its inhabitants exhibit the broad faces, high cheek-bones, and oblique eyes of the Mongolian type. From amongst them are drawn the Gurkhas who enlist very freely in the Indian army and powerfully add to its fighting strength. East of Nepál the Mongolian type continues. Whether of Indian or Mongolian type, the people of the hills are generally of much shorter stature than those of the plains; and this is also the case with their cattle.

At either end of the Himalayas there is an abrupt change in the trend of the mountains. They run north and south instead of east and west, and form with the Himalayan chain a three-sided barrier, shutting in the plains of India from Afghanistán and Baluchistán on the one hand and from China on the other. The strain which produced this gigantic contortion may have forced up two subordinate hill-ranges,—the Punjab Salt Range within the western angle, and, within the eastern angle, the Hills of Assam,—which jut out, like a promontory, into the plain. In both these ranges earthquakes are of very frequent occurrence, and may indicate a subsidence which accompanies a gradual relaxation of pressure.

Burma

Burma lies outside the Indian region, and owes its connection with India mainly to its recent history, and to its administrative arrangements. It was conquered at the expense of India, and in great measure by Indian troops; and, had it not been for the assistance of Indians in garrisoning it, policing it, and constructing its public works, its annexation and government would have been exceedingly difficult. The province consists of the valleys of the Irrawaddy, the Sittang and the Salween rivers, and of a series of parallel hill ranges which separate them from one another and from the sea. These ranges are, geologically speaking, of recent origin. They run for the most part north and south. On the side of the Bay of Bengal they break up the country into a number of long narrow ridges drawn as if it had been furrowed by a gigantic plough. Across these ridges, from west to east, progress is exceedingly difficult, and hence the Burmese railways have as yet not been connected with the Indian system. These hills are sparsely inhabited by tribes of the Tibeto-Burman race, which have hardly emerged from a condition of primitive savagery and until recently found their chief interest of life in inter-tribal conflicts and the practice of head-hunting. Further east, beyond the Irrawaddy, the hill summits become broader and flatter, widen in fact into plateaux which contain much cultivable land, and support an intelligent people known as the Shans. In origin "Shan" is the same word as "Siam," and these hillmen are closely allied to the Siamese. By far the most important of the valleys of Burma is that of the Irrawaddy, with its affluent, the Chindwin. In its upper reaches bays of rice fields are formed by the recession of the fringing hills. But some 200 miles above the river mouth the valley opens out into a broad cultivated plain, which gradually expands into a delta of remarkable fertility. The valley of the Irrawaddy is the principal home of the Burmese people, who, while connected by racial affinities with the wild tribes of the hills that surround them, have developed under the influence of a fertile soil a civilisation which ranks high by the Asiatic standard. Buddhists by religion, they have conserved the doctrines and observances of their faith in a simplicity which presents many admirable traits. The Indian caste system is unknown: women are completely emancipated, and life is viewed with a demonstrative appreciation which contrasts very markedly with the sombre pessimism of the Hindus.

The Rainfall

A description of the physical aspects of India would be incomplete without a reference to the rainfall, the fluctuations of which bring happiness or misery to millions of the people. It is peculiar because it is markedly discontinuous. In Europe a rainy day, or a succession of rainy days, may be expected during any month, or week, of the year. In India rain falls only during certain definite seasons. From February to May the skies are practically cloudless, and dryness gradually develops into parching heat: violent dust storms may sweep the country: draughts from the hills may at times bring a few drops of rain or a fall of hail; but these are casual occurrences, not reckoned upon in the economy of the country, which during this period of the year depends for its moisture upon what is stored in the soil, or flows down the rivers. Towards the end of May banks of clouds appear upon the seaward horizon, and, heralded by violent thunderstorms, there occurs what is known as the "burst of the monsoon." Thence onward to October the atmosphere is saturated with moisture, and rain falls at frequent intervals. In October the clouds withdraw and the air becomes dry, crisp and invigorating. In December clouds should again appear, coming this time from the north, across the barrier of the Himalayas; and during a fortnight or three weeks there should be falls of rain, which, but two or three inches in aggregate amount, are of inestimable benefit to the standing crops. The clouds again draw off and a fresh cycle commences in the drought and heat of the five months following. This general description needs of course many qualifications before it can be applied to the weather of so large a country. It is most nearly typical of the conditions of the upper portion of the Indo-Gangetic plain, where the seasonal contrasts attain their maximum. In tracts that lie near the sea—the deltas of Bengal and Burma, and the littoral of the peninsula—the air always contains moisture and hot winds do not blow. In the northern part of the peninsula height above sea level compensates for loss of latitude: frosts are not unknown during the cold season, and during the rainy season there are breezes which mitigate the exhausting effect of moist heat. Further south we are beyond the limits reached by the cold weather rain: we enter the zone of continuous heat, and there is no marked difference between the cold and hot seasons. The country round Madras receives its heaviest rainfall in October and November, when the monsoon winds are retiring seawards. Here January differs from July only in degrees of oppressiveness.

It will have been gathered that the rainfall varies very greatly from place to place. Precipitation is heaviest where the current of the monsoon winds is opposed by abrupt scarps which compel it suddenly to ascend. On and below the steep cliffs of the western coast range the rainfall commonly exceeds 150 inches. On the other side of India, north of the Bay of Bengal, the Assam hills offer a precipitous barrier, 4,000 feet high, to the progress of the clouds that drift from the sea over the lowlands, and here the rainfall is the heaviest in the world,—normally 450 inches, and having been known to amount to 50 feet. The greater part of the country ordinarily receives amounts ranging between 30 and 75 inches. Over the western portion of the peninsula the rainfall generally decreases from west to east, possibly by reason of the drying of the west sea winds by the extraordinarily heavy condensation that takes place upon the west coast range.

Poona, on the plateau above Bombay, receives only 25 inches, not more than a fifth of the quantity which falls on the scarp of the plateau twenty miles away. In the eastern portion of the peninsula and throughout the Indo-Gangetic plain the rainfall diminishes in a contrary direction—from east to west. In the country at the head of the Bay of Bengal the rainfall is nowhere less than 75 inches; progressing up-country westwards, at Patna the fall is 50 inches, at Allahabad 40 inches, at Delhi 25 inches, and at Lahore 20 inches. West and south of Lahore it rapidly diminishes, and vestiges of cultivation can hardly be traced in a sandy desert which extends over 60,000 square miles in the Punjab and Rajputána. Beyond this desert lies Sind, the lower valley of the Indus, which is also rainless, but is irrigated from the river by such a network of canals as spreads the waters of the Nile over the fields of Egypt.

India owes its monsoon rainfall to the condensation of a mass of vapour which drifts northwards from the equator, and hangs for some months over the Indian continent. Normally winds blow towards the equator from north and from south to supply the place of ascending currents. Towards the end of spring the south wind gradually overpowers the north wind, presses it back and advances upon its traces. The causes of this conflict are obscure, and apparently depend upon the timeliness of certain changes in atmospheric pressure. Should the south wind fail in moisture, famine descends upon the land; and man learns that his struggles only reach the outworks of Nature, and that, behind them, she stands, spear in hand, unmoved by his efforts or his entreaties.

CHAPTER II

NATURAL HISTORY

Flora

INDIA extends over so wide an area and range of latitude, and is varied by such differences in elevation, climate and soil, that it offers to the botanist an extraordinarily diversified collection of vegetable life. The ascending slopes of the Himalayas are an epitome of the earth's surface between the tropics and Siberia, and conduct the traveller in a few days' time from the atmosphere of a palm house to that of a refrigerator. The perennial vegetation of the plains is fitted to endure the most violent seasonal changes, from parching drought to saturating moisture, and (in Northern India) from frosty cold to burning heat. Forests are evergreen where the air is moistened by sea breezes all the year round. But over the greater part of the country the forest trees are, as a rule, deciduous, shedding their foliage in January and February, and during the two following months presenting the leaflessness of an English winter. In this season, surveyed from a hill-top, an Indian forest is a sombre expanse of brown, softened by the hot weather haze that overhangs it ; through this expanse narrow meandering lines of dark green mark the beds of streams along which some evergreen species can still find moisture. The trees do not, however, await the advent of the monsoon rains before putting forth their new leaves. Their buds open towards the end of April, exactly as if moved by the impulse of an English spring—two months before rain can be expected—and it is an extraordinary and beautiful sight to watch the Indian forests blush in delicate shades of green, silver-grey and pink at a time when Nature is a desiccating force, when the ground is as hard and dry as a roadway, and when the rocks amongst which the trees grow are too hot at midday to be touched without discomfort. The trees send their roots deep into the rock, to the underlying stores of subsoil water. In the plains of Northern India there is an inconspicuous little plant, allied to the English groundsel, which comes up and flowers in dense patches when the hot winds are at their fiercest. Its roots, like thick whipcord, have been traced to a depth of 30 feet below the surface. In Northern and Central India, above the latitude in which Nagpur is situated, the climate is suitable for the growth of a double set of annuals—of temperate plants during the cold season, and of tropical plants during the rainy season. But in a wild state only tropical plants can flourish. Their seeds lie dormant during the cold weather, whereas the seeds of temperate plants cannot resist the stimulating effect of the summer rains, and germinate only to perish in the heat. Man has, however, filled in the blank left by Nature. By preventing the seeds from germinating during the rainy season, he preserves uninjured many cultivated species of temperate annuals, which are sown at the beginning of the cold weather and reaped in the early spring. Thus it is that the fields of Northern India, during the cold weather, bear crops such as wheat, barley, peas and linseed, which give them a familiar appearance to European eyes.

The Himalayas

Of the botanical regions into which India is divided, the Himalayas, with their wide ranges of climate, naturally offer the most varied flora. At different elevations it is tropical, temperate, and arctic. The eastern Himalayas, receiving a much heavier rainfall than the western, differ very markedly from the latter in vegetation. The forest growth on their lower slopes is exceedingly luxuriant. A rank and tangled undergrowth of coarse grass,

3—(2134)

bushes and cane-brake, embroidered here and there with the delicate fronds of tree-ferns, is overshadowed by bamboos or tall forest trees bearing on their branches thick clusters of orchids. There are, indeed, more species of *Orchideæ* than of any other Natural Order. As one goes west the vegetation of the outer hills becomes sparser: it is characterised by forests of a pine[1] which can withstand great heat. Still further west, the hillside is imperfectly clothed with low scrub jungle, and is bare, except for a growth of prickly candelabra-shaped *Euphorbias*. On the upper slopes also of the mountains the vegetation will be observed to change its character very markedly, as one passes from east to west. In the eastern Himalayas, owing to the humidity of the air, dense forests of tall magnolias can flourish at an elevation of 6,000 feet. Oaks of four kinds appear. The forest trees are hung with long festoons of pendulous lichen, which in appearance resemble the "Spanish moss" of the southern States of America. Conifers do not flourish until a height of 9,000 feet is reached. Above the forest there are dense masses of rhododendron, decorating the hill slopes in spring time with banks of pink, crimson and mauve. They are the most characteristic plants of this region, and no less than twenty-five species occur, some of which extend up to 16,000 feet. In May and June grassy slopes are brilliantly carpeted with flowers of an Alpine type, violets, primulas, and gentians. In the western Himalayas tropical trees do not extend so high up the slopes. The general character of the forests above 5,000 feet is markedly coniferous. Firs, pines, and cypresses abound, and at a higher level the hill sides are often shadowed by forests of deodars, the glory of the Himalayas. Six species of oak occur, but only one species of rhododendron. Amongst herbaceous plants balsams are very conspicuous. The Alpine flora of the higher slopes is curiously European

[1] *Pinus longifolia*.

in character and includes over 400 species that are British. Amongst the butterflies that flutter over the high pastorages in early summer, many kinds may be recognised as British, or as differing from British kinds only in a few inconspicuous markings.

Along the foot of the Himalayas, between them and the cultivated plain, there stretches a level belt of jungle, which occupies land that is too gravelly for cultivation. Amongst its typical trees are the *sāl,*[1]—a valuable timber tree,—a species of myrobalan,[2] and the *khair,*[3] growing gregariously, each apart from the others. From the wood of the *khair* is extracted the catechu of commerce. At intervals the forest is interrupted by savannahs of long grass, the favourite haunt of the tiger, and, until recent years, of the rhinoceros.

The Indo-Gangetic Plain

Of the Indo-Gangetic plain so large a proportion is under tillage that the most interesting features of its botany are the cultivated trees and crops. In former days large areas of waste were covered with a leguminous shrub known as the *dhāk* or *palás,*[4] which is gay in spring time with sprays of large flame-coloured flowers. Its bark supplies the cultivator with rough cordage, and its branches are the favourite habitat of the insect that produces lac. But it is vanishing before the plough. On low ground adjoining streams and rivers, and on islands in river beds, there still remains a thick jungle of tamarisk[5] which gives a flush of verdure to the hot-weather landscape. Another characteristic tree is the *shisham* or *sissu,*[6] of the leguminous order, which grows freely on light soil and yields excellent timber. But the tree of spontaneous growth which most generally

[1] *Shorea robusta*
[2] *Terminalia tomentosa.*
[3] *Acacia catechu.*
[4] *Butea frondosa*
[5] *Tamarix articulata.*
[6] *Dalbergia sissu.*

pervades the western plain is the *babul.*[1] Thorny and small-leaved, it is indifferent to heat, and is equally at home in Southern Persia, Arabia and Egypt. Babúl wood, being very hard, is in request for wheel-axles and ploughs. Going eastward, as the rainfall increases, the babúl gives way to the bamboo and to palms[2] which introduce a tropical air into the scenery. But throughout the length of the plains it is the cultivated trees which principally strike the eye. They are generally of noble proportions. Perhaps the commonest of them is the mango[3] which may be planted either in irregular clumps near the village houses, or in regularly spaced groves. Its fruit is small, and distinctly flavoured with turpentine—very different to that which is produced by the smaller mango tree of irrigated gardens. But it provides the poorer classes with food at a time when work is slack and they are greatly in need of it. Equally large, and almost equally profitable is the *mahua*[4], sometimes called the Indian olive. It bears large, fleshy flowers, which abound in sugar and are commonly used for the manufacture of spirits. Its fruit yields an oil of value. Still more conspicuous are the trees of the fig order—the *pipal*[5] and the *banyan,*[6] which are regarded in some measure as sacred. Against their broad trunks there is generally set a little rustic shrine, and you will often see saucers hanging from the boughs, in which curds are offered to haunting spirits. They commonly overshadow the little open spaces where the villagers meet for their evening gossip. The tamarind, which attains very great size, and the *nim*[7] are also widely domesticated. These trees are grown in sufficient numbers to give the plains' landscape a well-wooded appearance. In the

[1] *Acacia arabica.*
[2] *Phœnix dactilifera* and *Borassus flabelliformis.*
[3] *Mangifera indica.*
[4] *Bassia latifolia.*
[5] *Ficus religiosa.*
[6] *Ficus bengalensis.*
[7] *Melia indica.*

Punjab, at the western end of the plain, trees are much less general than in its central region. In Bengal, at its eastern end, the peasants' cottages are embowered in clumps of bamboos, plantains,[1] and betel palms.[2] Of the wild herbaceous flora of the plains the most interesting plant is a wild cotton,[3] occurring in Sind, from which the Indian cultivated cottons are not improbably derived.

The Peninsula—North

In the peninsula the tracts that remain under forest are generally hills or stony slopes of poor natural fertility. The tree growth which they support is rarely luxuriant and often sparse and stunted. There is no such dense undergrowth, whether of grass or bushes, as would make the forest impassable on foot. The trees are deciduous, except for a few species that are generally confined to beds of streams. Their character depends more upon rainfall and height above sea-level than upon the composition of the soil. Hills, whether of trap or sandstone, will bear forest of the same kind at a like elevation. The stony slopes of low hills generally carry mixed forest in which the common bamboo,[4] *Boswellia thurifera, Terminalia tomentosa, Sterculia urens, Oegle marmelos* and *Bombax malabarica* are characteristic. Below them is frequently a belt of the palás,[5] which, when in flower, girdles the forest with a ring as of fire. Higher up, on the plateaux, the trees grow larger. The finest specimens commonly belong to the Natural Order *Combretaceæ,* including, besides *Terminalia tomentosa, Terminalia belerica* and *Terminalia chebula* (the trees which produce the myrobalans of commerce), and the graceful *Anogeissus pendula.* Forests of sál[6] are very characteristic of these localities and produce valuable timber. They do not occur south of the Godávari. Of

[1] *Musa sp.*
[2] *Areca betle.*
[3] *Gossypium Stocksii.*
[4] *Dendrocalamus strictus.*
[5] *Butea frondosa.*
[6] *Shorea robusta.*

herbaceous plants the most noticeable are *Acanthaceæ* of various kinds. Towards the west, in the part known as the Deccan, where the rainfall is at its lightest, the hills are exceedingly bare ; and during the hot weather, when grass is off the ground, there is often little to be seen on them but a few stunted teak trees, standing in a wilderness of loose stones. In the valleys, amidst the fields, dense thickets of palm bushes, a favourite cover for wild pig, are perhaps the most characteristic natural vegetation.

The Peninsula—South

Further south, towards and beyond the Godávari river, where night frosts are unknown, the teak[1] flourishes, and satin wood[2] and sandal wood[3] give a special value to the forests. In the open country barren land is frequently occupied by masses of prickly pear (*Opuntia*). The western coast range rises to a very high elevation, 8,000 feet above the sea, and changes the character of its vegetation. There is much undulating grass land, with evergreen coppices in the hollows that are brightened by the flowers of a tree rhododendron. On this high plateau the eucalyptus and wattle have been introduced from Australia, and grow more luxuriantly than the trees of the locality. The low hills which lie between this high range and the western sea—on the Malabar coast—receive an extraordinarily heavy rainfall, and are densely clothed with vegetation of the tropical type, such as that of the low slopes of the eastern Himalayas. This is the country in which the spices are grown which first attracted western nations to a trade with India.

Burma

In Burma (which from a botanical point of view includes Assam), with a rainfall almost as heavy as that of

[1] *Tectona grandis.*
[2] *Chloroxylon swietonia.*
[3] *Santalum album.*

the eastern Himalayas and Malabar, we find a flora closely akin to the flora of those regions, but including many links with China. Orchids are exceedingly numerous : there are over 700 species. Other characteristics are the abundance of the *Laurineæ*, of palms, and of bamboos. Some distance up the valley of the Irrawaddy there is a zone in which the rainfall diminishes to 32 inches, owing to the intercepting effect of mountains between the river and the sea, and there is accordingly a patch of deciduous forest in the midst of a vast expanse of evergreen vegetation. The *khair* grows here abundantly, and the production of catechu is of importance. The most notable forest tree of the Irrawaddy valley is the teak,[1] which attains fine proportions. The exports of teak from Rangoon are worth over a million pounds annually. They represent the only considerable business in timber which India transacts with foreign countries. The mountain vegetation is tropical up to a height of 3,000 feet : at this altitude its character changes ; pines[2] appear, and oaks, with an undergrowth of bracken, give quite an English appearance to the landscape. At 5,000 feet the country may open out into undulating grassy downs, with groves and coppices, in which the tree branches are covered with ferns, and studded with brilliant orchids. The Khasi hills in Assam offer a charming illustration of this type of scenery : it is repeated in the Shan hills, between the Irrawaddy and the Salween, 500 miles to the south. Between Burma and Assam the hillsides have commonly been usurped by bamboos which, springing up after forest fires, have choked all other vegetation. In this locality, and eastwards towards the Chinese frontier, is the home of the tea-tree from which the cultivated plants of Assam, Ceylon and Java are derived. It attains a quite considerable size, and frequently grows gregariously in patches.

[1] *Tectona grandis* and *T. Hamiltonii*.   [2] *Pinus khasya*.

Fauna

The variety of Indian conditions has naturally developed a great variety of animal life, and the Indian fauna is much richer in number of species than that of Europe. But in India proper—the plain and the peninsula—animals are by no means numerous, since, during the annual five months of drought, drinking water is scarce, and apart from the big rivers, is only to be found in scattered pools in the beds of forest streams and in such of the village ponds as do not dry up entirely. Birds can pick their climate by changing their homes, and during the cold weather India is visited by hosts of migrants from the north, which press their way through the icy winds of the Tibetan plateau. There are animals which can support the seasonal changes of India proper and also the continuous moist heat of Malabar, Assam and Burma. But these differences in circumstances have commonly produced differences in development ; and in a large number of cases a species occurring in the former locality is represented in the latter by another species that differs only in what appear to be trifling details of colour or marking. On the other hand, there are a few animals which succeed even better than the varieties of mankind in adapting themselves to their surroundings and live unaltered in Europe and in India. Such are the house sparrow, the cuckoo, both kinds of English rat, the otter, and that common English butterfly known as the " painted lady." It would be impossible to give an adequate idea of the Indian fauna within the limits of this chapter and all that can be attempted is to indicate the animals which commonly impress themselves upon the observer in the open country of India proper, in the forests of the peninsula, Malabar, Assam, and Burma, and in the Himalayas.

Mammals

The Open Country.—The fine mango grove which lies outside a typical village of the plains is commonly inhabited by a tribe of brown monkeys [1] whose social life is regulated by some of the observances of savage man. Living for the most part on grain, they are destructive to the crops, and exceedingly mischievous. But their lives are safeguarded by their likeness to mankind, and the severest penalty that can be considered is to catch them alive and deport them across the nearest big river. Where scrub jungle adjoins cultivation large monkeys of another kind, the *hanuman*, [2] may often be seen in the mornings, seated in the fields and scampering off to the jungle when approached. They are black, with a fringe of white whiskers that gives them a ludicrous resemblance to an old man ; and, since they are supposed to be the monkeys that assisted the epical hero Ráma in his invasion of Ceylon, they are protected by superstitious as well as by sentimental scruples. At morning and evening time stray jackals [3] are to be seen slinking about the fields ; when it grows dark they roam the country in packs, uttering the wild cries, which, with the responsive barking of the village dogs, break the windless quiet of an Indian night. They are useful scavengers, but they also eat fruit and vegetables and are fond of poultry. The Indian dog has undoubtedly jackal blood in him : jackals interbreed with dogs, and, since they are liable to hydrophobia, they preserve this disease against all efforts for its extirpation. In early morning one often hears the snappy bark of the Indian fox, [4] small, grey-coloured, with black-tipped tail. In wilder localities river-side ravines may be infested with wolves [5]—smaller than those of Europe—which carry off goats and sheep and occasionally dare to attack and kill children. The only other *Carnivora* of the open country are a civet cat, [6] the palm civet [7] and the mongoose, [8] a

[1] *Macacus rhesus.*
[2] *Semnopithecus entellus.*
[3] *Canis aureus.*
[4] *Vulpes bengalensis.*
[5] *Canis pallipes.*
[6] *Viverra.*
[7] *Paradoxurus.*
[8] *Herpestes.*

grey weasel-like animal, well known for its antipathy to snakes and its skill in catching them. The most noticeable *insectivorous* animal is the small shrew known as the musk rat,[1] which at night enters houses, scurrying round the rooms with shrill squeaks in search of cockroaches and other insects. A large fig tree (pipal or banyan) may often be seen laden with what appear to be enormous brown fruits. They are large bats, known as flying foxes,[2] which hang head downwards from the branches, and at evening-time launch themselves into flight. Amongst *rodents* the little striped squirrel[3] gives life to every grove and garden : it commonly feeds on the ground, finding something worth investigation in horse and cattle droppings. Four kinds of rat are common, the black and the brown rats of Europe (the latter a recent immigrant and so far confined to sea-ports and towns on the main lines of traffic), and the gerbil of North, and the soft-furred rat[4] of South India, both of which at times suddenly multiply in swarms and cause widespread distress by eating up the grain crops. Houses are often visited by the bandicoot,[5] a variety of rat over a foot long. Grass land beyond the village fields gives shelter to hares, distinct species of which are localised to Northern India, to the peninsula, and to Sind. Fortunately for the cultivator there are no rabbits. The *Ungulata* are most commonly represented by the Indian antelope or black buck,[6] small herds of which are occasionally to be seen feeding in the fields throughout the length and breadth of the plains and the peninsula. In some districts they are exceedingly numerous and roam the country in hundreds. According to Hindu ideas this animal is typical of Hindustan, and an ascetic is most appropriately seated when the skin of a black buck is beneath him. Bushes on the edge of cultivation often

[1] *Crocidura cærulea.*
[2] *Pteropus medius.*
[3] *Sciurus palmarum.*
[4] *Mus multadus.*
[5] *Nesocia bandicota.*
[6] *Antelope cervicapra.*

shelter a much larger antelope, the *nilgai*,[1] bearing a handsome coat of blue-grey. Barren ravines may harbour a few graceful little gazelles (*chinkara*[2]). And wild pig[3] lie up in scrub jungle or coarse grass, from which they emerge at night to a revel of wasteful feeding. They are especially destructive to rice and sugar-cane. They differ from the domesticated pig in some inconspicuous details, but the two races will interbreed. The wild boar is the most courageous of animals and to ride him down with a spear is the most characteristic, and the most exciting, of Indian sports.

The Dry Forests

Leaving the open country for the forests the most interesting animal is the tiger which, although generally becoming scarcer, is still common on the borders of hill pasturages to which cattle are driven in summer. It has the curious habit of postponing for several hours the eating of an animal which it kills. Meanwhile it lies up near by, and the sportsman knows where to drive for it, or can sit over the kill until it returns. Were it not for this habit, the bagging of a tiger would be far more difficult than it is, since the animal is of roving habits and covers large distances in its nightly wanderings. Tigers do not attack men in cold blood. Those which take to man-eating are generally old and infirm; but they will terrorise the country side, and sometimes indeed cause villages to be deserted. Leopards (or panthers) favour rocky forest. They are malicious and desperately revengeful when wounded, but at times show a curious familiarity, taking up their abode amidst human habitations. The hunting leopard or *chita*[4] is much less common: its claws are only partially retractile; it can run with extraordinary speed, and in semi-domestication will hunt antelopes for its master. Fifty years ago the Indian lion ranged the

[1] *Portus pictus.*
[2] *Gazella bennettii.*
[3] *Sus cristatus.*
[4] *Cynæ lurus.*

deserts of the western Punjab and Rajputána : it is now only to be found in a corner of Kathiawar and in very small numbers. The hyæna not uncommonly disappoints the sportsman who is beating for tiger. The lynx is seen more rarely. There are several species of wild cat. The so-called wild dog [1] is in reality not so close a connection of the dog as is the jackal. It is of a rusty red colour with large shell-like ears. It hunts in packs and will clear a forest of all other animals, tigers not excluded. Forest rivers are haunted by otters undistinguishable from the English kind. They can be tamed, and are trained by fishermen to drive fish into their nets. The badger tribe is represented by the ratel, [2] a handsome animal with silver-grey back. A black bear [3] is very common in forests that contain rocky hills. It has smaller teeth but stronger claws than the typical bears. Its favourite food is the combs of white ants (termites), and to obtain them it excavates the ground to the depth of several feet. The place of the little striped squirrel is taken by a larger and very handsome kind, [4] chestnut and black above, buff beneath, which is one of the most easily tamed of animals. Wild elephants still haunt the dry forests of Central India in small numbers, but their home is in the damper forests of Assam and Burma, where they occur in large herds, and are terribly destructive to rice and sugar-cane crops. To catch them, either by riding them down with tame elephants or by driving them into corrals (kheddas), is a regular industry. Wild buffaloes [5] are not uncommon in the open grass jungles of the peninsula ; they will interbreed with domestic buffaloes, but cannot, it is said, be tamed. On higher ground there may be sighted that noble beast, the *gaur*, or Indian bison, [6] standing six feet at the withers and with horns sometimes

[1] *Cyon.*
[2] *Mellivora indica.*
[3] *Meliursus ursinus.*
[4] *Sciuropterus indicus.*
[5] *Bos bubalus.*
[6] *Bos gaurus.*

three feet in length. He is a species of ox, but has no hump. The Indian domesticated cattle are humped, and their origin is obscure. The dry hill forests give shelter to a four-horned antelope[1] and to three species of deer, the sambhar,[2]—the finest of Indian stags—the pretty spotted deer,[3] and the barking deer,[4] which bears its horns upon long pedicels as long as the horns themselves. The long grass of open swampy ground conceals the *barasingha*,[5] —a fine stag with six tines on each antler—and the small hog-deer.[6]

The Damp Forests

In the damp forests of Assam and Burma occurs the monkey which in structure is most nearly allied to man,—a small black gibbon[7] known from its call as the "*hoolak*." In Burma there are no hyænas or wolves, and the jackal is rare. The civet cat and brown squirrel have each developed two species peculiar to the moist climate of Malabar on the one side and of Burma on the other. The *barasingha* is also represented in Burma by a peculiar species. The dense grass jungle of Assam is the home of two kinds of one-horned rhinoceros, now becoming so rare as to be verging upon extinction. A smaller two-horned rhinoceros occurs in Burma. The most peculiar animal of the Burmese region is perhaps the bear-cat,[8] a species of tree civet that possesses a prehensile tail. It is the only animal of the old world that is so endowed.

The Himalayas

Wild sheep and goats characterise the fauna of the Himalayas. The giant sheep[9] only just cross the frontier of Tibet and the Pamirs. But six species of sheep, goat, or goat-antelope are not uncommon, including the ibex,[10]

[1] *Tetracornis graducornis.*
[2] *Cervus unicolor.*
[3] *Cervus axis.*
[4] *Cervulus muntjac.*
[5] *Cervus duvauceli.*
[6] *Cervus porcinus.*
[7] *Hylobatis.*
[8] *Arctitis binturong.*
[9] *Ovis Hodgsoni* and *O. poli.*
[10] *Capra siberiaca.*

and that fine goat the *markhor*.[1] There are two kinds of bear—a variety of the European bear,[2] living at higher, and the black bear[3] living at lower levels. The cat-bear[4] is peculiar as a species of racoon,—an animal which is typical of the American continent.

Birds

The Open Country.—During the cold season India is visited by hosts of European birds. Ducks of many species arrive in multitudes from Siberia, and assemble in large flocks on all considerable sheets of water. Other winter visitors of European kinds are snipe, storks, cuckoos, plovers, quails, the hooded and carrion crows, the sparrow-hawk, and swallows.

Of resident birds the most conspicuous in village life are the Indian crow[5] and the house sparrow. A little owl commonly lives under house rafters, and of evenings the pair may be heard suddenly breaking into loud cackles, as if delighted by the telling of a *risqué* anecdote. Overhead at midday kites[6] hover in large circles, and on the village refuse ground some scavenger vultures,[7] white with yellow neck and bill, will surely be seated. From the grove hard by comes the loud note of the *koel*,[8] a species of cuckoo, and (in summer) the agonised repetitions of the brain-fever bird[9] and the metallic chirping of the little barbet,[10] commonly known as the "coppersmith." Some low throaty warblings betray a flock of green pigeons,[11] seated upon the upper branches but hardly distinguishable among the leaves. Through the foliage the golden oriole flashes, while overhead flocks of green parrots[12] scream as they sweep in long undulations between the trees and

[1] *Capra falconii.*
[2] *Ursus arctus.*
[3] *Ursus torquatus.*
[4] *Oïlurus fulgens.*
[5] *Corvus splendens.*
[6] *Milvus govinda.*
[7] *Neophron gingimiensis.*
[8] *Eudynemis honorata.*
[9] *Hierococcyx varius.*
[10] *Xantholœna hœmatocephala.*
[11] *Crocopus.*
[12] *Palœornis torquatus.*

the grain crops. In the freshly watered fields starlings and *mainas*[1] with some hoopoes[2] are eagerly searching for insects; above them hovers the little green bee-eater[3] in chase of flies; he is joined from time to time by a handsome black-plumaged bird with long forked tail, the *drongo.*[4] Watching them from a low tree hard by is the beautiful blue Indian roller,[5] with some doves, ceaselessly murmuring. All suddenly fly off as a *shikra*[6] hawk appears, oppressing their gaiety with the shadow of death. Further afield in the bushes, a family of babbling thrushes[7] are chattering with a garrulous intimacy that has earned them the name of the "seven brothers." The crow-cuckoo or *coucal,*[8] rustles in the dry herbage. On the branches may be seen the bulbul, a handsome little bird, black with red tail coverts—a favourite pet—some Indian shrikes, and a pair of minivets—gay, the cock in black and crimson, the hen in black and yellow. From a thorn-tree or palm, there hang a number of long, flask-like nests, neatly woven of fine roots by the little *báya,*[9] or weaver-bird. Overhead larks are singing. From a ruined temple a pair of blue pigeons take their flight, hardly distinguishable from pigeons of Europe. Still further away from habitation, where the untilled land is covered with coarse grass, you may flush grey partridges[10] or some quail; if black-breasted[11] it is the resident species. The black partridge or francolin[12] is less often seen. It is localised to Northern India; in the south its place is taken by the painted partridge.[13] Wastes of large area are sometimes frequented by bustards,[14]—difficult to discover, still more difficult to approach—and, in Bengal, by the commoner florican.[15]

[1] *Acridothera tristis* and *Sternopastor contra.*
[2] *Upupa indica.*
[3] *Merops viridis.*
[4] *Dicrurus.*
[5] *Coracias indica.*
[6] *Aster badius.*
[7] *Crateropus canorus.*
[8] *Centropus sinensis.*
[9] *Ploceus.*
[10] *Ortygiornis.*
[11] *Coturnix coromandelicus.*
[12] *Francolinus vulgaris.*
[13] *Francolinus pictus.*
[14] *Eupodotis edwardsii.*
[15] *Sypheotis bengalensis.*

As we draw near the large pond or lake, at which the pasturing cattle are watered, the wailing cries of lapwings are around us. Along the margin of the water flit bands of sandpipers.[1] Small heron-like birds, sitting inconspicuously by the water's edge, suddenly rise with a flash of brilliant white. They are the "paddy-birds"[2]—victims by thousands, when in their breeding plumage, to their effectiveness in the adornment of ladies' hats. Moorhens,[3] sometimes of a splendid blue kind,[4] and grebes[5] push their way through the reeds; and in the open water there may be duck of four resident species—the *nukta,*[6] the whistling teal,[7] the little cotton teal,[8] and the spotted bill.[9] If it be the cold weather, duck and teal of half a dozen migratory kinds will be amicably swimming about together, and from the reeds you may put up two kinds of snipe and the jack snipe. In the shallows stand a pair of splendid cranes, quite five feet high, slate-coloured with red heads, the *sáras*:[10] there is no Indian sportsman who can remember without emotion the clanging screams with which these birds salute the cold weather sunrise, heralding to him the dawn of many a happy day.

The Dry Forests

The most characteristic birds of the dry forests of the peninsula are gallinaceous—the pea fowl, jungle fowl, and spur fowl. Pea fowl may be seen at early morning in hundreds, feeding in the forest glades. There are two kinds of jungle fowl, the red and the grey. The former is no doubt the ancestor of the domestic fowl; it is widely distributed through south-eastern Asia, giving place, however, in the south of the peninsula to the grey jungle fowl. Spur fowl[11] are peculiar to India proper and Ceylon.

[1] *Totanus glareola* and *T. ochropus.*
[2] *Ardeola grayi.*
[3] *Gallinula chloropus.*
[4] *Porphyris poliocephalus.*
[5] *Podiceps capensis.*
[6] *Sarcidiornis.*
[7] *Dendrocygna.*
[8] *Nettopus.*
[9] *Anas pœcilorhynca.*
[10] *Grus antiqua.*
[11] *Galloperdix.*

Two beautiful green parroquets are common, one[1] large, the other[2] small, with plum-coloured head. The small hornbill[3] is also to be frequently seen. The bill of this curious bird is surmounted by a large horny casque, resembling in some ways an inversion of the bill that is below it. During incubation the female is imprisoned in the hole which forms her nest, the entrance being blocked with mud by the male bird save for an opening through which he feeds her. A large horned owl[4] may often be seen sitting motionless on rocks or trees.

The Damp Forests

The damp forests of Malabar, Burma and Assam are extraordinarily silent. The numerous birds which they shelter seem to be oppressed by their gloom. In the Burmese region a number of Indian birds are replaced by kinds of trifling specific difference; this is the case with the swift, the *sáras* crane, the paddy bird, the pea fowl, and the jungle fowl. Malabar, the Eastern Himalayas and Burma are connected by a little parrot[5] which is elsewhere unknown.

The Himalayas

The eagles of the Himalayas include the lammergeyer of Europe. Finches and warblers are much more abundant than in the plains. Three kinds of pheasant are common and are peculiar to this locality—the *chir,*[6] the *koklas,*[7] and the lovely blue *monal.*[8] A partridge, the *chikor,*[9] is to be found in large numbers on grassy slopes.

REPTILES

During the dry season, when the Indian rivers are low, crocodiles[10] (generally miscalled alligators), crawl out upon the sand banks and bask in the sun. Not

1 *Palæornis Alexandri.*
2 *Palæornis cyanocephalus.*
3 *Lophocerus birostris.*
4 *Bubo bengalensis.*
5 *Loriculus.*
6 *Catruus wallichii.*
7 *Pucraria necrolophus.*
8 *Lophophorus.*
9 *Caccabis chucar.*
10 *Crocodilus palustris.*

infrequently they travel across country by night and find their way into village ponds. They will seize goats, if occasion offers, but are as a rule harmless to man. But a crocodile, like a tiger, may take to man-eating; lying in wait at bathing places he may kill large numbers of women and children. The sharp-nosed crocodile, or *gharidl*[1] is exclusively fish-eating. It occurs only in the rivers of the Indo-Gangetic plain, the Mahanadi in Orissa, and the Keladon in Arrakan. Small lizards are amazingly numerous. The gecko is semi-domesticated, and may be seen on the walls of most Indian rooms catching the insects which flock to the wall lamps. The "blood-sucker"[2] is also very common: the males during the breeding season are brilliant in red and black. Small scaly lizards abound where an old wall or a rock offers them shelter. The chameleon may be found in the jungles of the peninsula. Nowhere else in India does this typically African animal occur. The Indian monitors[3] are lizards of very large size: one of them grows to a length of six feet. But the snakes are the reptiles with which Indian life is ordinarily associated. There are more than 280 species. A European rarely comes across them. But poisonous snakes annually cause the death of at least 20,000 persons. One of the commonest is the carpet snake,[4] which is harmless, but has a frightening resemblance to the deadly *karait*,[5] whose sluggish habits render it particularly dangerous. The *dhāman*[6] alarms one by its size; it is often six feet long, but it is harmless and indeed useful to man since it feeds on rats; it not uncommonly takes up its abode amongst the rafters of dwelling-houses. The cobra[7] hardly needs description. It is *par excellence* the typical snake of India—deadly but an object of veneration

[1] *Gavialis.*
[2] *Calotis versicolor.*
[3] *Varanus.*
[4] *Lycodon aulicus.*
[5] *Bungarus cœruleus.*
[6] *Zaminis mucosus.*
[7] *Naia tripudians.*

and indeed of worship. Other poisonous snakes of common occurrence are Russell's viper and the *kappa*.[1] In the jungles sportsmen come across the python which grows to a length of 12 feet and over. Another species of python, peculiar to Burma, is said to attain a length of 30 feet. The damp forests of Assam and Burma are haunted by the king-cobra, or hamadryad,[2] which is sometimes 12 feet long, is as deadly as a cobra, and is so fierce as sometimes to attack men unprovoked. It ordinarily feeds upon other snakes.

Batrachians

The chorus of the frogs is an unceasing accompaniment to the discomfort of a night in the rainy season : a frog which has crept into the house will suddenly lift up his voice from under a corner of the carpet. The Indian species of frogs and toads are very numerous indeed. A very familiar kind is a little frog[3] which lives along the margin of ponds, and, when alarmed, jumps away in shoals across the surface of the water. The "chunám" frog, not uncommon in Southern India, by means of expansions on its fingers and toes, can climb over walls and ceilings. Tree frogs[4] are limited to the south of the peninsula and to Assam and Burma.

Fishes

Fish are of immense importance in the economy of the rice-growing districts of the Bengal delta and Assam, since they supply the inhabitants with the nitrogenous food which, in the drier parts of India, is derived from pulses. These do not flourish in moist heat, and hence in Eastern India the Brahminical prohibition of animal food does not apply to fish, and the people, Brahmins included, are all fish-eaters. In Burma and parts of Assam dried and half-cured fish is largely consumed.

[1] *Echis carinata.*
[2] *Naia bungarus.*
[3] *Rana cyanophlyctis.*
[4] *Ixalus.*

Its smell is deterrent, but it seems wholesome enough. Europeans are introduced to it in the bummalo,[1] or "Bombay duck," which is commonly eaten as a relish with curry. The lower castes all over India eat fish when they can get it ; and during the rainy season every little stream is set with fish traps, often of most ingenious construction.

The Indian seas contain a great variety of fish but no organised attempt has been made to exploit their resources. Sharks, saw-fish and rays occur, and one species of shark[2] ascends the Ganges for some hundreds of miles. Of the tribe of catfishes the *pofta,*[3] which frequents muddy rivers, is a recognised delicacy. The rivers contain no salmon or trout. Their place, from the sporting point of view, is taken by fish of the carp tribe, which include the *mahseer,*[4]—a game fighter, which has been caught up to 95 lbs.,—and the well-known tank fishes, the *rohu*[5] and the *cotta,*[6] which also run to heavy weights. Three species of pomfret[7]—sea fish—adequately supply at breakfast the place of the English sole. Other well-known edible fishes are the *hilsa,*[8] a migratory fish of the herring tribe ; the *begti,*[9] a species of perch which runs up to 200 lbs. ; and the mango fish,[10] a small fish of most excellent flavour, which is caught in tidal waters. The *murral* is another fresh-water fish of repute : it belongs to the ophio-cephalous tribe, which is distinguished by breathing the air direct, instead of taking it from water by means of gills. Fishes of this kind die if unable to obtain air by periodically rising to the surface. They can exist for some months in dried mud; and ponds that are completely dried up in the hot weather will swarm with fish when refilled at the setting in of the rains.

[1] *Harpodon neherius.*
[2] *Carcharias gangetica.*
[3] *Callichrous.*
[4] *Barbua tor.*
[5] *Labas rohita.*
[6] *Cotta buchananii.*
[7] *Stromateus.*
[8] *Clupea ilisha.*
[9] *Letea calcarifer.*
[10] *Polynemus paradoxus.*

INSECT LIFE

Insects

Immediately the hot air is moistened by the fresh breath of the monsoon, insect life springs into activity. As evening approaches, insects issue forth and take possession of the land, and were they not for the most part merely irritating, they would render human life impossible. Beneficially and injuriously they influence human economy very greatly indeed. The ubiquitous white ants (termites) take the place of the earth worms of Europe in aërating the soil and promoting its fertility. The lac[1] insect secretes upon the twigs to which it clings the lac that is one of India's most typical exports. The dried bodies of the insects yield the lac dye (lake). The mulberry silkworm is cultivated in Bengal, but, breeding several times over during the year, it has degenerated and produces silk of inferior quality. In the forests of the peninsula the *tassar* silkworm is grown, semi-domesticated, on several kinds of trees; and two other species of silkworms are cultivated in Assam, one the *eri*, feeding on the castor-oil plant, and the other the *muga*, on various kinds of laurels.[2] To this list of insect utilities there is much to oppose. Insects constantly threaten the cultivator with ruin and not infrequently achieve it. A descending horde of locusts will eat up in a few hours the crops of a country side. Swarms of caterpillars appear, which crawl across the fields in dense lines leaving nothing but stalks behind them. But for injury to mankind no insect can be compared to the *anopheles* mosquito, which by spreading malaria has profoundly affected the condition of the Indian people, and is probably accountable for much in their history. In some parts of the Indo-Gangetic plain malaria has been found present in the blood of four-fifths of the children. From time to time it breaks out into violent epidemics causing mortality compared to which that from cholera is trifling. In some

[1] *Coccus lacca.* [2] Principally *Machilus odoratissima.*

localities it appears actually to have emasculated a large proportion of the men ; and where its permanent efforts are less evident, it is reasonable to assume that it weakens the energy and perhaps taints the character of the people.

Minerals

The increasing mineral production of India remains insignificant for so large and varied a country. In view of the striking developments in winning coal, manganese, gold and oil, that have occurred during the last twenty years, it would be rash to dogmatise ; but it does not appear that the country is richly endowed with mineral resources. It may be that it has been insufficiently explored. And it is certain that under free trade conditions the manufacture of iron and steel has hitherto enjoyed little chance of surviving the dangers of infancy. Specimens are to be found of all the principal industrial minerals. But only coal, petroleum, gold, manganese and mica are worked on a large scale. The rocks of the peninsula contain masses of iron ore, and the enterprise of a Parsi capitalist has just succeeded in establishing large well equipped iron and steel works. But in the past the history of the Indian iron industry has been the decline of native manufacture under competition from outside, and this although the Indian iron workers produce iron of exceedingly good quality, and have indeed for long time past used some of the processes that are now employed in Europe for the manufacture of high-class steel. There are immense deposits of the bauxite from which aluminium is extracted. Copper ore occurs in several localities ; it was formerly smelted, but is now neglected. Efforts have been made to work tin and chromium ; but they are still in the stage of experiment.

The principal source of Indian coal is the Gondwána system of rocks, the relics of the continent which in mesozoic times extended across the Indian Ocean. These rocks underlie the chain of hills which stretches across the north of the peninsula; and they are mined in six localities at its eastern extremity (in Bengal), in four localities in Central India, and at one place in the Native State of Hyderabad. The Bengal collieries are by far the most important, yielding six-sevenths of the total output. The Indian coal industry is of quite recent growth. Twenty years ago only 1½ million tons were raised, and the requirements of the Indian railways were met very largely by English coal. The output has now risen to 12 million tons, and importation has practically ceased. The extension of railway communication has, of course, stimulated coal mining greatly. But so also has the establishment of factories, chiefly of cotton and jute, which now consume 70 per cent. of the output. There are two other sources of coal,—tertiary beds, commonly including nummulitic limestone, and beds of still more recent origin, probably of the miocene age. Tertiary coal is mined, but to no very considerable extent, at various places in Baluchistan, the Punjab, Rajputána, and Assam: miocene coal at a more important colliery at the eastern extremity of the Assam valley, which is distinguished by the possession of a seam 80 feet thick. Speaking generally, the tertiary and miocene coal contains very much more moisture than the Gondwána, and is therefore less esteemed. But the Assam coal is of high calorific value.

Petroleum occurs in the hill ranges which run southward from each end of the Himalayas at (roughly speaking) right angles to them,—that is to say, in the north-eastern corner of the Punjab and in Baluchistan at one end, and in Assam and Burma at the other. In the former tract, owing to dislocation of the rock *strata*, the oil has not accumulated in large quantities, or has drained off. The latter tract includes the oil district of Upper Burma which now produces 215 million gallons a year, and despatches its oil to the seaport of Rangoon down a pipe line 275 miles in length. In eastern Assam oil wells produce 2½ million gallons. But the Indian supply does not suffice for the needs of the country, and over 50 million gallons are annually imported from Russia and the United States.

Deserted gold workings of unknown age have for long past attracted attention to a reef of auriferous quartz occurring at Kolár in the Native State of Mysore, and thirty years ago mining operations were undertaken on a large scale. The annual output has risen to 600,000 ounces, and economies in working, due in part to the use of the water power of some falls on the river Cauvery, have rendered it possible to crush quartz of lower grade than at first would have yielded a profit. There are gold-bearing rocks in the north of the peninsula, in the Hyderabad State, and in Upper Burma; but, so far, except in one locality, attempts at extraction have not been profitable. The sands of very many rivers of the peninsula, and of Assam and Burma, are explored for gold by native gold workers, who make, however, but a small and precarious income. The sands of the upper Irrawaddy offer greater possibilities; but they have disappointed the costly efforts of a gold-dredging company.

During the last twelve years an export trade has grown up in manganese, which occurs in large quantities at several places in the peninsula and can be secured by shallow quarrying. The annual output has risen to 800,000 tons. Mica is also quarried for export to the value of about £100,000. It occurs in veins of pegmatite, and is worked in the hills at the north-eastern corner of the peninsula and at Nellore in the Madras presidency. Its extraction is in the hands of local Indian capitalists, and the mines are driven unsystematically and wastefully.

Of the salt used in India about 44 per cent. is extracted

from sea water, and 30 per cent. imported from England. The balance is obtained partly from deposits of rock salt, which occur in the north-western corner of the Punjab, and partly from the water of some shallow lakes in Rajputána, the beds of which are so deeply impregnated with salt that they saturate the fresh water that flows into them during the rainy season.

Until forty years ago the manufacturers of explosives were very largely dependent upon Indian saltpetre, and, reduced though its importance has been by discoveries in industrial chemistry, it is still exported to the value of £250,000. During the hot weather it occurs as an efflorescence in parts of Bengal where, owing to density of population, the soil is saturated with ammonia, and the range of temperature is peculiarly favourable to the action of nitrifying microbes.

Amongst gems the rubies of Upper Burma are well known. They are raised by an English company to the value of about £100,000 per annum. For diamonds India has been celebrated since the time of Pliny. But such beds as were then worked appear to have been exhausted; and at present diamond mining is confined to one locality in the north of the peninsula—in the Native State of Panna—with a yield that is quite inconsiderable.

Taking all Indian minerals together, the value of the annual production has risen to £7¾ millions. Twenty years ago it was under £2 millions.

CHAPTER III

AGRICULTURE

In India crops can be cultivated all the year round. During the fiercest heat of the dry months you may see, clustered about the wells, patches of small millet[1]—oases in a desert—which, so long as they are watered, can defy the hot wind. Vegetation luxuriates in the warm moisture of the rainy season that follows. The night frosts of the Northern India cold weather do not injure—or greatly retard—the growth of young wheat. It is possible, then, to take two crops off the ground within the year, if they be crops of rapid growth, requiring no more than five or six months between sowing and harvest; so, by double-cropping his land, a cultivator may practically double the area of his holding. In Northern India wheat often follows a crop of maize or indigo, and in Southern India rice follows rice within the year. When a crop requires more than half a year to come to maturity, a second crop may be gathered by sowing it amidst the growing plants. Pulse, for instance, may be sown in standing rice, and rape in standing cotton. In this way nearly an eighth of the area under tillage is cropped twice within the year.

Soils

The alluvial soil of the vast plain that is drained by the Indus, the Ganges and the Brahmaputra is not generally of great natural fertility. The Himalayan *strata* from which it is derived contain no volcanic rock, and are largely composed of shales and slates. But the land is easily worked and responds with some generosity to irrigation and manuring. Moreover, in seasons that are

[1] *Panicum frumentaceum* and *P. italicum.*

specially favourable to bacterial growth in the soil, unmanured and over-cropped land will produce astonishingly. The texture of the soil varies from clay to loam, and from loam to sand, with the sudden irregularity of a river current which in its swirl lets only coarse sand drop, but deposits fine silt where its flow is checked. Clay may rest upon fine sand, and, so to speak, platforms of clay may be suspended beneath a surface of loam or sand. Upon the existence of these platforms the construction of wells in Northern India very greatly depends. The masonry well-ring is sunk to the clay and rests upon it; the clay is pierced, and water springs up with no risk of undermining the masonry. In the northern and western parts of the peninsula the soil is as a rule black—the *detritus* of trap rock, which is naturally of greater fertility than the alluvium of the Indo-Gangetic plain, but is stiffer to work and much less responsive to irrigation and manure. In the valleys it is often accumulated to a depth of 20 feet and more. In beds of such thickness it becomes during the rainy season an unworkable morass, but can be sown at its close, and, being retentive of moisture, will yield a crop even should the weather be rainless up to harvest. Where it is thinner—on plateaux and slopes—it can be cropped during the rainy season, and it may be irrigated and manured with advantage. In the south and east of the peninsula yellow or red soil predominates, derived from crystalline rocks. When occurring *in situ*, on elevated ground, these soils are as a rule thin and poor. But, as one approaches the eastern coast, they increase in depth and fertility, and collected by river action in the deltas of the Mahanadi, the Godavári, the Kistna and the Cauvery, they support sheets of magnificent rice cultivation.

Agricultural Regions

The Indo-Gangetic Plain.—From the agricultural point

of view, India may be divided into seven distinct regions, each characterised by differences of temperature and rainfall that involve differences in the character of the cropping. But for purposes of general description it will suffice to give some account of these varied conditions as they occur in the three geographical areas of the Indo-Gangetic plain, of the peninsula, and of Burma. Wheat is the characteristic crop of the western portion of the Indo-Gangetic plain : rice of the eastern portion. The climatic differences which are represented by this striking distinction, shade into one another as one travels along the plain, but a convenient dividing line between the western and the eastern regions may be drawn about the longitude of Patna. In the *western* region there is a marked cold weather and some cold-weather rain is expected ; temperate crops such as wheat, barley, oats and peas can accordingly be grown during the, so-called, winter season, and cover about two-fifths of the cultivated area, the proportion rising as one goes west-wards. These crops are reaped towards the middle of March or beginning of April, and until the monsoon arrives, three months later, the country is barren save for a few irrigated patches of millet. During the rainy season the crops are tropical, such as maize, millet and cotton. So, within the course of a year, the face of the country changes from the similitude of Canada to that of the Soudan. We may find a similar contrast in the valley of the Nile. But there wheat ceases to grow south of the 25th parallel of latitude ; in India it is cultivated as far south as the 21st parallel. The winter air of Northern India is chilled by the snows of the Himalayas ; a fall of snow in the upper ranges sends a cold wind over the plains as far south as Nagpur. The rainfall of this western region, during both monsoon and cold-weather seasons, is vari-able and uncertain ; the land is suitable for irrigation, and there are facilities for the construction of wells and canals. Here it is accordingly that irrigation works have attained their widest development. In the *eastern* portion of the plain the cold weather is less marked and wheat does not flourish, although mustard and rape are grown to some extent. The country is practically given up to rice. Heavy showers mitigate the heat of April and May, and permit of the sowing of early rice (broadcasted), to be harvested before the flood time of July. The main crop of rice is put in two months later—on the breaking of the monsoon. This is mostly grown from transplanted seedlings, and is not ripe much before the end of the year. The continuous sheet of rice is broken only by fields of tall jute,—a crop which is of immense economic importance to India, but is only grown in this region.

The Peninsula

The upper portion of the peninsula, as far south as Nagpur, enjoys a cold season and may hope for some cold weather rain. Temperate crops—wheat and linseed—are widely cultivated. The soil is mainly of the black variety and is seldom irrigated. With the coming of the monsoon, tropical crops—millet, cotton and the sesame[1] oil seed—are sown save where the soil is too deep for tillage when saturated with moisture. In the districts which approach the Bay of Bengal much rice is grown. Further south, on the western half of the peninsula, we enter the arid region known as the *Deccan*. This is also black-soil country, but the soil is generally shallow, the monsoon rain light and uncertain, and no cold weather rain to speak of falls after the withdrawal of the monsoon. Little can be grown between November and June, and the country is mainly dependent upon tropical crops cultivated between June and November. Below the western coast range there is a strip of land which receives a

[1] *Sesamum indicum.*

heavy rainfall and grows rice. In the south-east of the peninsula, where the soils are of crystalline origin, the weather is affected by a peculiar feature, the heavy rain that during November and December is yielded by the retiring monsoon. This is particularly marked in the districts round Madras. Here there are, as in Northern India, two seasons, one commencing with the onset and the other with the retirement of the monsoon. But owing to increasing heat both seasons are devoted to tropical crops. On the uplands the principal crop is a small millet known as *ragi*;[1] towards the east rice takes possession of the land, being irrigated very extensively from tanks and canals. Still further south, towards the extremity of the peninsula, extensive stretches of red soil are cultivated with cotton. In some localities in the Madras presidency there is much garden cultivation irrigated from wells.

Burma

In Burma, as elsewhere round the Bay of Bengal, agriculture mainly consists in the growing of rice, and the lower valley of the Irrawaddy is a vast rice field, one of the world's most important granaries. Rice is exported from Rangoon to Europe and America up to a value of £10 millions a year. In the delta, the crop is generally raised from broadcasted seed and not from transplanted seedlings; but as one advances up the valley transplantation becomes more general. In the dry belt of Upper Burma (in which the town of Mandalay is situated) there is more variety of cropping: the rice crop is here greatly benefited by irrigation and the Government has constructed two large canals which supply water to 157,000 acres. Beyond this belt heavy rain recommences and rice may be cultivated early or late, as in the adjoining districts of Assam.

[1] *Eleusine coracana.*

CHANGES IN AGRICULTURAL ECONOMY

Economic Isolation

Until recent years the agricultural system of India has been extraordinarily self-contained. Each tract, indeed each village, endeavoured to provide for the whole of its wants, growing not only its grain but its sugar, tobacco and cotton; and where, as in Eastern Bengal, cotton would not flourish, the poor found a rough substitute for it in jute. The produce of each field was distributed without the intervention of money. The landlord took his rent, the labourer his wages, in kind; and even the artisans—the village blacksmith and carpenter—were supported by subscriptions of sheaves of wheat or cakes of coarse sugar. Each locality accordingly grew not only crops that were suited to it, but crops that were needed for its consumption. During the last half-century the Indian railway system has grown in length from 300 to over 30,000 miles; commodities are interchanged between distant localities, and the people have begun to specialise—to cultivate in each locality only such crops as are suited to it, and to rely upon importation for other products. One result, it may be observed, has been the serious decline of sugar-cane cultivation. Some crops, such as jute, indigo, tea and coffee, are grown entirely for export; and, apart from these special products, the influence of the export trade upon agricultural production is very considerable. Taking *all* food grains together, the proportion that is exported is quite inconsiderable except in Lower Burma, which sends more than a third of its rice crop to the seaports. But in years of brisk trade a sixth of India's wheat crop, and as much as half of the oilseeds crop may be despatched to Europe, while practically the whole of the cotton crop is bought up for export or for being spun in the Indian cotton mills. But, so dense is population in proportion to produce, that the export business in agricultural produce, absorbing although it does so large a share of the more valuable products of the land, hardly amounts in value to 6s. a head.

Effect of Social Conditions and Prejudices

India is a country of very small holdings. In the most thickly populated areas of the Indo-Gangetic plain the average size of a farm does not exceed three acres: anywhere in India fifteen acres would be considered a substantial tenancy. There are large proprietors, "zemindars" or "talukdars," as they are called; in some provinces, Oudh and Bengal, for instance, the greater part of the land belongs to comparatively few landed magnates. But they concern themselves but little with the actual farming of their estates, which are mostly parcelled out amongst a multitude of small tenants, so that the landlord's intervention or control hardly extends beyond the collection of his rents. Early marriages are the rule: there have been no industrial outlets to draw the increasing population off the land; holdings have been subdivided till they provide little beyond a bare subsistence. Families, and sometimes whole villages, rateably divide the produce of the land on a system which takes the life out of individual effort. Enterprise is blunted by poverty, and by the respect that is felt by the poor for traditional custom—the force which regulates their lives and protects them from outrageous oppression. And in India agricultural development has been retarded by a special and very peculiar obstacle. The Hindu Scriptures regard cultivation as a degrading pursuit, to be avoided by men of scrupulous morality. The reason given for this prejudice is that in tilling land insects are killed and pain is inflicted upon the plough bullocks. Centuries have passed since the laws of Manu were composed in which these reflections occur. But at the present day very few men of the two highest castes—the Brahmin and the Rajput—will do so much as lay hands on a plough; not

E. H. Blakesley

CATTLE TREADING OUT THE CORN

only does their example lower the dignity of farming, but the very large area of land that is held by them is farmed in slovenly fashion by hired labour. Some of the lower castes have become infected by the idea that it is respectable to be particular; and large numbers of common people will, for instance, not sow lentils because the red colour of the grain reminds them of blood. Such curious prejudices would be ridiculed by a people of industrious habits. Speaking generally, Indian cultivators are not industrious. They have not turned the smallness of their holdings to advantage, like the Japanese, by discarding the plough for the hoe, and increasing the outturn of their fields by hand cultivation. Ridging and trenching require manual labour; in Japan fields are prepared in this way for irrigation, but the Indian is content to flood the surface of his land, wasting the water, and injuring the crops by the subsequent caking of the soil around them. He leaves to his women the laborious task of transplanting rice seedlings, alleging that to women stooping causes less fatigue than to men. This excuse has not occurred to the men of China and Japan, who transplant rice as well as tend it. Cattle dung is used as fuel—a practice which would be regarded in those countries as shockingly wasteful, although in many parts of them coal or wood is not more easily obtainable than in India. Nor would the Chinaman or Japanese be less surprised to discover that the vast majority of Indian cultivators will have no concern with sewage, and will make no arrangements for collecting or applying to their land a manure which in the Far East is the life-blood of agriculture. That such prejudices should be permitted to impoverish the people is the more remarkable as there are some castes of cultivators who are free from them—who in the minuteness of their cultivation, their use of sewage, and the productiveness of their fields are not surpassed in any Japanese village. But these castes are low down in the social scale, and in the opinion of their neighbours the fertility of their land has been purchased by a degrading sacrifice of human dignity. Except amongst the higher castes the Indian cultivator is painstaking so far as his customs will allow him ; and he is steeped in the experience that contributes so much to successful farming. But he is afraid of trusting to it, and submits his judgment as to ploughing or sowing time to be guided by the calculations of priests and astrologers. The Indian fields would yield far more to the people were their fertility not blighted by overshadowing prejudices—were they permitted by custom to be cultivated with more industry and with the intensity that is feasible in a densely populated country.

Varieties of Crops

A larger variety of crops is cultivated in India than in any other country of the world. There are fourteen cereals, of which rice and millet are most characteristic of the Indian climate, since, if uncultivated by man, they could survive in a wild condition and indeed are represented in the wild flora of the country. The varieties of rice are almost infinite in number, but they can all be referred to a single species.[1] The coarser and quicker growing varieties are grown from broadcasted seed : the finer kinds from transplanted seedlings. In one locality, where broadcast sowing is the rule, the plants are thinned by being ploughed up when a few inches high. The crop appears hopelessly ruined, but in a few days' time the plants for which there is space assert themselves. Rice generally needs to stand in water during a period of its growth, and rice fields are accordingly levelled and embanked, and lose, therefore, little of their fertility by surface drainage. Maize, the " corn " of America and the " mealies " of South Africa, has been introduced from

[1] *Oryza sativa*.

America within the last three centuries, and has taken an important place in agricultural economy. Three other cereals—wheat, barley and oats—have been introduced from more temperate regions, possibly brought by the races which for at least 3,000 years have periodically invaded India from the north. Their cultivation is limited to Northern India where the cold season offers them favourable conditions for growth. There are nine distinct species of millet, two growing to a height of 5 or 6 feet, the others not overtopping wheat or barley. The large millets are *juar*,[1] or *cholam*, bearing its grain in compact, generally pendulous, heads (each of which sometimes weighs as much as a pound), and the spiked, or bulrush, millet—*bajra*[2] or *cumbu*. The former is the durra of Egypt, the kaffir-corn of South Africa, and the broom-corn of America. Of the small millets the most important are *mandwa*,[3] or *rági* (the bird's-claw millet), and *kodon*,[4] in appearance resembling rice. These are, respectively, the main staples of the hilly country in the south and centre of the peninsula, and are the food of the tribesmen who, pressed back into the hills, are purest in descent from the indigenous inhabitants. Five other kinds of small millet are less widely cultivated.

For the supply of nitrogenous food there are thirteen species of pulse. The most characteristic of these is the pigeon pea (*arhar*[5] or *tur*), a sub-tropical shrub, perennial, but cultivated as an annual, being very commonly sown in lines through cotton or millet fields. Three species of *phaseolus*[6] are widely cultivated, generally as a creeping undergrowth to cotton or millet. The hardiest of the three is also grown as the sole crop on poor sandy land, of which, like lupins in Europe, it improves the fertility. Its grain is chiefly used as cattle fodder. In

[1] *Sorghum vulgare.*
[2] *Pennisetum typhoideum.*
[3] *Eleusine coracana.*
[4] *Paspalum scrobiculatum.*
[5] *Cajanus indicus.*
[6] *Phaseolus mungo, P. radiatus,* and *P. aconitifolius.*

Southern India its place is taken by Madras horse-gram.[1] Four pulses are cold-weather crops. The principal of them is gram[2]—the garbanzo of Spain—a vetch-like plant, yielding a pea, of immense importance in the dietary of Northern India, that curiously resembles a ram's head. The others are lentils,[3] field peas, and the chickling vetch.[4] The latter is grown principally for cattle food; but it is also eaten by the poorer classes. It contains a poison (which has not yet been isolated), and produces paralysis in man if eaten in quantity for any length of time; and one of the most distressing heritages of an Indian famine is the permanent disablement of large numbers of labourers who have been driven to subsist upon the cheapest kind of grain available. All kinds of pulse are commonly grown as a mixture with another crop, to which the association is as beneficial as in English farming clover is to the wheat that follows it.

For a people of simple tastes a diet of cereals almost suffices if it is supplemented by pulse or (as in Eastern India and Burma) by fish. Some oleaginous food should be added, and this is supplied partly by the clarified and preserved butter known as *ghi*, and partly by vegetable oils. Oil-yielding plants are then of great importance to the subsistence of the people; and they also contribute materially to the exports of the country. Seven kinds are grown, two of which, linseed and rape, are European. The former is in Europe of more repute for its fibre (flax) than for its seed. In India its fibre is not of value. The broadest area of its cultivation is in the black soil country of the peninsula, where it not infrequently follows rice within the same year. Rape is a characteristic cold-season crop of Eastern Bengal and Assam, where it is sown on low land as the river floods subside. It is also grown very

[1] *Dolichus biflorus.*
[2] *Cicer arietinum.*
[3] *Ervum lens.*
[4] *Lathyrus sativus.*

largely in the western region of the Indo-Gangetic plain, being sown in lines across wheat-fields, which in spring time are striped by it with broad bands of yellow flowers. The safflower[1] yields flowers which can be used, and sometimes are used, for dyeing; but imported aniline dyes are cheaper than carthamine and the plant is principally valued for the oil of its seed. The oil-seeds, which are most typical of India, are, however, tropical plants—the sesame[2] (*til* or *gingelly*), and *niger-seed*[3] produced by a small plant of the Composite order with brilliant yellow flowers. The former is cultivated on land of the better classes; the latter grows readily on stony ground, and during the rainy season enlivens the hillsides with broad patches of flaming yellow. The tall broad-leaved castor-oil[4] plant is during the rainy season a prominent feature of the Indian landscape. It is grown in cottage gardens, and as a border to crops of cotton and millet. Its oil was, until the introduction of kerosine, the common luminant of the country. In the peninsula the earth[5] nut is cultivated for export with rapidly increasing popularity. It is of the leguminous order and has the curious habit of plunging its seed pods in the ground as they ripen.

Four plants are cultivated for their fibre. Chief of them is cotton, which appears to be a typical Indian plant and to have been derived from a wild cotton that is indigenous to the country. Cotton was hardly known in Europe during the classical days of Rome, and for several centuries later Indian muslins and calicoes remained expensive luxuries which gave the attractions of fashion to the Indian trade. Introduced by the Arabs into the Levant, the cotton plant found in Egypt a soil and climate that were excellently well suited to it, and it grows and yields

[1] *Carthamus tinctorius.*
[2] *Sesamum indicum.*
[3] *Guizotia abyssinica.*
[4] *Ricinus communis.*
[5] *Arachis hypogœa.*

there far more luxuriantly than in its original home. The cotton exported from Bombay is vastly inferior in quality to that which comes to market at Alexandria. The very numerous Indian varieties can conveniently be grouped into two classes, differing very materially in rapidity of growth—the one needing eight months, the other five months, between sowing and maturity. Cottons of the former kind yield the longest and finest fibre ; but since in India sowing must await the arrival of the monsoon in June, and cannot be effected in the spring as in America and Egypt, these varieties can only be grown in the southern portion of the peninsula, where growth is not checked by the chill of the cold season. In Northern and Central India only varieties of the rapid growing kind can be cultivated, and these generally yield a short, coarse fibre. The cultivation of jute[1] is localised to Eastern Bengal, where in tall, dense masses of vegetation it stands out above the level sheet of rice. The stalks are steeped in water for about three weeks, when the bark can readily be stripped off by hand. Practically the whole of the jute crop is exported. In a single year it has commanded in Calcutta £24 millions. Two other fibre plants, *sonai*[2] and *patsan*,[3] supply the cultivators with materials for ropes.

The sugar-cane has been cultivated in India from the earliest times. Up to the beginning of our era cane sugar was unknown in Europe. We owe to the Arab conquests of the eighth century the spread of sugar-cane cultivation to the countries of the Mediterranean and thence to the western hemisphere. Indian sugar is in its most characteristic form as a mixture of sugar crystals and molasses, obtained by boiling down the cane juice; and, although for some centuries past refined sugar has also been manufactured by straining off the molasses, the name by which it is known (*chini*) appears to indicate that this process

[1] *Corchorus* sp. [2] *Crotalaria juncea.* [3] *Hibiscus cannabinus.*

was introduced from China. Sugar refineries on modern lines have been established; but they have not been conspicuously successful. Indian sugar has in fact for some time past been giving way before the competition of imported sugar, and in the course of the last ten years the area under sugar cane has shrunk by nearly a million acres. During the centuries when India enjoyed a monopoly of the sugar-cane, its cultivation spread over tracts that are much less suited to it than the lands in which it has since found an adoptive home across the seas. It extended in particular to the Indo-Gangetic plain, where its growth may be assisted by irrigation but suffers from the chill of the winter months. South of Nagpur it is not injured by cold; but in this tract of country it is less easy, and more expensive, to provide the irrigation which the crop requires.

Three narcotics deserve mention—the opium poppy, tobacco and hemp.[1] The poppy is a cold-weather crop requiring very careful cultivation, and in British India can only be grown under licence on behalf of the State, which takes over at a price the whole of the produce. The opium exudes as a juice from the seed capsules when scored by scratches. Tobacco was introduced into India by the Portuguese three centuries ago, and the spread of its cultivation throughout the land indicates that the conservatism of the people will not reject a novelty that adds to the pleasure of life. In some localities the tobacco plant grows exceedingly well, though without acquiring the finest flavour, and Indian cigars have of late years secured a market in England. But more tobacco is imported than is exported. The narcotic yielded by the Indian hemp plant is preserved in two different ways—by simply drying the leaves (*bhang*), of which an infusion is made for drinking, and by gathering and pressing the female flowers (*ganja*). The plant can only be grown

[1] *Cannabis sativa.*

under licence and its cultivation is narrowly restricted.

Spices give some variety of relish to the monotony of a vegetarian diet. Many kinds are grown, the chief being the betel leaf, the betel nut, pepper, cardamoms, chillies, and turmeric.

Betel leaf (*pān*) is yielded by a pepper[1] vine, the pungency of which is distributed through its foliage. It is cultivated throughout India, generally under sheds of fine trellis work to protect it from the dry heat, and its leaves, mixed with some betel nut, catechu and lime, are chewed even more universally than are tobacco or gum in America. The betel nut is the fruit of a palm[2] which is cultivated in the moister parts of the country. Pepper is the seed of another pepper[3] vine which is trained up the stems of the betel palm in the tropical gardens of the Malabar coast. In this locality, and in the valleys behind it, cardamoms[4] are also cultivated. They are the seed of a species of lily. Chillies[5] are grown in most cottage gardens throughout the country. So also are the little umbelliferous plants which yield the seeds known as carraway, coriander and cummin. With turmeric[6] they are the ingredients of the well-known Indian curry.

Tea, coffee, cinchona and indigo are mainly the fruits of European planting enterprise; they are grown under European supervision with capital supplied from Europe. Efforts to introduce tea-planting into India date from the commencement of last century; for many years experiments were made with Chinese seed in ignorance of the fact that the tea tree grows wild on the hills of Assam. From this indigenous stock the Indian cultivated teas have been derived. Given a warm moist climate the tea-plant will thrive at exceedingly different elevations. In

[1] *Piper betle.*
[2] *Areca catechu.*
[3] *Piper nigrum.*
[4] *Elettaria cardamomum.*
[5] *Capsicum.*
[6] *Curcuma longa.*

Assam it flourishes at little above sea-level ; it also flourishes in the eastern Himalayas up to a height of 7,000 feet and over. A high elevation improves the flavour but lessens the produce. Tried at first in various localities, tea-planting has concentrated itself in Eastern India—in the two valleys of Assam and on the slopes and at the foot of the eastern Himalayas. It has extended to an area of 500,000 acres, and affords employment to about 1,500 Europeans and to three-quarters of a million labourers, who have mostly immigrated from densely populated tracts further west, and owe to the industry material comfort which they could not have expected at home. Coffee was introduced some two centuries ago by a Mohammedan pilgrim returning from Mecca. Its cultivation has succeeded only on the hills of Southern India and is contracting under the competition of cheaper produce from Brazil. The cinchona tree (introduced from South America) is grown for the production of quinine and cinchona in the eastern Himalayas near Darjeeling and in the Nilgiri hills of Madras. Most of the area planted in both localities is owned and is worked by the State for the provision of quinine for the medical department, and for distribution to the people at a price very much below that which private manufacturers would accept. The history of indigo-planting is peculiar. The Europeans who took up its production rarely cultivated the plant themselves — that is to say, with hired labour, as is the case with tea and coffee. The plant that was required for their indigo factories was grown by tenants holding either from the planters or from neighbouring landowners. They were generally induced to undertake its cultivation by the grant of advances, and sometimes, through these advances, became hopelessly involved in debt to the planter. Friction between creditor and debtor has on several occasions engendered serious disturbances which have threatened the life of the industry. But the extinction to which it now appears to be doomed is due, not to these causes, but to the competition of the artificial indigo which German enterprise has succeeded in manufacturing. During the last ten years the area under indigo has fallen from nearly 1,000,000 to 300,000 acres.

CATTLE

The production of meat does not enter into Indian agriculture. The peasant's cattle are for the tillage of his land ; milk is consumed, but far less than in Europe, and the clarified butter (*ghi*) which is an important article of diet is generally obtained from professional graziers. Large herds are kept by these men in localities where grazing is available, and in their hands some excellent breeds have developed, notable some for their size and strength, some for their milking qualities, and some for their activity. The trotting bullocks of Central India rival the speed of a pony. The Mongolian races of eastern Asia have a curious dislike of milk and butter : the cows that they keep are for breeding plough cattle only, with udders that have not enlarged under domestication. These are the circumstances in Burma and in the hills of Assam. Throughout India the character of the village cattle depends with curious exactness upon the food supply, and illustrates very forcibly the connection between diet and physical development. In rice districts the plough cattle are exceedingly small and feeble : the rice straw which is their diet is the poorest of fodders. In wheat districts there is a great improvement : wheat straw is much more nutritious than rice straw. In districts that grow large millet and cotton (these crops flourish under similar conditions) the cattle are very fine indeed : millet stalk is the best of all straw-fodders and cotton seed is, of course, a strengthening addition. In the wheat and millet districts well-to-do farmers stall-feed their cattle, but as a general rule the cattle of a village, when off work, are herded together on the village common, and since none are killed for food, the herd includes a very large proportion of old and useless animals. Castration is not practised, and no breeding improvements are possible when cows are liable to be covered by immature or ill-bred bulls. Buffaloes as well as bullocks are used for ploughing ; the conditions under which they are bred and kept are generally similar to those described above. Most peasants keep a milch goat or two ; but goat-keeping and sheep-keeping are pursuits distinct from agriculture, and are in the hands of special castes, although the owners will not infrequently add to their income by herding their animals, for a consideration, upon fields which need heavy manuring.

Manure

India is generally pictured as rich in its agriculture. But it is doubtful whether this view can be maintained. Wheat that is irrigated and manured does not yield on an average much more than twenty-four bushels to the acre ; if irrigated without manure the produce will rarely exceed twenty bushels, and over the large area which receives neither water nor manure—quite one-third of the total—the average outturn falls to ten or eleven bushels. Cotton is only a quarter as productive as it is in Egypt ; sugar-cane only a third as productive as it is in the West Indies. The country suffers grievously by surface denudation at the time when the heavy rain of the monsoon, falling upon land that is unprotected by vegetation, scours the fine particles of the soil into the rivers. The land urgently needs manure, but is inadequately provided with it. In a country of vegetarians cattle are, of course, not so numerous or well-fed as where meat is eaten. They are, however, infinitely more numerous than in China or Japan, since (as already stated) Mongolian races dislike cows' milk and employ bullock power very sparingly in their cultivation. But in India the cattle dung is mostly consumed as fuel, and the people have no idea of resorting to the shifts by which food is cooked in Chinese or Japanese villages. Over the extensive wheat-growing area of the peninsula manure is not applied at all except to vegetable gardens. In the Indo-Gangetic plain such manure as is available is applied to the fields that are close at hand. There are no such systematic and exhaustive arrangements for the application of sewage to the land as marks the agriculture of China and Japan. Fields near the village houses cannot, however, but be fertilised by the daily offices of the people. Accordingly each village is surrounded by a belt of fine crops; and, in densely populated localities, where the villages are within half a mile of one another, field succeeds field in an uninterrupted sheet of fertility. But where the village areas are larger, the crops fall off very markedly from centre to circumference. The fertilising effects of leguminous crops are recognised and they are cultivated, not merely in rotation with cereals, but in association with them. Green manuring is practised in some localities. But a very large proportion of the land is never manured, and has worn down to a condition of impoverished stability, from which, however, it will now and again make a surprising start if the seasonal conditions are exceptionally favourable to bacterial action in the soil.

Scope for Expansion

There is an idea that much waste land remains to meet the necessities of a growing population. Generally this is incorrect. Statistics exhibit large areas of unreclaimed waste. But, except in the remoter tracts of Assam and Burma, or in the case of expanses of desert—mostly in the Punjab—which may be rendered irrigable by the development of the State canal system, comparatively little

PLOUGHING IN BENGAL

of this waste is agriculturally an asset, and over the greater part of India the land can feed a larger population only by the better cultivation of the fields which exist.

Implements

The implements of agriculture are ingenious but of very rough construction and depend for their efficiency upon the assiduity with which they are used. In a country of small holdings,—where, moreover, a field labourer can be hired for two or three pence a day,—money will hardly be spent upon labour-saving appliances, and during the three generations of British rule the agricultural methods of the country have remained practically unaffected by European example or influence. The cultivator ploughs his field with a wooden grubber,[1] fixed by a long pole to the yoke of the bullocks. He harrows his land with a log of wood, cuts the crop with a little ineffective sickle, threshes it by the treading of his bullocks, and winnows it by pouring the grain and chaff out before the wind. The ploughs, scarifiers, and drills in use vary a good deal from place to place in weight and details of construction ; and they illustrate in some cases the ingenuity of man in fitting things to his environment, and, in other cases, his reluctance to change the good for the better when the former can appeal to his sentimental regard for ancient custom.

[1] The "swing" plough, having a *short* beam attached by a rope or chain to the drawing power, is to be seen everywhere in China, but has not been adopted by Western Asia.

CHAPTER IV

FAMINE AND IRRIGATION

A COMMUNITY which trusts only to the land for its subsistence, and is sufficiently numerous to consume the whole of the produce, must inevitably starve should the land cease from bearing. The Irish famine of 1863 was a terrible illustration of this necessity; and in earlier centuries, when in Europe, as still, in India, surplus resources were expended, not in the purchase and manufacture of things, but upon the maintenance of hosts of servants and dependants, the countries of Europe were famine-stricken when harvests failed them. Conditions may be less primitive; there may be accumulated resources which may be exchanged for food. But they are useless should means of transport be lacking. Until half a century ago the Indian provinces were land-locked in isolation from one another. Trade now passes freely between them. A network of railways enables one part of India to respond immediately to the needs of another; and since (so far as is known) a failure of crops has never extended over the whole of the country, famines cause no more than a rise in prices and widespread unemployment. No longer do they inflict the supreme calamity of a lack of food grain. Should Indian stocks run short, grain can be drawn from other countries. But its price in India is ordinarily so exceedingly low that it is not till it rises to double the normal that any profit can be made upon importation from outside.

Crops may be ruined by an excess as well as by a deficiency of moisture. Floods are very destructive; and in 1893 the wheat crop in Central India was destroyed by rust over hundreds of thousands of acres. There are, however, two seasons of harvest in the year; over-abundant rain which may spoil one of them will generally be of benefit to the other. But a failure of rain may be disastrous to both, and India suffers from famine when the skies have been cloudless.

The rainfall of India is liable to catastrophic fluctuations. In places which expect annually no more than 50 inches, as much as 25 inches have fallen within twenty-four hours; in Calcutta 7 inches—a tenth of the annual normal—once fell within the space of a single hour. On the other hand, the monsoon rain, which should spread itself over three and a half months, may be limited to a few showers, falling within a fortnight, and may allow the parching heat of May to continue throughout what should be the rainy season. And, to complete the disaster, the cold-weather rain may also fail, so that both the winter and the summer crops are ruined. In the western part of the Indo-Gangetic plain an average annual rainfall of 30 inches represents a mean between such extreme limits as 15 inches and 45 inches. Indeed over a very large portion of Northern India it is an even chance that the rainfall will exceed or fall short of the average by at least a fifth. In the experience of the past century a failure of rain, resulting in famine, is to be expected in one part or other of the country in one year out of every five. But there is no reason to believe that famines are becoming increasingly frequent. They attract more attention than in former years because each of them occasions a strenuous effort to save millions of lives that are threatened by Nature. It is only within the last half-century that the State has systematically undertaken this responsibility. In earlier days—and during the centuries of Native rule—famines were accepted as irresistible calamities which were too hopeless to merit practical attention. Histories of Native rule concerned themselves with the fortunes of dynasties not of peoples. But they offer incidental glimpses of terrible calamities, which depopulated whole provinces and startled the most indifferent of observers by instances of cannibalism.

Some parts of India are, so to speak, famine proof. In the eastern portion of the great plain—in eastern Bengal, Assam, and parts of Burma—the ordinary rainfall is so exceedingly heavy that the crops can sustain a large deficiency. This is also generally true of the low-lying strip which forms the littoral of the peninsula. For a different reason famine cannot affect the extreme west of the Indo-Gangetic plain, where good rain is so little expected that the country is abandoned to a few wandering graziers. Irrigation protects some 65,000 square miles of cultivation against vicissitudes of season. There remains an enormous area—some 180,000 square miles of cultivation—no part of which is absolutely immune against famine. But the liability is much greater in some tracts than in others. Risks are largest in the north-western corner of the peninsular plateau—in the tract known as the Deccan—where the people can hardly expect two good crops out of five. The frequency of their losses has inured them to privation. When oppressed by famine they support it hardily, and leave their homes without reluctance in search of work. Very different is it with tracts that are normally productive but suffer from famine at rarer intervals. There is no ever-present shadow of disaster to check the increase of the population, and the people lose *morale* under the calamity, and hold back from relief works until weakened by privation. In such conditions a heavy mortality is inevitable. During the past generation there have occurred four widespread famines the effects of which lasted over seven years, and cost the State, in direct expenditure for the relief of distress, over £25 millions. Southern India suffered in 1877–1878 and again in 1896–1897; Central India in 1896–1897 and in 1899–1900; Western India in

1877–1878, 1896–1897 and in 1899–1900; Northern India in 1877–1878 and 1896–1897.

Railways blunt the edge of famine by transporting grain; but they tend to equalise prices, so that scarcity in one part of the country is reflected generally throughout it. This result may be profitable to farmers and traders in the exporting localities, but weighs hardly upon others, who find their expenses increased because crops have failed elsewhere. They would like to see their abundance safeguarded by the check of exportation, and this expedient has not infrequently commended itself to the rulers of Native States. But it has been unflinchingly opposed by the British Government—and with success, for the experience of the last thirty years has proved that, if trade be left unfettered, it can be trusted to supply the needs of any province, however remote and however afflicted. In the tracts that are actually famine-stricken the rise in prices may double, or even treble, the cost of living; and moreover, in these circumstances of hardship, the great mass of the people suffer the extreme calamity of losing the whole of their income. Landlords collect no rents; farmers gather no produce, and labourers are without employment. It is not too much to say that during an Indian famine two-thirds of the population lose their means of livelihood. The problem of famine relief is then in chief measure the provision of work for millions of people that are thrown out of employment. But this is not all. There are those to be considered who by reason of age or infirmity are unable to work. No poor relief is ordinarily provided by the State in India. Incapable paupers are generally supported by private charity, impelled sometimes by a desire for ostentation, more often by feelings of religion or kindliness, and, in respect of relatives,—however remote,—insisted upon by the obligations which bind together the caste and the family. But in time of famine parents cannot be expected to give in alms what their children require from them: the springs of private charity run dry and the aged, the infirm and the crippled wander forth to seek the vague chances of casual beggary. Their only hope is in the State. Famine relief, then, includes the provision not only of work for the able-bodied, but of charity for those who are destitute and incapable.

It is no light task, at short notice, adequately to relieve the distress of hundreds of thousands of people, without demoralising them, or wasting the public money. Road-making and the excavation of tanks offer simple means of giving employment. But when people flock to them by thousands it is difficult, without some semblance of harshness, to ensure that a tale of work is completed; yet, if no work test be exacted and wages, however small, be distributed unconditionally, few people will be able to resist the temptation of making a little money at the expense of the State; in these circumstances experience has shown that half the numbers receiving relief may be in no real necessity. Similarly with those who are incapable of working; if relief is granted them without scrutiny, the well-to-do will send their dependants to seek public charity. Famine relief administration is then beset by two serious dangers—the risk of sacrificing life to over-scrupulous strictness, and the risk of sacrificing economy to over-indulgent sympathy; and the difficulty of avoiding one or the other is immensely increased by the suddenness and the irregularity with which famines occur, and the consequent impossibility of providing any permanent organisation for dealing with them. Speaking generally, the initiation and control of an enormous system of poor-relief falls upon the shoulders of the ordinary official staff of the country.

The foundations of the present system of famine relief were laid by a Commission in 1880; some changes of principle and method were introduced by two later

Commissions, and it was not until 1901 that the scheme of relief now in force was finally settled. So soon as the prevalence of famine is officially recognised, the State concedes to the unemployed the " right to work " at a subsistence wage, provided that they will resort to a public relief work, and will execute a task the amount of which varies with the capacity of the labourer and is always less than would be exacted by a contractor. The wage is paid in cash, but is calculated according to the current price of necessaries. It is an individual wage—that is to say, it suffices for one person only ; relatives or dependants, who accompany the labourer but are unable to work, receive relief gratuitously. A question which has been earnestly debated is whether a labourer who refuses or fails to perform his task should be given a " minimum " wage, that might just support him. This concession was formerly allowed, but was very greatly abused. It has now been withdrawn, and experience has shown that it can be withdrawn without risk, provided that the relief works are opened when need first presses. Even so, however, it has been found that the light task which is exacted does not suffice to exclude hosts of the undeserving, especially if they live near the work and have not to leave their homes to attend it. Most provincial governments have then reserved power to exclude persons whose condition is shown by enquiry not to be necessitous. There should ordinarily be a separate relief work for every 5,000 persons, but this number is often greatly exceeded. Elaborate arrangements are made for sanitation, and the provision of drinking water. But they do not prevent the occasional outbreak of epidemics of cholera, which cause great mortality. As soon as the rains set in, relief works are gradually closed, since labour is then in demand for field work. Gratuitous relief is, however, then distributed with increased liberality until private charity revives with the gathering of the crops.

In former days gratuitous relief was mainly afforded in "poor-houses," in which food was provided for those who would take refuge in them and submit to something of the discipline of prison life. Most of their inmates arrived in the last stage of destitution: they sought shelter by thousands and no care could avert terrible mortality. Moreover, the provision of these asylums stimulated the wandering which is now recognised as the most desperate feature of famine, and their employment is now discouraged except for the relief of immigrants from elsewhere. The present policy is to keep the destitute and incapable in their villages by granting them relief at their homes. This is, of course, a far more difficult task than the opening of "poor-houses" at various centres; and it would indeed be impossible were it not for the existence of village officials whose business it was originally to maintain rental accounts between landlords and tenants, but who are now paid by the State and organised into a staff of village notaries-public. These men prepare lists of the destitute, and on their lists, after such check as is possible, doles are distributed at regular intervals. This procedure is, of course, open to much abuse, and its working requires close supervision. But it is infinitely more-effective in preventing mortality than the "poor-house" system; and, as for supervision, it is essential to the success of every branch of famine relief. Large numbers of Indians of respectability are enlisted in temporary employ, officers are borrowed from the army, and during the currency of a famine it is hardly too much to say that every young Englishman lives in the saddle.

Special measures of relief are required for children, who, when distress is acute are neglected by their parents even when the parents are given special allowances for them. Children will only be fed properly if the State feeds them, and children's "relief kitchens" are opened in the villages (in charge of the police, village schoolmasters or private individuals who will assist in this charity) where a sufficient meal is given daily to all children that are listed as in need of it. They attend by thousands, and the success and the popularity of this simple and direct expedient have become one of the most striking features of famine experience. Similar kitchens are opened on relief works for the children and infirm dependants of the labourers.

To give some idea of the magnitude of these operations it may be mentioned that during each of the famines of 1876–77 and 1899–1900 the numbers in receipt of relief, at their maximum, exceeded four millions. In some districts a quarter of the population was at one time or another on the hands of the Government.

Successful as these relief measures have been in saving human life, they have not altogether averted deplorable mortality. During a famine the ordinary machinery for collecting statistics is thrown out of gear, and the published death-rates are not reliable. A safer clue to the effects of recent famines upon population is afforded by the results of the decennial censuses. During the ten years 1891 to 1900 Northern, Central and Western India were affected by two severe famines. The State spent £11·5 millions upon direct measures of relief. Yet the population of the British districts that were famine-stricken decreased by two millions. This loss, severe as it must appear, was however inconsiderable when compared with that suffered by the adjoining Native States, which, although assisted by loans of over £2 millions from the Imperial Government, had not the resources, nor the machinery, for combating famine on British methods. Of a much smaller population five millions disappeared. Had the mortality in British India been on this scale their population would have decreased by seven millions, and the State may thus safely take credit for having saved at least five million lives. It should be added that the excess mortality which occurred in British India during these two famines was due in great measure, not to privation, but to sickness. Cholera broke out virulently. And in India a year of drought is generally succeeded by a year of fever, of very fatal type, which attacks not only the poor, who may have been weakened by hunger, but well-to-do families who have suffered no hardship. Moreover, Indian famine administration may take credit for two encouraging facts. In the first place, the people are not demoralised by the charity of the State: a couple of months after the closure of relief works one may ride about the country unassailed by the entreaties of a single beggar. Indeed there is good ground for believing that the distress of a famine, as now mitigated by the State, is actually a helpful experience, and that the people have gained in enterprise from calamities which may be disciplinary, though no longer destructive. Secondly, there is no such retrogression of cultivation as formerly marked for many years the track of a famine. Two years after the famines of 1896–97 and 1899–1900 the cropped area had practically recovered its full extension. The State assisted the cultivators by liberal advances at a low rate of interest. And of the money subscribed by private generosity to the Indian Famine Fund a large portion was most usefully expended in providing resourceless cultivators with plough cattle and seed grain. The subscriptions to the Fund on the occasions of the two last famines amounted to over £2 millions, mostly remitted from the United Kingdom. Not only did it offer a new lease of life to many thousands of ruined families; in providing petty luxuries for the sick, and clothes for the destitute, it fulfilled purposes which lay outside the scope of State interference.

The truest safeguard against the effects of a great agricultural catastrophe is the development of industrial as opposed to agricultural employment. In this matter India is infinitely behind Europe and will long remain so. But a catastrophe which results from drought may be limited by irrigation, and in the extension of irrigation there have been notable achievements.

Irrigation

In the extreme west of the Indo-Gangetic plain—in country which is practically rainless—irrigation is essential. Sind depends as much upon the Indus as Egypt upon the Nile. On the other hand, in the extreme east—in Eastern Bengal and Assam—the rainfall is so exceedingly heavy that the land needs no water beyond what it receives from the clouds. Between these limits irrigation would everywhere be useful for some crops and in some seasons; as one passes from east to west it becomes desirable for all crops in all seasons. In the peninsula, throughout the black soil region, irrigation is but little used, partly because it is difficult to secure, and partly because in ordinary years the land yields with fair certainty without it. In the crystalline area to the south of the peninsula it is almost as useful and as widely practised as in the centre of the Indo-Gangetic plain. In Sind, as already stated, the whole of the cultivated area is irrigated; in the Punjab two-fifths; in the United Provinces between a quarter and a third, and in Madras a quarter.

In British India as a whole about one acre in six is irrigated. But in some years irrigation is practised much more widely than in others, especially in tracts, such as the United Provinces, which lie midway between regions of heavy and of scanty rainfall. Here, in a favourable season, irrigation is hardly used during the rains except for crops that are sown before the monsoon sets in, or for transplanted rice or sugar-cane which require water at regular intervals. And, during the cold weather, although generally useful for valuable crops such as wheat or opium, it is not needed by the hardier grains, if the winter rains are not disappointing. But if (as frequently occurs) the monsoon is light, or the winter rains fail, water is in urgent demand, and no source is left unutilised. Temporary wells are sunk wherever possible; streams are dammed, and even the village ponds are emptied upon the land. In other provinces the annual fluctuations are much less striking.

Irrigation works may be distinguished according as their source is the subsoil water, surface drainage water, or large rivers—that is to say, they may be classed as wells, tanks or canals. Wells provide water for twelve million acres;[1] tanks, ponds and small private canals for thirteen million acres;[1] large canals, constructed by the State, for seventeen million acres.[1] The people owe then to the Government the means of irrigating two out of every five acres watered by them.

WELLS

In the upper portion of the Indo-Gangetic plain the well has for ages been literally the life-spring of mankind, providing the inhabitants not merely with drink but with subsistence. Without irrigation-wells this tract could never have supported half its dense population in the days before British engineers led canal water on to the land. Wells must have been used here for irrigation from remote antiquity. Where the soil is closely compacted it is unnecessary to line them with masonry: water is seldom more than 30 feet from the surface, and a well 6 feet in diameter will provide for the irrigation of four or five acres of wheat. But there are fine masonry wells by hundreds of thousands. The masonry cylinders which line them are sunk into the ground by dredging away the

[1] Taking into account once only the large area which bears two irrigated crops within the year.

earth and water from within them until a bed of clay is reached; a hole is pierced through the clay and water springs up without endangering the stability of the masonry. When the cold weather rains fail, inexpensive surface wells are dug in vast numbers. In the peninsula wells have to be sunk through rock, costing more and yielding less abundantly.

Well-irrigation entails the raising of water. This is effected by human or bullock labour, without, save in rare cases, the assistance of pumps. From small wells, in which water stands within 15 feet of the surface, the water is commonly raised by a man working the "lever" or "pole and bucket" lift. From deeper and larger wells water is drawn by bullock power. The simple appliance in most general use is a large leather bucket attached to a rope which passes over a pulley, above the well-head, and is fastened at its other end to the yoke of a pair of bullocks. They drag up the bucket by rushing down an inclined ramp, of length approximately equal to the depth of the well. The apparatus varies in some of its details in different parts of the country, but within each tract there is absolute uniformity of construction, although no reason may be discoverable in local conditions for the adoption of the particular pattern in use. In some tracts a self-emptying bucket is used, discharging its contents through a leather pipe, which by an arrangement of cords is held up, alongside the bucket, while the latter is ascending, but is stretched out on reaching the well-head. This device saves the labour of a man, but its use is strictly localised to certain parts of the peninsula. Another contrivance, worked by bullock power—the Persian wheel or *Noria*—is common to several distinct localities. Well irrigation provides very extensive employment for labour. During the cold-weather months not less than four million men earn their livelihood by raising water.

So many temporary wells are sunk in Northern India

when the rainfall is insufficient that it is difficult to estimate the normal number of wells in the country, or to compare their present with their past numbers. When most numerous they have approached two millions. In Northern India the construction of permanent wells is undoubtedly advancing, although, viewed statistically, progress is masked by the abandonment of old wells in tracts to which canal irrigation has been extended. In Southern India the number of wells is reported to have increased by as much as 40 per cent. during the twenty-five years 1876 to 1900. It is generally admitted that well-water yields better crops than canal water : it is warmer, it is used less extravagantly, and it not infrequently contains nitrous salts in solution. The extension of well irrigation is eminently desirable. For many years past the State has offered to assist cultivators to construct wells by lending them the necessary capital at a low rate of interest. Advantage is taken of this offer, but not so generally as might have been anticipated.

Tanks

The crystalline area of the peninsula is distinguished by the abundance of its irrigation tanks. The uneven surface of the country, and its rock formation, facilitates the impounding of water, and every valley contains a chain of tanks—one above the other—constructed by throwing embankments across the bottom. Most of them are of small size and irrigate less than 100 acres ; but some are imposing sheets of water, resembling large natural lakes in the irregularity of their contour and in their effect upon the scenery. Certain of these large reservoirs are known to be over 1,000 years old, and the system of tank irrigation has undoubtedly come down from a very early period of Native rule. Where the land is in the hands of cultivators holding directly under the State, the repair of the village tanks is undertaken by the Government. In the Madras presidency alone 40,000 tanks are so maintained. Where the ownership of the land is vested in proprietors, intervening between the State and the cultivators, the tanks have very generally been neglected and cultivation has suffered. Tank irrigation is used for rice, and to a less extent for sugar-cane. It assures a regularity of supply without which, even in tracts of heavy rainfall, the better kinds of transplanted rice cannot be cultivated; and with its assistance two, and sometimes three, crops of rice are grown on the same land within the year.

Canals

The most impressive irrigation works are, however, the State canals, which are comparable with large rivers in the volume of water they carry. Indeed the discharge of the Chenáb canal in the Punjab is six times that of the Thames at Teddington. There are a considerable number of petty canals that have been made by private enterprise. Two of the existing canals from the river Jumna were initiated by Moghal rulers for the irrigation of their demesnes. But, speaking generally, the canal system of India is the creation of the State, and is an asset with which the country has been endowed by the British Government within the last two generations. Canals owned and managed by the State irrigate an area of about seventeen million acres: their construction has cost over £35 millions and it is calculated that the value of the crops that are raised by them *annually* returns to the country four-fifths of this large sum. Taken together, the State canals yield a revenue of about 7 per cent., obtained by the levy of water-rates, which vary according to the crop that is grown (upon the nature of which depends the number of waterings), the productiveness of the soil, and the market facilities of the locality. Generally they may be taken to represent about 10 per cent. of the value of the produce, and in the peninsula (where watering is less profitable) considerably less than this. They are collected in the main from occupiers; but landlords contribute (when landlords intervene between the occupier and the State) since they are enabled by the irrigation to exact higher rents.

The circumstances of the peninsula are unfavourable to the construction of large canals, since the ground surface is not even, and the river-beds lie deep below the level of the country. There is an appealing contrast between the assured and heavy rainfall that occurs on the seaward face of the western coast range, and the uncertain and scanty supply that reaches the hinterland, and three considerable experiments have been made in supplying the deficiency of one place from the surplus of another. Two canals in the Bombay presidency are fed by rain that is impounded on the coast-range. A more ambitious undertaking in the south of Madras diverts eastwards, by a tunnel through the hills, the water of a river that flowed down their westward slope. But these canals, however valuable in famine time or for the cultivation of special crops such as sugar-cane, do not affect very widely the agriculture of their localities; and the most notable of the peninsular canals are those which give water to the level deltas of the Godávari, Kistna and Cauvery rivers. The Cauvery system is of ancient date, the cross-river anicut upon which it depends having been constructed 1,500 years ago. But it owes its development, and the other two systems their initiation, to British engineers. The three canals irrigate two and a half million acres of productive rice land, and support a population in such circumstances of well-being as are rarely enjoyed by Indian cultivators.

The typical canals of India are, however, those of the Indo-Gangetic plain. They are of two classes—inundation and perennial. The former simply draw water from the rivers on to the land during the monsoon season, when the rivers are in high flood. Of this type are most of the canals which give life to Sind and to large tracts of arid country in the south of the Punjab. They are generally serviceable only for crops that are grown during the monsoon. Perennial canals are more elaborate undertakings. Their object is to provide water during the dry season as well as the monsoon, and for this purpose it is necessary that the level of the river's dry-season supply should be raised very considerably by a large masonry dam, or *barrage*, which is constructed across the river-bed. During flood time the current overtops the dam, and flows on seaward; during the dry season the effect of the dam is to convert the river-bed above it into a reservoir. Below the dam the river channel is dry; but water springs up into the river-bed again, and some way down its course there is a fresh supply which may be impounded, and taken off into another canal. In this manner three canal systems are fed by the river Jumna, and two by the river Ganges. The canal takes off from the river above the dam. The canal slope being less than that of the river-bed the water is gradually raised to ground level as it passes down its channel, and can ultimately be delivered flush with the surface. But, over large tracts of country, a lift of two or three feet is required; and the water is raised by various simple appliances, the principal of which is a basket swung backwards and forwards on cords by a couple of men. Ten large perennial canals, irrigating eight million acres, are fed by Himalayan rivers, flowing through the Punjab and the United Provinces; and, since these rivers are partly snow-fed and rise in the spring with the melting of the snows, they replenish the canals at a time when the plains are at their driest. Two of the most recently constructed Punjab canals have within the last ten years practically created new countries. Their courses traverse land which was originally uninhabited desert; they have covered it with cornfields, having attracted settlers in multitudes. The Chenáb canal has in this way reclaimed two million acres of land, and supports a new population of nearly a million. There is, of course, a risk in interfering with Nature on so stupendous a scale. Water poured across a country through many thousands of miles of distributing channels soaks into the subsoil and raises very greatly the subsoil water-level. In the Punjab the river-beds are not deep enough to act as drains: large areas have become water-logged and a problem has arisen which will tax very greatly the ingenuity and the resources of the State engineers.

Further east—in the province of Bengal—three systems of canals have been constructed. The area which they irrigate is not inconsiderable—nearly a million acres—but in ordinary seasons their water is not in great demand, and they have, so far, failed to earn full interest on their capital. Within recent years two large canals have been made in Upper Burma. They irrigate 175,000 acres situated in or near the dry zone, and return 4 per cent. on their cost of construction.

It appears that no very wide field remains for the construction of canals which would be profitable to the State as well as protective to the people. In the Punjab there is scope for two more great reclamation canals, such as the Chenáb canal; and a project is under consideration for increasing immensely the use that is made of the river Indus in Sind. These schemes affect the extreme west of the Indo-Gangetic plain; elsewhere the engineers seem to have exhausted the possibilities of irrigation as a profitable State investment. But in the circumstances of India there is no waste of public money in constructing a canal which secures a countryside against famine and in ordinary years adds greatly to its productiveness, even although, after meeting its working expenses, it may provide no adequate surplus for the payment of interest. The scope for protective irrigation works has recently been exhaustively considered by a special Commission, and a very extensive programme has been elaborated which makes liberal provision for the needs of the peninsula. In this area some large canals have already been commenced which may not improbably revolutionise the local system of agriculture, although offering no profit to the State for very many years to come.

CHAPTER V

MANUFACTURES

Two centuries ago India, in the development of manufacturing industry, compared favourably with many countries of Europe. Weaving and dyeing, artistic working in wood, stone and metals, had after centuries of experience reached a high pitch of excellence ; architecture displayed itself in buildings which are still amongst the notable monuments of the world. But she has stood aside from the current of industry which has changed the face of Europe. Her people have remained untouched by the desire for possessions which is the ultimate foundation of manufacturing enterprise ; to them the estimation of their fellows has appeared more desirable than belongings, and, the needs of life once satisfied, they have been unwilling to toil for the obtaining of superfluities. Moreover, they have not felt the spur of female extravagance. The industries of the West owe most of their life to the desires of women. In the East woman has never been permitted to use or even to feel her influence. There has then been little reason for the establishment of the large factories, which in Europe have revolutionised the conditions of manufacturing industry. Nor have the old-established handicrafts developed with the agricultural growth of the country. Many of them have indeed lost ground. Hand-made goods cannot withstand the competition of imports from Europe. In some directions the country is fitting itself to the new order of things. Cotton and jute mills mark Bombay, Calcutta and Cawnpore with multitudes of chimneys. But, generally, India is still only feeling her way between mediæval and modern methods of manufacture, and suffers the inconveniences that attend a state of transition. It follows that the industries of the present day can suitably be distinguished according as they represent old-time handicrafts or modern factory organisation.

Handicrafts

The simple wants of the Indian villager—that is to say, of nine-tenths of the Indian people—hardly exceed some cotton clothes, shoes, some ornaments for his wife and daughters, some metal vessels and platters for cooking and eating, some earthenware pots and, for furniture, a few stools. There are, in addition, the implements used in his cultivation. His village is a little self-supporting community which has grown up in independence of its neighbours, providing itself with its manufactures as well as with its food. Indian handicrafts are then village industries, in so far as they are concerned with the primary wants of life. The carpenter and the blacksmith are, like the priest, the barber and the washerman, village servants, who may earn something extra by special work, but are generally remunerated by receiving from each cultivator a small share of his produce, and are responsible for keeping his ploughs and harrows in repair. Every village of any size has its own weavers and potters. It is only handicraftsmen who make objects of art or luxury that have tended to congregate in towns.

Cotton Weaving

The weaving of cotton cloth is the most characteristic of the Indian industries. India is the home of the cotton plant, and it was not until the Arab conquests of the eighth century that its cultivation spread westwards, beyond her boundaries. Weavers generally belong to one or other of four Hindu castes, or to a particular class of Mohammedans. But they form only part of these communities and their numbers are uncertain. Including

7—(2134)

their families they probably number between five and six millions. Within the last half century, looms have certainly been abandoned very widely for other means of employment. As for the preliminary processes of carding and spinning, they are now almost extinct as hand industries, and the weavers generally use machine-made yarn. Hand-made fabrics are supposed to be more durable than those made by machinery; but they are less attractive in appearance and dearer in price, and they are losing ground in the market. Thirty years ago the imports of British-made cotton fabrics amounted to 1,333 million yards, and (deducting exports) about 83 million yards were contributed by Indian mills. The imports have risen to 2,500 million yards, and the output in Indian mills, for consumption in India, to 850 million yards. This large increase has been partly evoked by a real increase in demand; population has increased by 24 per cent., and the poorer classes are infinitely better dressed than they were a generation ago. But making every allowance for this, and for the fact that large numbers of weavers have secured employment as factory hands, there has been a great displacement of labour which must have been accompanied by much hardship. It does not appear that hand-looms now supply more than a third of the cotton fabrics which are used in the country.

The mass of hand-woven fabrics is of the unbleached cotton known in trade as "grey." In towns, to meet a demand for finer and more decorative clothing, hand-weaving has developed into an ornamental art on lines which are generally special to the locality and represent the peculiar tastes of its inhabitants. The inclination of old-fashioned Hinduism is for white, especially for men's wear; but weaving in patterns, with coloured yarn, has been elaborated with great skill and tastefulness, especially in the Punjab, Central Provinces and

Hoffmann, Calcutta

NEPALESE WOMEN WEAVING

Southern India, where the simpler fashion has given way before tastes that were introduced by the Mohammedans from Central Asia, or that represent the warmer temperament of the Dravidian races of the peninsula. And Indian hand-looms produce fabrics not only of elaborate design but of exquisite fineness. Indian muslins, plain and flowered, have been famous for centuries. They are made in several provinces—in Southern as well as in Northern India—but those of the highest reputation are produced in Eastern Bengal, chiefly in the town of Dacca, where yarn has been spun so finely that a pound's weight runs to 250 miles. The muslins may be flowered in cotton, silk, or gold, being in fact cotton brocades. In making elaborate or fine cotton fabrics hand-looms have some chance of resisting the competition of machinery. But the hands can make little that machinery cannot imitate, and Manchester now annually consigns to India about 500 million yards of coloured cloth and muslins. Some well-known crafts have already perished. It is difficult now to procure a piece of Dacca muslin of the traditional fineness. . . .

In India proper weaving has become a caste profession. But on its eastern border—in Assam and Burma—it is still a domestic occupation. The women of the household weave for the family, using a small, portable loom, pegged at one end to the ground and secured at the other end to the waistband. Such looms are also used by the hill-tribes of the north-eastern frontier, and produce in the hands of their women striped cotton fabrics of real artistic merit.

Silk Weaving

The mulberry silkworm is grown in parts of Bengal, but it does not appear to be indigenous to the country, and was probably introduced from China. In the climate of the Indian plains it yields silk of poor quality. In the eighteenth century, before silk cultivation was widely established in France and Italy, Indian silk under the fostering care of the East India Company became an export of much importance. Its growth is now a declining industry, and the silk-weavers generally use imported material. Their skill has been well known for centuries. Indian silken fabrics have attracted traders to her gates from remote antiquity. They are worked up with gold thread into the magnificent brocades known as "kincobs"; these often contain more gold than silk, and appear to be—indeed sometimes are—fabrics of wrought gold. Twenty centuries ago they excited the admiration of the Greek envoy, Megasthenes; and the rich stuffs brought from India to Babylon and Jerusalem were probably such as are now made at Ahmedabad, Benares and Murshidabad. Plain silk fabrics, and mixtures of silk and cotton, are woven in every variety of colour and pattern. But India no longer exports them in any quantity.

Wool Weaving

The wool of the Indian sheep—particularly in the peninsula—is short-stapled, of a hairy character and felts badly. Coarse blankets and felts are made throughout the country, but the only woollen fabrics which have gained reputation are Kashmir shawls and pile carpets. Both represent Persian influences. The former are made at some places in the Punjab (to which Kashmiri workmen migrated in time of famine) as well as in Kashmir. The material used for them was formerly the soft under-coat of the Tibetan goat (known as "pashm"), which was imported across the Himalayan passes. But the small available stock of this has been amplified by a number of inferior substitutes, and the general quality of the shawls has declined. They are no longer exported in any considerable number. The weaving of pile carpets has for long time past been an industry of importance in Kashmir and Northern India, whence it spread down the west coast to Madras. The vegetable dyes formerly used gave tones of soft brilliancy which were combined with much artistic skill. But the present output, where at all considerable, meets a demand in Europe for cheap, showy carpets; and, outside a few special factories, the best specimens are produced in Indian jails, which have very generally adopted carpet-making as an employment for prisoners.

EMBROIDERY

Specimens of the needlework embroidery of India are commonly to be seen in modern drawing-rooms. It has attained great excellence in various directions, although, so far as colours go, it has suffered from the very general substitution of chemical for vegetable dyes. The *phulkáris* made by women in the Punjab are admirable specimens of darn-stitch needlework; so also are the table-cloths and table centres made in Kashmir, the manufacture of which is a new and growing industry. At Delhi and Agra satin-stitch embroidery on silk also successfully meets a modern demand for export. Chain-stitch is used in Kashmir for embroidering small felt carpets which command a ready sale. But its most characteristic employment is in Kathiawar—in the Bombay presidency—where it is applied effectively and artistically to women's garments, handkerchiefs and curtains. The open "button-hole" embroidery known as "chikan-work" is produced at several places, notably at Lucknow, Calcutta and Dacca. It is in great demand; and, generally, it may be said that embroidery work, utilising, as it does, the meticulous care and patience of the East, is one of the few Indian handicrafts that modern trade and fashion have actively supported. The most splendid and costly products of Indian needlework are the gold embroideries of Delhi, Agra, Benares and Hyderabad. These, when light, are founded upon silk or muslin; when heavy, upon velvet, and in the latter case, the gold work is generally supported by cotton lining and stands out as if heavily embossed. This costly work was employed for the decoration of State trappings, such as canopies and elephant cloths; and its survival, like that of most other ancient Indian handicrafts of luxury, reminds us of the numerous royal courts between which, in the vicissitudes of history, the government of the country has shifted.

Dyeing

Except in Bengal, gay colours are fashionable—everywhere for women, in a less degree for men, but in Southern India for the whole population. The arts of dyeing and calico-printing are very ancient and are very widely practised. The country produces a large number of vegetable dyes of very delicate colouring. Most of them are fleeting, no mordants having been discovered for them. But this has been an advantage, since the fashion of colour varies at different festivals and the poor are glad to be able to wash out one colour and substitute another. Two notable Indian dyes are fixed—indigo and madder. The import of cheap chemical dyes (aniline and alizarine) from Germany has increased sixteen-fold during the last thirty years, and the indigenous dyes of India are doomed to extinction. Madder has practically disappeared from cultivation, and during the last five years the exports of indigo have decreased by a half. Little use is now made of the colours yielded by safflower and turmeric. Chemical dyes are easily applied, giving a glaring brilliancy of tone which public taste does not condemn. Indian dyers are acquainted with the processes of "tie-dyeing" and "waxing" in order to isolate part of the fabric from the effect of the dyeing vat, and so to produce patterns. But the patterned calicoes and "palampores," which three centuries ago were amongst the most attractive specialities of the Indian trade, are produced either by block-printing or by painting. The former art is practised in every province of India except Bengal, the style of designs used in each part of the country being curiously distinct. Generally, colours are printed on a white or pale ground, but in Western India a ground colour is given by hand-washing after the design has been printed. In Southern India, whence the calicoes once so popular in Europe were mainly derived, designs are produced by brush-painting, wax being used as a resistant to limit the spread of the colour. The export trade in Madras calicoes and bandanas has shrunk to nothingness ; and, as already stated, India now looks to England for a large supply of coloured cotton goods.

Leather Working

Leather-working is confined to men of the lowest caste, since to Hindu ideas the touching of raw hides is abhorrent. So far as it supplies a domestic demand, it extends little beyond shoe-making. There is a colony of shoemakers in every large village. Here and there leather is stamped or embroidered for such articles as gaiters, saddle-cloths and powder-flasks. But these handicrafts are commercially of very little account.

Perfumery—Ivory—Paper

The extraction of perfume is an industry of importance in some districts of the United Provinces ; amongst the scents that are made are attar of roses, patchouli, and ylang-ylang. Paper-making was introduced by the Mohammedans, who learnt it from the Chinese ; the Hindus wrote upon birch bark in the north and upon palm leaves in the south—indeed, the latter are still in use. But machine-made paper is driving the hand-made article from the market. Ivory carving is practised effectively.

At Delhi little ornaments are made for the European market; in Southern India the craft retains stronger traces of Hindu religious influences; from Southern India it has crossed to Moulmein in Burma. On ivory tablets are painted the delicate miniatures which are sold as souvenirs of Agra and Delhi. They are a development from the Persian illuminative painting, which was as formal, as brilliant, and as pleasing as that which was employed to illustrate the books of mediæval Europe.

Iron

Iron occurs abundantly at many localities in the peninsula, and the skill which Indian ironworkers attained is shown by the admirable temper and finish of ancient arms. The art of carving in steel still survives. But Indian iron is not as cheap as the imported metal; and iron-smelting is dying out, even in places where good ore is abundant, and where the workers possess the art of making fine steel.

Brass and Copper

The casting and hammering of vessels in copper, brass and bell-metal is still a living industry of much importance. There are prejudices against taking food or drink from glass and china, and save in Europeanised households metal vessels are universally used at meals as well as in cooking. Hindus prefer brass, the Mohammedans tinned copper; but of recent years a large import trade has sprung up in cups and platters of white metal and enamelled iron. Indian water-vessels are of graceful shapes; the one in commonest use, the *lota*, is modelled on the lines of a flower calyx with recurved lips, Very elaborate ornamentation is applied to brass platters by hammering; those made at Benares have caught the fancy of Europe. Metal platters, tinned or plain, are also decorated by working black or coloured lac in minute patterns into their surface. Brass and copper are encrusted very effectively with silver; and silver, inlaid flush with the surface, is used to decorate vessels of base metal. The damascening of steel with gold wire was in former days used extensively for the ornamentation of arms; the art still survives in a few places.

Jewellery and Plate

To the Indian woman jewellery is a necessity; if she cannot afford gold and silver, she covers her neck with beads, and her arms with bangles of glass, gilt lac, or base metal. No village of any size but has its goldsmith, to whom is taken from time to time some portion of the family savings to be converted into gold and silver ornaments. Jewellery can be secreted as readily as bullion or coin, and the privilege of wearing it on occasions may reconcile woman to the many disabilities which she suffers in the East. In the larger towns there are skilful workmen, and in jewellery (as with other Indian art handicrafts) certain styles or fashions of make are localised to certain places. Indian jewellery exhibits tastefulness in design and minuteness in execution; but it is not carried to a good finish, where finish is not effective, and is disappointing in the roughness of hinges, fastenings and under-sides. Enamelling on gold and on silver is characteristic of North-Western India. It has suffered from being cheapened to the resources of the tourist market. Silver plate is made in half a dozen districts in decorative styles which were formerly localised but are now generally copied. Most admirable of all is perhaps the deeply chased silver work of Burmese artists.

Woodwork

Wood-carving is distinctively used for the decoration of house doors, windows, and balconies, and it is only the very poor who do not attempt to embellish their homes in this fashion. In Northern India the style shows Persian influence, affecting geometric figures in flat relief ; as one goes southward the ornamentation increases in depth, and in liveliness of imagery ; in the pagodas of Burma these qualities are at their highest, heavy teak beams being carved (or under-cut) throughout their thickness—showing, for instance, in minute detail an ox-cart progressing up the middle of the beam. These arts have been applied to furniture, made for the most part for sale to Europeans. The carved wooden screens of the Punjab are well known, and so was, at one time, the black wood furniture of Bombay. Decoration has been carried further in the case of articles suited, more or less, to the wants of the country, such as small tables, platters and boxes. These are at various places prettily inlaid with brass wire, or with strips of ivory, decorated with coloured lac, or made in carved sandal wood. A foundation of wood pasted over with strips of paper, printed and varnished, is the so-called *papier mâché* work of Kashmir.

Pottery

Earthenware vessels are held to be very easily polluted, and are broken up with little thought. The potter is then essential to domestic life ; but he lives in general contempt on the outskirts of the village. Vessels of glass or porcelain could not be cast aside so heedlessly, and they are not manufactured or used except by Indians of Europeanised habits. House decoration has been then the only possible purpose which could stimulate the development of the potter's art, and for this end the making of painted pottery has grown up under Hindu and of rough glazed ware under Mohammedan influences. The former is coloured after the process of firing. The glazing of pottery was introduced from Central Asia, and in its original use was applied to decorative tiles which are largely and

Bourne and Shepherd, Calcutta

THE HALL OF AUDIENCE IN THE MOGHAL PALACE AT DELHI

effectively used in Mohammedan architecture. The general colouring is in shades of blue. Glazed vessels ornamented in colour are made in several localities. But they are rough in design and in finish.

Stone Work

Where good stone is available, as in Rajputána, it is used for windows and balconies, being elaborately and beautifully carved, generally on the lines followed in woodwork applied to this purpose. The pierced stone lattice-work is particularly effective. Hindu temples are, as a rule, profusely decorated with stone carvings of figures which exhibit a grotesque and sometimes lascivious imagination. In no case do these carvings approach in skill or tastefulness those executed under Greek influence during the two centuries that followed Alexander's conquests, such as have been discovered in great numbers on the sites of ancient Buddhist monasteries in the north-western corner of the Punjab. The elaborate inlaying which was employed by the Mohammedans in decorating their palaces, tombs and mosques limited itself generally to verses from the Koran or to geometric figures. But some of their buildings—notably the Táj at Agra—are profusely inlaid with floral designs in stones of various colours, which, though claimed by some for Indian inventiveness, by their close resemblance to Florentine mosaic assign themselves to Italian artists, several of whom are known to have found employment at the court of the Moghals.

General

In meeting the tendencies that have worked to depress them, Indian handicraftsmen have not been assisted by any active vitality of their own. Generally they are successful only when they adhere to traditional patterns, and vulgarise their designs if they attempt to change them. In this respect they compare unfavourably with the artisans of China and Japan, and there is also a marked inferiority in the finish of their goods,—in details which mark the workman's pride in his accomplishment. Art schools have for some years past been maintained at Calcutta, Lahore, Bombay and Madras. Their scope does not altogether exclude modern art; but they are principally concerned with the art handicrafts of the country, which it is their object to strengthen and revive by the elaboration of design upon traditional lines and the improvement of technique. They can claim some gratifying successes. But it has not been easy to induce men of the artisan class to attend them; and the students drawn from other classes have commonly made use of their diplomas simply in order to obtain employment as clerks.

Modern Factories

So far, this sketch of Indian manufactures has generally illustrated a melancholy loss of ancient vitality, skill, and good taste; we now come to modern developments which although, perhaps, less interesting, are of more importance to human comfort, and at all events display progressive activity. Judged by European standards, manufacturing enterprise is in India still in its infancy; new wants come to the people very slowly, and it is only in textile manufacturing—in the making by machinery of the fabrics that are indigenous to the country—that the progress of the last half century has been at all commensurate with the numbers and intelligence of the population.

Cotton Mills

Cotton mills have grafted themselves intimately upon the life of the country. Fifty years ago there were but two. There are now in British India 217 with 6 million spindles and 75,000 looms, representing a capital of about £12·5 millions. Four-fifths of them are situated on the west coast—mostly at Bombay—where their establishment has attracted the wealth and the talents of the Parsi community. In Upper India there are groups of mills at Delhi, Cawnpore and elsewhere, but in Bengal and Madras they are still remarkably few in number considering the large demand for cotton fabrics. In yarn the aggregate output amounts to 600 million lbs., of which about a third is exported to China and Japan. About a fifth of the yarn is of fine quality—of higher counts than 20's—but for the spinning of these counts it is necessary to import a good deal of cotton from Egypt. The import of English yarn is falling rapidly. In woven (piece) goods the annual output is about 900 million yards. This may still hardly exceed a third of the English piece-goods that are imported; but the Indian mills are becoming formidable rivals to those of Manchester, and in India it is generally suspected that it was owing to the apprehensions of Lancashire manufacturers that when, owing to financial exigencies, customs dues at 3½ per cent. were imposed upon imported cotton piece-goods, an equivalent excise was levied upon Indian manufactures.

Jute Mills

Next in importance come jute mills. Jute fibre anciently provided a clothing material for the poorer classes of Bengal; at present there are none so humble as to wear it. Its value as a material for sacking (gunny) was demonstrated by experiments made in Dundee eighty years ago, and it now furnishes the world with bags and packing cloth. Bengal has, so far, a monopoly of its production. The larger portion of the crop is exported raw to Dundee and places in Germany. But nearly half of it passes through jute mills in Calcutta. There are now sixty such mills with a capital of about £7·5 millions annually turning out cloth and bags to a value of £11 millions.

Other Factories

Of woollen mills there are only four with 25,000 spindles, and 678 looms. The people of Northern India are appreciating the comfort of woollen fabrics for cold-weather wear, and manufacture is expanding rapidly. But Indian wool is unsuitable for cloth of the better kind, and part of the raw material is imported from Australia.

There are a number of iron and brass foundries but they are mostly small businesses, and hardly afford a quarter of the employment that is provided by the State railway workshops. During the last five years the imports of iron and steel have risen from £13 millions to £22 millions in value. It seems probable that at least a quarter of this could be produced locally. But ventures that are unsupported by a protective tariff are risky, unless on a very large scale; and it is only quite recently that large iron and steel works, on modern lines, and with a capital exceeding a million sterling, have been established in the mining districts of Bengal by the enterprise of a Parsi capitalist.

Potteries and tile works are numerous, but are generally small concerns. At least five of them are, however, of industrial importance. Their aims are limited to the coarser manufactures, and their leading output is in glazed drainage pipes.

Leather working has for many years been associated with the important mercantile town of Cawnpore, where the establishment of a Government military harness factory stimulated private enterprise to undertake the manufacture of saddlery, harness and boots. A large number of Indian firms are now engaged in the business, but the lead is taken by some English capitalists who obtained, in a Government contract for army boots, the initial security which free trade denied them. The industry has extended to Bombay and Madras, and India has actually developed a considerable export business (chiefly with South Africa) in boots and shoes. . . .

There are eight paper mills with a capital of £300,000, and an annual output which in value approaches the amount of their capital. But paper is imported in at least double this amount. Printing presses have multiplied exceedingly. They are as a rule petty concerns, and by far the most considerable are those maintained by the Government for its own purposes. . . .

Manufacturing industry, strictly so called, has then little to show beyond cotton and jute mills. Indeed, these mills engage quite 80 per cent. of the total capital invested in mills of all descriptions. But there is a very large business in the preparation of raw produce for export. The oil refineries of Burma are on an American scale, leading the raw product from the wells through 275 miles of pipe line. Cotton and jute presses, rice-husking mills, saw mills, tea factories, sugar refineries, indigo factories, and silk filatures together give employment to a quarter of a million men. Including workshops of all kinds, there are about 2,500 factories inspected under the Factory Act, employing about three-quarters of a million hands. But if we deduct the operatives in cotton and jute mills, those employed in preparing raw produce for export, and the employés of railway workshops, less than 40,000 remain to cover the staff of all other factories. The mass of the people are indebted to modern industrial developments for but little more than the substitution of machine-made cloth for hand-made cloth, of kerosene for vegetable oil, and for their introduction to the conveniences of matches and cigarettes. Factories for the making of both of these have been established. The better classes are less conservative; they have, for instance, discovered that biscuits, ice and aërated water are too attractive for caste prejudices to resist, and these small luxuries are made in very large quantities at prices which to Europeans appear exceedingly low.

General Prospects

The factory system owes its introduction to the capital and enterprise of Europeans; and in Calcutta European capitalists and companies are still by far the largest mill-owners. In Western India they have not remained so prominent; the profits of cotton milling have here attracted large investments of Indian capital, and the Parsis in particular have shown much aptitude not merely for the financing of mills, but for their management and the control of their machinery. Throughout the country there is an increasing disposition to adventure money in starting industries; and small concerns are growing rapidly in number. During the last ten years factories of all kinds that are inspected under the Factory Act have increased in number from 1,207 to 2,051, and employ 40 per cent. more workmen. To provide capable management is the great difficulty, and outside Bombay undertakings of any size rarely attract Indian investors unless they are controlled by a European. Six years ago, under the influence of the cry of "India for the Indians," a large number of purely Indian companies were hastily started in Bengal for the manufacture of pens, pencils, matches, hosiery and soap. They have practically all disappeared, and their failure will discourage Bengali investors for some time to come. Elsewhere industry is advancing, although with timid steps. Enterprise is hampered by the customers' prejudices; there are glass factories, owned by Indians, that are failures because Indians will not drink out of glass. But the country could make a great deal that it now imports, and its existing consumption would doubtless support a wider and more varied industrial enterprise. There, are, however, serious risks in attempting to compete with a well-established line of imports that is prepared to cut prices in order to stifle a rival industry. Undertakings which may thrive at economic prices may perish in infancy unless these prices are assured. Indian manufactures have enjoyed no such security, and it is probable that they would have covered a far wider field had they, like those of almost every other country of the world, been assisted in their enterprise by a protective tariff.

Factory Labour

The wages paid to the ordinary run of Indian factory hands run from threepence to eightpence a day. When they exceed the lower rate they provide the coolie with a balance which he not infrequently values as a means of providing a holiday from work. The conditions of factory employ differ very greatly from those of western countries: the employés work less strenuously, less continuously and have a far lower standard of comfort. But serious abuses have compelled the State to legislate for their protection in 1881, in 1891, and in 1911. Under the law, as last amended, the factory day is limited to thirteen and a half hours for all classes of labour in textile mills, and in other mills for women and children, and the maximum number of working hours is fixed at twelve hours, eleven hours, and six hours for men, women and children respectively. The employment of children under seven is prohibited. Sunday labour is disallowed except for industries of a specified nature, and there are provisions to ensure proper water supply, ventilation and cleanliness, and the protection of the workpeople against injury.

8—(2134)

CHAPTER VI

COMMERCE

THE caravans which slowly trail their way through the passes of Afghanistán are following the oldest of the trade-routes between India and the Mediterranean Sea; by it, in remote antiquity, specimens of Indian treasures reached the courts of Assyria and Egypt. In less ancient days, but centuries before the commencement of our era, land carriage was shortened by the use of the sea, either to the head of the Persian Gulf or to Aden, whence goods were carried, respectively, across the desert to Damascus, or up the east coast of the Red Sea. The navigation of the Red Sea was not attempted till later: its accomplishment made Egypt the principal *entrepôt* for the Indian trade during the period of the Roman empire. The conquests of the Arabs advanced commerce. Those of the Turks extinguished it; and the Turkish annexation of Mesopotamia in the thirteenth, and of Egypt in the sixteenth century, closed the Persian Gulf and the Red Sea. Thus shut off from India the nations of Europe found a new passage round the Cape of Good Hope. But, with the piercing of the isthmus of Suez, the traffic has returned to its ancient channel.

So long as the trade was conducted by caravan, either wholly or partly, it was necessarily limited to valuables of small bulk. With the opening of the Red Sea, silk and cotton fabrics and spices reached the Mediterranean in considerable quantities, and these were the attractions which excited the commercial rivalry of the Portuguese, Dutch, French, Danes, Germans and English in the sixteenth, seventeenth and eighteenth centuries. The English trading company which emerged victorious from the conflict took pains to give a wider scope to the commerce: notable additions were indigo, sugar and raw silk.

Its transactions were very profitable; but, judged by present standards, their extent was small. In 1834, the earliest year for which a record is available, the Indian trade was worth no more than £14 millions—less than an eighteenth of its present value.

Within the last half century the trade has grown very largely and has changed its character. India is no longer a curiosity shop; she has become a corn exchange, and her exports consist in the main of raw produce. The opening of the all-sea route round the Cape made the carriage of bulky goods possible; but the profits from their transport were diminished by the length of the journey and the risk of damage. In these respects commerce benefited enormously by the opening of the Suez Canal in 1870; and, to turn this route to best advantage, there has been a revolution in the character of the shipping. Twenty-five years ago there were over 7,000 sailing vessels engaged in the foreign trade of India, with a tonnage equal to half that of the steam vessels. Their numbers have fallen by 54 per cent. and their tonnage by 85 per cent. On the other hand, steam vessels have doubled their number and trebled their capacity. Over 6,000 are employed in the Indian trade with a capacity of 13 million tons.

But these developments would not have sufficed completely to change the character of the Indian trade had they not been accompanied by the active construction of railways. Fifty years ago there were only 300 miles of railway in the country, and the total value of its foreign trade was less than £40 millions. The railway mileage is now over 32,000, and the value of the trade exceeds £260 millions. Until the interior of the country was opened out, heavy masses of raw produce could not be brought to the seaboard, except where the ports were served by a river,—and this advantage is only possessed by Calcutta and Rangoon. The mileage of the

Indian railways now exceeds that of every European country except Germany and Russia, and in either of these is out-distanced but little. In proportion to population the comparison is not, of course, so favourable; to every mile of railway there are in India five times as many people as in England, and three times as many as in Russia. The Indian ratio corresponds very nearly with that of Japan. Indian railway rates are exceedingly low. Goods are carried at an average rate of two-fifths of a penny per ton per mile; a third-class passenger can travel five miles for a penny. The railways are served by a network of roads, 37,000 miles of which are metalled. But there is little transport by water. The Indian rivers, at any distance from the sea, run very low during the dry months. The irrigation canals were generally so constructed as to be serviceable for navigation, but, except upon the eastern coast, they are scarcely used for the purpose. They rarely connect with trade centres, and they are liable to be closed periodically for repairs. River navigation is, however, of importance in Eastern Bengal, Assam and Burma, where the Brahmaputra and Irrawaddy rivers carry fleets of steamers.

The statistics on the next page give some idea of the growth and conditions of Indian foreign (sea-borne) trade during the past twenty-two years.

The exports do not consist entirely of Indian produce: they include some imports that are re-exported. But the amount of this passing trade is relatively small; it does not contribute more than 2 per cent. of the value of the exports. The imports include consignments from England to Government departments: these consist in the main of railway material, and have in some years amounted to over £5 millions. In 1910–11 they were valued at £2,900,981, constituting about 3 per cent. of the total.

The business in treasure is also complicated by Government transactions. Ordinarily the State has exported

Bourne and Shepherd, Calcutta

MOON-LIT VIEW OF THE RIVER HOOGLY AT CALCUTTA

	Annual Averages of the Seven Years:			Actuals of 1910–11.
	1889–90 to 1895–96.	1896–97 to 1902–03.	1903–04 to 1909–10.	
	£	£	£	£
Exports—				
Merchandise	71,251,304	74,810,512	111,260,297	140,111,850
Treasure	2,939,227	5,981,889	6,756,261	4,752,307
Total	74,190,531	80,792,401	118,016,558	144,864,157
Imports—				
Merchandise	47,651,780	52,634,735	77,581,482	89,136,992
Treasure	10,717,800	13,622,993	24,458,785	26,514,690
Total	58,369,580	66,257,728	105,040,267	115,651,682
Grand Total	132,560,111	147,050,129	225,056,825	260,515,839
Net Import of Treasure	7,778,640	7,635,770	17,702,524	21,762,382
Excess of Exports over Imports	15,820,951	14,534,673	12,965,291	29,212,475

or imported little ; but during the second and third septennial periods it purchased silver in very large quantities (in one year to the amount of £11 millions) for being minted into rupees. These purchases practically ceased in 1910–11. In this year the exports and imports of treasure were almost wholly on private account.

Within the twenty-two years the gross amount of the trade has almost doubled itself. The second septennial period was disturbed by two severe famines which seriously delayed the expansion of commerce ; but thenceforward the increase has been fairly steady and exceedingly rapid. The Indian trade now exceeds by 30 per cent. that transacted by China and Japan, taken together. But, in proportion to the population of the whole of India, its value is still very small, falling at an average of only 17s. per head. The import traffic provides each head of population with goods or treasure to the amount of 7s. only. It is worth remark that in Burma, where caste does not prevail and the women are free, the people import to a value of 17s. per head. This agrees very nearly with the rate of importation into the Philippines (where also expenditure is not restricted by caste and the *zenana* system), if we exclude consignments of food-stuffs from our calculation. These islands are not, like India, self-supporting.

The exports of merchandise in normal years exceed the imports very largely indeed. A portion of the excess is balanced by the importation of gold and silver, which as a rule disappears into private hoards. India has always used her commerce to draw the precious metals from the countries of the West ; so far back as the time of Pliny, the Indian trade was reproached with its accompanying loss of gold and silver. The Indian people have never found the commodities of Europe so attractive as Indian products are to European households, and they have always exacted part payment in cash. The people of

Eastern Bengal, for instance, annually realise about 10s. per head by the sale of a single product—jute—and put by much of the price in hoards of gold or silver. For a country of so vast a population as India the annual absorption of the precious metals is perhaps not very large; but it has been continuing for centuries, and in spite of the disbursements occasioned by famine, the people's hoards must in the aggregate be enormous. The annual imports of treasure have risen in twenty years from £7 millions to £17 millions; during 1910–11 they actually exceeded £21 millions.

But, after taking into account importations of treasure, a balance remains; the exports still exceed the imports in value by an amount ranging from £12 millions to £20 millions a year. This excess is, generally speaking, covered by the cash payments which are due from the Indian Government in London; merchants who owe money in India for goods consigned to them pay into the India Office in London instead of remitting to Bombay or Calcutta; and receive orders for rupees on the Indian Treasury. The process by which this adjustment is effected is the sale of bills in London by the Secretary of State. The amount that is annually payable in London by the Indian Government—the "home charges," as they are termed—may be taken as £18 millions. About half of this sum is owed for stores, and for interest that is due on Indian Government loans, contracted in sterling. This much represents actual cash value received, for, although India might profit more largely could she raise her loans locally, she cannot do so, and is no worse off in using British capital than is, for instance, the Argentine Republic. The balance of the home payments are for Army charges, pensions and the maintenance of the India Office. These obligations may seem expensive; but deliberations inspired by the sincerest of purposes have been unable to find means of retrenchment which would not prejudice the efficiency of government. And India, it must be remembered, is charged nothing for the protection she receives from the British fleet.

Two tables are appended to this chapter stating in some detail the export and import trade of the year ending on the 31st March, 1911, and comparing it with the trade that was transacted five years previously.

Export Trade

During these five years the export trade in Indian merchandise has increased by 30 per cent.—equivalent to £32 millions. Agricultural produce enters into it so very largely that its volume is liable to great and sudden fluctuations according as harvests are short or plentiful, and the crops of 1910–11 were decidedly good. But if we compare the exports not of single years but of seven years' periods, we need not exclude years of famine to find that they have progressed substantially; and this indicates an increase in the productive resources of the country, since, taking India as a whole, the development of its export business does not ordinarily entail the importation of food grain. Indeed India generally exports food grain largely. This is not, however, the case with every part of the country. The cultivation of jute in Bengal and of tea in Assam is in great measure dependent upon the importation of rice from Burma.

Of the £137 millions that express the total value of the Indian merchandise exported, not more than £23 millions represent manufactured goods, and, if the production of cotton and jute mills are excluded, the share which manufacture contributes to the exports hardly amounts in value to £2 millions. The exports of manufactured cotton and jute are of much importance, the former being worth £8 millions, and the latter £11 millions. But 50 per cent. of the cotton goods consist of yarn, mainly consigned to China, where it is losing ground before the competition of the mills of Shanghai and Japan. In woven cloth the trade has better prospects, since it supplies countries in Asia and Africa where, as yet, no cotton mills have been established. The export trade in manufactured jute is in a stronger position. The principal customers are the United States, Australia, and Argentina, which use this material for bagging their exports of raw produce.

But 84 per cent. of the exports are of unmanufactured goods, and India under present conditions may be likened to a reservoir of raw produce which is drawn upon by all the countries of the world. Some portion of the produce undergoes a process of preparation which affords employment to industrial labour: cotton, for instance, is ginned and pressed; indigo, opium, tea and sugar are all manipulated in factories. But articles of this kind constitute no large proportion of the exports, which for the most part are consigned as received from the hands of the cultivators. An export trade of this character is consistent with the prosperity of a thinly populated country such as Canada and Argentina. But for the dense population of India it leaves much to be desired.

In 1910–11 the exports of raw produce were headed by grain (£25 millions), mainly consisting of wheat (£9 millions) and rice (£15 millions). The former was consigned for the most part to the United Kingdom; the latter was distributed over the four quarters of the globe. Next in importance was cotton (£22 millions), for which the principal customer was Japan. But large consignments were made to the chief countries of Europe. Oilseeds followed (£16 millions), being, like rice, very widely distributed. Raw jute was exported to the value of £10 millions: less than half was consigned to Dundee, Germany taking the largest share of the balance. For hides (£8 millions) the American demand is considerable. Opium and tea each were valued at £8 millions: the former was mainly for consumption in China and in countries of the Far East where there is an immigrant Chinese population: of the latter the United Kingdom received rather less than two-thirds. The growth of the export of tea to Russia is a satisfactory feature. Other exports of some magnitude are: wool (£2 millions), lac (£1·4 million), fibres (£0·8 million), fruits (£0·6 million), spices (£0·5 million), myrobalans (£0·4 million), and indigo (£0·2 million). Sugar, silk and tobacco were exported, but were at the same time imported in larger quantities. The excess is remarkable in the case of sugar, anciently a typical Indian product, which was imported to a value of over £8 millions, nineteen-fold the value of the exports. The growing dependence of India upon other countries for its sugar is one of the most curious features of its economic condition.

Import Trade

Turning now to the import trade, we find that during the five years it rose by £30 millions, an increase which in amount is a little less, but as a percentage is considerably more than the increase in the export trade. Imports consist almost wholly of manufactured goods, and there is at present very little demand for foreign raw materials to feed local manufactories. Some portion, no doubt, of the metals that the country receives is imported in an unfinished condition, and much of the copper goes to maintain the industry of Indian coppersmiths and brass-workers. But apart from this, very little is imported in order to be made up in the country. This is, however, only to be expected. India possesses raw material in abundance, and could develop factory industries upon her own resources.

Cotton yarn and piece-goods amount in value to nearly £30 millions, and dwarf into comparative insignificance all other imports. They are almost wholly the product of Lancashire cotton-mills, foreign mills hardly contributing a tenth; and the assistance which this business yields to English manufacturing industry is perhaps the chiefest of the material advantages that England derives from the Indian Empire. The importation of yarn has been declining before the rivalry of Indian mills and now amounts to no more than £2 millions. The business in woven fabrics (piece-goods) is still growing. During the five years 1903–04 to 1905–06 it expanded rapidly—at the rate of 10 per cent. per annum. It then received a set-back—possibly owing to political unrest, which endeavoured to maintain a boycott of British goods. But it has since recovered much of the ground then lost. Of the countries which compete with England in the trade—at a great distance behind her—Japan, Germany, Holland, and Belgium are gaining ground rapidly. But their consignments remain comparatively insignificant.

If metals are taken to include machinery, railway plant and hardware, the imports reach the high value of £16·8 millions. They have doubled within the last ten years and are at present in more progressive demand than cotton goods. The purchases of railway material have trebled within this period, owing to the energetic development of railway communication. The imports of machinery have lately been fluctuating between £3 millions and £4 millions in value, but are twice as large as they were ten years ago; in these years the number of jute mills in Calcutta has grown from thirty-six to sixty. Both railway material, and machinery are almost wholly supplied by British makers. The imports of hardware (£2·2 millions) have also doubled. Two-thirds of these are supplied by the United Kingdom. Metals that are not covered by these three headings amount in value to £9·6 millions. Ten years ago their value only just exceeded £5 millions. The principal, in order of importance, are iron, steel and copper. Four-fifths of the iron is British, and the imports from Belgium—Britain's chief competitor—are not increasing. To the imports of steel the United Kingdom contributes much less considerably—something over a half; but here again British factories are gaining ground. Ten years ago they supplied less than those in Belgium; since then Belgian consignments have risen by 50 per cent., but the British consignments have doubled. Germany contributes only a twentieth. Within the ten years the imports of copper have risen in value from £0·7 million to £1·7 million. Half of them are British. Germany contributes substantially—about a quarter; and her consignments have increased with extraordinary rapidity—by no less than twenty-five-fold—and are growing steadily.

Sugar is imported to a value of £8·7 millions, and here again we find that within the last ten years the consignments to India have doubled. The character of the trade has changed remarkably. Four years ago beet-sugar was imported from Germany and Austria to a value of about £2 millions. It has now given place to cane-sugar from Java and from Mauritius in the proportion of about 3 to 1. In ancient days Indians do not appear to have been familiar with the refining of sugar, and the ordinary product of the Indian cane is still a conglomerate of sugar crystals and molasses. Some portion of the refined sugar that is imported is actually reduced to this condition before it is placed on the market.

Woollen fabrics and apparel are each imported to a value of £2 millions, and silken fabrics to a value of £1·8 million. Other considerable imports are provisions (£2 millions), spices (£1 million), liquors (£1·2 million), books and stationery (£1·3 million), kerosene oil (£1·7 million), and glassware (£1 million). The trade in all of these goods, except in liquors, has been increasing rapidly. The imports of liquor stand almost alone in showing no response to increasing prosperity. The consignments of beer and wine have actually decreased; and there has also been a considerable fall in the production of the breweries that have been established in India on European lines. On the other hand, imported spirits have increased by 24 per cent. during the last ten years, and their increased consumption is due in some measure to the growing disregard by educated Indians of the obligation of caste rules. Japan contributes most of the silk. The kerosene oil is almost wholly American; a few years ago Russian oil held the market, but it has now lost it almost entirely.

General Condition of British Trade

For many years the British merchants who were engaged in the Indian trade endeavoured to safeguard their profits by closing the door against not only foreigners but countrymen of their own. But for a long time past, under the less interested policy of the British Parliament, the Indian markets have been thrown open to the world; the British have retained for themselves no special privileges, and merchants from other European countries—in particular from Germany—have settled freely in Calcutta, Bombay and Rangoon. It is interesting to examine how far in these circumstances of free competition British merchants have retained the advantages which they have gained by their priority in the field, and the prestige of their flag.

Of the total trade of India, export and import, only two-fifths is now transacted with the United Kingdom. But this is a fact of little significance. The raw produce which India exports can in great measure be obtained from other countries with equal profit, and British merchants have no particular object in securing a large portion of it. India supplies the United Kingdom with the greater part of its tea; but Indian wheat only supplements the despatches which are made from temperate countries, and British factories hardly require more cotton, jute and oilseeds from India, at current prices, than they receive. Accordingly the share taken by the United Kingdom in the Indian export trade is no more than a quarter. Even so it is much larger than that of any other country. It is three times the share of Germany, and four times the share of Japan, the two countries which are India's next largest customers. Nor do British purchases of Indian products show any sign of declining. They are increasing quite as rapidly as the purchases of all other nations taken together. It is true that the export business transacted with some other nations has increased still more rapidly; the purchases of Belgium, Austria, and Italy have doubled within the last ten years, and those of Germany and the United States have increased by 75 per cent. But these increases have not been secured by any reduction of the British share, which remains substantially as large, in proportion, as it was ten years ago.

The import trade touches British interests more nearly, since its conditions directly affect the profits of British factories, and the employment of British workmen. Here the British share is much more considerable. It is 62 per cent. of the total import trade, but it rises to 80 per cent., if we exclude lines of commerce in which the United Kingdom cannot pretend to compete,—that is to say, the imports from all African and Asiatic countries except Japan, and the import of kerosene oil from America, of silk from the continent of Europe and Japan, and of horses from Australia. British factories, then, supply India with four-fifths of the goods which they could possibly expect to supply, leaving only a fifth for the factories of all the other manufacturing countries of the world. British consignments show no sign of losing ground: they increase *pari passu* with the general increase of the Indian import trade—indeed, during the past ten years they have gained a little. The United Kingdom is not even distantly approached by any other country. Java, which owes to her sugar the next largest share, holds only 7 per cent. of the import trade. Next comes Belgium with 4 per cent., and Germany with 3 per cent. Belgium has increased her trade more rapidly than the United Kingdom, but this is not the case with Germany. Austria, having ceased to despatch beet-sugar, now supplies only 2 per cent. of the imports. France supplies less than Austria. Russia has lost the trade in kerosene oil and her share is negligible. By gaining this trade the United States have trebled their Indian business during the last ten years. But it amounts to only 4 per cent. of the total. Of Asiatic countries Japan holds, after Java, the largest share; she sends silk, metals and cotton hosiery, and her consignments have increased far more rapidly than those of any other country. But so far they form only 2 per cent. of the total.

British manufactures then dominate the Indian market, and at present show no signs of losing ground before those of continental Europe. The most dangerous rivalry they may apprehend appears to be from Japan. But, so far, it exists in apprehension only.

To its profits on trading with India the United Kingdom adds very large earnings made in carrying for other countries. Transacting two-fifths of the total trade of India, export and import, it owns in tonnage nearly four-fifths of the shipping that enters and leaves Indian ports. Here it has been losing ground. Ten years ago British shipping was even more in evidence than at present. Within this period it has indeed increased by nearly 80 per cent. But German and Austrian shipping engaged in the Indian trade has doubled, that of Japan has trebled, and that of Holland increased by twenty-six-fold.

TRANS-FRONTIER LAND TRADE

The mountains which guard the Indian frontier on the north-west, north, and north-east permit some trade to cross their passes. Compared with the sea-borne traffic it is of quite inconsiderable amount. The value of the land trans-frontier trade is about £9 millions ; but more than half of this is transacted with open country in Nepal, and the Shan States of Siam, which lie within the mountain chain. The traffic with Afghanistán and Turkestán that follows the Khyber Pass does not amount in value to £1·5 million a year ; and this is six-fold the trade which Tibet affords to Indian markets.

Exports from British India by Sea to Foreign Countries during the Years 1905–06 and 1910–11: Quantities and Values

Articles.		1905–06. Quantity.	1905–06. Value.	1910–11. Quantity.	1910–11. Value.
			£		£
Animals	no.	254,817	140,296	466,583	160,067
Apparel		—	225,826	—	252,211
Bristles and Fibre for brushes and brooms	cwt.	93,873	143,402	99,938	160,436
Candles	lbs.	6,057,566	111,267	5,503,876	104,297
Caoutchouc and manufactures		—	87,570	—	112,755
Carriages and Carts, and parts thereof		—	23,551	—	38,002
Coal and Coke	tons.	836,188	436,628	889,610	513,408
Chemicals		—	274,126	—	269,267
Coffee	cwt.	362,408	1,109,512	273,230	890,124
Coir and manufactures of (excluding cordage)		—	368,594	—	472,164
Cotton, Raw	cwt.	7,399,723	14,227,816	8,686,400	22,703,718
Cotton Twist and Yarn	lbs.	298,524,567	8,299,963	184,394,436	5,805,277
Cotton manufactures		—	2,256,955	—	2,607,036
Total Cotton and Cotton Goods		—	24,784,734	—	32,316,032
Drugs and Medicines		—	146,767	—	201,594
Dyes and Tans—					
Indigo	cwt.	31,186	390,918	16,939	223,529
Cutch	,,	55,070	57,591	90,988	111,318
Myrobalans	,,	1,206,398	297,245	1,658,895	465,097
Other sorts	,,	82,291	56,723	113,104	96,180
Total Dyes and Tans (except Lac)		—	802,611	—	896,125
Fodder, Bran, and Cattle Food—					
Oilcake	cwt.	1,474,912	346,613	1,184,536	315,274
Rice bran	tons	189,142	369,455	188,939	454,049
Other sorts	cwt.	350,200	71,627	195,454	46,431
Fruits and Vegetables		—	248,635	—	677,526
Grain and Pulse—					
Rice (including Paddy)	cwt.	43,042,965	12,425,571	48,017,376	15,497,682
Wheat (including Flour)	,,	19,649,523	6,115,150	26,728,054	9,059,797

EXPORTS FROM BRITISH INDIA BY SEA TO FOREIGN COUNTRIES DURING THE YEARS 1905–06 AND 1910–11: QUANTITIES AND VALUES (*continued*)

Articles.		1905–06.		1910–11.	
		Quantity.	Value.	Quantity.	Value.
Grain and Pulse (continued)—			£		£
Pulse	cwt.	2,136,517	537,019	2,485,654	667,853
Gram	,,	417,672	97,680	909,012	242,356
Other sorts	,,	1,941,564	513,519	1,120,797	263,251
Total Grain and Pulse	,,	67,188,241	19,686,274	78,660,893	25,737,608
Gums and Resins	,,	93,960	111,040	99,460	130,229
Hardware and Cutlery (including Plated Ware)	..	—	103,086	—	125,685
Hemp, and manufactures of	..	—	361,437	—	410,155
Hides and Skins	cwt.	1,823,822	9,171,554	1,695,689	8,723,681
Horn and Hornmeal	,,	73,728	123,173	85,444	162,103
Ivory, and manufactures of	..	—	29,442	—	31,828
Instruments, Apparatus and Appliances, and parts thereof	..	—	18,637	—	33,837
Jadestone	cwt.	1,796	50,975	2,737	57,997
Jewellery and plate, and precious stones	..	—	99,586	—	76,307
Jute, Raw	cwt.	14,480,407	11,417,109	12,732,460	10,326,649
Jute Manufactures—					
Bags	no.	233,326,201	4,052,260	360,880,236	5,709,361
Cloth	yds.	658,671,353	4,203,340	955,300,737	5,571,742
Other kinds	..	—	43,095	—	48,816
Total Jute and Jute goods	..	—	19,715,804	—	21,656,568
Lac dye, Shell, etc.	cwt.	274,445	2,120,077	421,629	1,428,038
Machinery and Millwork	..	—	19,893	—	32,612
Manures	tons	131,656	473,136	159,659	686,150
Metals—					
Copper	cwt.	9,301	35,094	12,016	46,996
Iron	,,	467,550	99,545	742,737	115,280
Tin	,,	1,270	8,512	4,509	26,783
Lead	,,	3,693	3,057	267,773	191,658
Manganese ore	,,	6,333,881	287,607	11,459,581	612,653

Other sorts	cwt.	77,885	£50,753	65,697	£79,973
Total Metals	,,	6,893,580	484,570	12,552,313	1,073,346
Mica	,,	131,554	159,627	42,593	188,983
Oils—					
Mineral	gals.	3,055,610	95,369	2,780,139	166,743
Paraffin wax	cwt.	56,795	77,226	241,505	368,008
Castor	gals.	1,432,108	114,139	1,203,007	112,697
Cocoanut	,,	1 508,424	148,445	1,934,608	232,643
Other sorts	,,	897,041	146,514	1,216,002	197,040
Total Oils	,,	—	581,694	—	1,077,131
Opium	chests	62,936	6,314,511	43,921	8,509,316
Provisions		—	589,846	—	818,069
Saltpetre	cwt.	336,429	256,861	327,657	248,153
Seeds	,,	17,575,951	7,072,949	30,983,753	16,750,192
Silk, Raw	lbs.	1,848,646	384,981	1,920,831	344,870
Silk, Manufactures of		—	90,860	—	88,433
Total Silk and Silk Goods		—	475,842	—	433,303
Spices	lbs.	38,801,748	625,775	34,086,324	557,613
Sugar	cwt.	442,201	257,575	522,112	320,315
Tea	lbs.	215,005,346	5,933,113	254,968,395	8,307,606
Tobacco	,,	14,284,780	157,355	19,553,814	234,517
Wax (excluding Candles)	cwt.	8,637	48,971	8,553	49,245
Wood and manufactures of		—	606,359	—	739,995
Wool, Raw	lbs.	47,559,123	1,581,885	64,060,283	2,087,398
Wool, Manufactures of		—	173,877	—	206,042
Total Wool and Woollen Goods		—	1,755,763	—	2,293,441
All other articles		—	647,057	—	1,150,964
TOTAL MERCHANDISE (PRIVATE)[1]		—	107,812,022	—	140,058,794
Treasure (private)—					
Gold		—	3,527,322	—	2,610,264
Silver		—	772,516	—	2,136,087
TOTAL MERCHANDISE AND TREASURE (PRIVATE)		—	112,111,860	—	144,805,146
Government Exports—					
Merchandise		—	78,392	—	53,056
Treasure		—	6,013,499	—	5,956
GRAND TOTAL OF EXPORTS		—	118,203,751	—	144,864,158

	£	£
[1] Indian	105,459,482	137,218,095
Foreign (Re-exports)	2,352,540	2,840,699

IMPORTS INTO BRITISH INDIA BY SEA FROM FOREIGN COUNTRIES DURING THE YEARS 1905-06 AND 1910-11: QUANTITIES AND VALUES

Articles.		1905–06.		1910–11.	
		Quantity.	Value.	Quantity.	Value.
			£		£
Apparel		—	1,477,559	—	2,065,117
Arms, Ammunition, etc.		—	146,897	—	216,348
Books, Paper, and Stationery		—	937,870	—	1,371,436
Building and Engineering materials		—	306,609	—	464,044
Cabinetware and Furniture		—	105,144	—	135,908
Carriages and Carts		—	512,075	—	854,271
Chemicals		—	459,475	—	584,098
Clocks and Watches		—	124,710	—	134,333
Coal, Coke, etc.	tons	179,935	214,119	334,181	381,414
Cotton, Raw	cwt.	161,476	360,205	45,291	128,509
Cotton Twist and Yarn	lbs.	45,776,742	2,283,593	32,503,657	2,091,503
Cotton Piece Goods and manufactures		—	26,011,798	—	27,801,689
Total Cotton and Cotton Goods		—	28,655,616	—	30,021,702
Drugs and Medicines		—	423,293	—	656,956
Dyes		—	631,520	—	842,820
Flax manufactures		—	137,599	—	175,169
Fruits and Vegetables		—	71,086	—	98,104
Glass and manufactures of		—	749,807	—	1,045,488
Grain and Pulse	cwt.	622,234	205,093	223,123	97,449
Gums and Resins	,,	153,772	130,285	139,153	137,366
Hardware, Cutlery, and Plate		—	1,510,488	—	2,231,274
Hides and Skins, raw and dressed, and Leather		—	361,277	—	416,291
Horses	no.	11,457	311,670	11,444	363,434
Instruments and Appliances		—	608,579	—	824,565

Ivory, and manufactures of		—	£112,938	—	£197,743
Jewellery and Plate, and Precious Stones		—	33,111	—	667,925
Jute manufactures		—	89,821	—	105,183
Liquors—					
Ale, Beer, and Porter	gals.	5,002,448	419,707	4,242,771	367,130
Spirits	,,	1,621,492	725,232	1,537,145	715,419
Wines and Cider	,,	350,578	200,267	343,082	182,895
Total Liquors	,,	6,974,518	1,345,208	6,122,998	1,265,444
Machinery and Millwork		—	3,283,787	—	3,153,640
Matches		—	392 083	—	559,411
Metals—					
Iron	cwt.	4,710,334	2,271,794	5,598,651	3,310,991
Steel	,,	5,700,274	2,157,478	7,256,363	2,983,899
Brass	cwt.	10,783	46,285	18,593	70,098
Copper	,,	271,517	956,495	732,914	2,473,978
Spelter	,,	74,672	99,328	95,289	125,394
Tin	,,	21,152	161,153	38,729	302,824
German Silver	,,	21,527	101,171	23,055	123,958
Lead	,,	143,844	126,717	136,501	119,335
Quicksilver	lbs.	256,562	26,641	352,856	39,608
Unenumerated	cwt.	22,370	74,940	27,302	108,669
Total Metals	,,	10,978,764	6,028,471	13,930,547	9,657,858
Kerosene	gals.	50,946,017	1,191,170	56,597,734	1,589,896
Other Oils	,,	11,707,095	438,577	24,213,135	814,155
Paints and Colours		—	328,357	—	443,889
Perfumery		—	19,263	—	23,594
Pitch, Tar, and Dammer		—	65, 584	—	77,381
Porcelain and Earthenware		—	224,052	—	309,448
Provisions		—	1,590,412	—	2,019,585
Railway Plant and Rolling Stock		—	1,081,745	—	2,830,221
Salt	tons	464,531	438,124	480,775	467,371
Ships, Parts of		—	70,753	—	66,357
Silk, Raw	lbs.	1,645,696	474,603	2,121,799	568,186
Silk manufactures		—	1,267,673	—	1,843,081
Total Silk and Silk Goods		—	1,742,276	—	2,411,268

IMPORTS INTO BRITISH INDIA BY SEA FROM FOREIGN COUNTRIES DURING THE YEARS 1905–06 AND 1910–11: QUANTITIES AND VALUES (*continued*)

Articles.		1905–06.		1910–11.	
		Quantity.	Value.	Quantity.	Value.
			£		£
Soap	cwt.	188,641	212,726	275,243	358,231
Spices	lbs.	117,034,410	733,725	156,845,355	1,027,767
Sugar	cwt.	8,271,129	5,183,013	14,782,038	8,777,977
Tallow	,,	34,126	54,447	42,569	79,933
Tea	lbs.	3,799,272	122,328	4,625,327	138,338
Tea Chests		—	127,868	—	252,178
Tobacco	lbs.	5,511,205	440,587	1,803,071	327,612
Toys and Games		—	194,104	—	258,085
Umbrellas and Fittings		—	227,461	—	267,587
Wood, and manufactures of		—	606,261	—	589,405
Wool, Raw	lbs.	2,908,039	61,226	3,140,255	107,398
Wool, Manufactures of		—	1,616,792	—	2,013,124
Total Wool and Woollen Goods		—	1,678,018	—	2,120,522
All other Articles		—	5,932,215	—	5,917,456
TOTAL MERCHANDISE (PRIVATE)		—	68,722,713	—	86,236,011
Treasure (private)—					
Gold		—	9,828,647	—	18,593,984
Silver		—	4,118,878	—	7,874,853
TOTAL MERCHANDISE AND TREASURE (PRIVATE)		—	82,670,239	—	112,704,848
Government Imports—					
Merchandise		—	6,019,781	—	2,900,981
Treasure		—	7,153,149	—	45,853
GRAND TOTAL OF IMPORTS		—	95,843,170	—	115,651,683

PART II
THE PEOPLE

CHAPTER VII

POPULATION, RACES AND CASTES

INDIA is the home of about a fifth of the human race. No other part of the world except China offers such ample facilities for leading a simple and frugal life of moderate industry. The climate reduces human wants to their fewest, and the land requires little labour and a trifling outlay for the bestowal of its produce. According to the last census (of March, 1911), the population of the country is 315,132,537, of which 244,267,542 inhabit British provinces and 70,864,995 Native States. On India as a whole this population falls at the rate of 170 to the square mile, but if uninhabited wastes, hillsides and jungles are excluded, the density is far greater. Indeed, two-thirds of the population is concentrated in a quarter of the total area. The Indo-Gangetic plain is much more thickly inhabited than the peninsula. Each square mile of it contains on an average from 500 to 600 inhabitants. Over large tracts the crowding is much closer, there being 800 people to the square mile, and even more. On an average three persons live upon the proceeds of two cultivated acres: in some very congested localities two persons make shift with the proceeds of a single cultivated acre. And this, moreover, with a population which is almost wholly rural. There are only thirteen towns with more than 100,000 inhabitants, and their contribution is lost in the immensity of the total.

The peninsula is less crowded with humanity. Cultivated stretches of black soil rarely support more than 200 persons to the square mile—usually not more than 160. The rice country lying along the seaboard is peopled more thickly. In some places it is inhabited as densely as the Indo-Gangetic plain. On the other hand, there are vast expanses of hill and jungle, each square mile of which hardly affords subsistence for twenty roving aborigines.

During the ten years 1902 to 1911 the population increased but moderately—by 7 per cent.; yet this increase represents an addition of more than twenty millions—a good-sized nation. The increase would have been far larger had it not been for the ravages of plague, which during the decade caused nearly six and a half million deaths. Fever was unusually malignant in the western portions of the Indo-Gangetic plain. Mortality resulting from these two diseases was so severe as to balance the increase from births: indeed the Punjab and the United Provinces, with a population of sixty-six millions, actually suffered a decrease of more than 1 per cent. The population of Burma increased by 15 per cent. and that of Eastern Bengal by 11 per cent. Elsewhere the largest increases were in the hilly tracts of the peninsula, and in many cases went to replenish losses which famine had occasioned during the preceding decade. Thus, the Central Provinces, which between 1892 and 1911 lost 8 per cent. of their population, during 1902–1911 added 16 per cent. to it. By a phenomenally high birth-rate (which in India often succeeds years of famine) the people of these provinces increased nearly as much in ten years as they would ordinarily have increased in twenty.

During the three preceding decades, the increase of the population was respectively 1½ per cent., 13 per cent., and 2½ per cent. The first and third of these periods were troubled by grievous famines which resulted in heavy mortality. Now the country is being scourged by plague.

The fecundity of the population and the destructive forces of Nature are in violent antagonism, and extraordinary oscillations are the result. Cholera is endemic in Bengal, and in some years sweeps through the country. Twelve years ago a disease which is believed to be communicated by the bed bug destroyed a fifth of the population in parts of Assam. Still more destructive is malarial fever. It is a persistent evil, with debilitating effects far worse than those of famine, ordinarily exacting a heavy toll of mortality, and in some years—particularly after an abnormal variation of the rainfall—almost decimating the inhabitants of regions that it attacks.

Racial Differences

It is a difficult and doubtful undertaking to discriminate the races which comprise a population, and in India not less so than in Europe. The race which is generally assumed to be indigenous to the country is characterised by rather low stature, very dark complexion, black (often curly) hair, and a very broad nose. These peculiarities mark the inhabitants of the hilly portion of the peninsula and of its southern districts—peoples which have collectively been termed the "Dravidian" race. They all speak languages that have no connection with Sanskrit. In places there occur vestiges of still earlier *strata* of humanity. But for practical purposes the Dravidians may be considered to form the original population of India. Upon them have fallen streams of immigrants from the north—from both the western and eastern extremities of the Himalayan barrier—who subjugated them, generally took wives from amongst them, but pressed them collectively towards the south. The most remarkable of these immigrations was that of a tribe, or tribes, allied to the nations of Europe, possessing a language—Sanskrit—which has its closest European affinity with the Lettish which is spoken on the shores of the Baltic.[1] These tribes are generally known as the *Aryans* (or "nobles") because in their own writings they so entitled themselves. They are supposed to have entered India before 1500 B.C., the epoch at which appeared (in the sacred hymns known as the *Vedas*) the beginnings of a Sanskrit literature which developed extraordinary wealth and brilliancy. It has exercised, and still exercises, enormous influence upon Indian ideas, customs and religion. A branch of the family settled in Persia. Their colonies in India were concentrated in the western and central portions of the Indo-Gangetic plain,—in the countries now known as Rajputána, the Punjab, and the United Provinces,—and although they sent off-shoots (especially colonies of missionary Brahmins) further afield, it is not believed that they materially influenced the population of Bengal or the peninsula. Aryan blood has remained purest in Rajputána, where it produces a refinement of feature at least equal to that upon which Europeans pride themselves. It is conjectured that the tribe which colonised this tract brought their women with them. Pure Aryan blood also appears in a considerable proportion of Brahmin families. For the rest the invaders seem to have interbred with the Dravidians around them, developing a mixed race which forms the greater part of the population of Northern India. But a Tartar element is also prominent here—especially amongst the Mohammedans—derived from the Tartar (or Moghal) invasions which during later centuries poured across the north-western frontier. The people of Western India (the Mahrattas) exhibit some peculiar physical features: they differ markedly from Aryans and Dravidians in the breadth of their heads, a feature which they are supposed

[1] The references to scenery in the early Vedic hymns give more than fanciful support to the theory that the Aryans came from Russia. Snow was familiar, and so were pine and birch trees.

Bourne and Shepherd, Calcutta

MADRASSI WOMAN

to have inherited from Scythian tribes which during the early centuries of our era are known to have penetrated India in large numbers and to have founded kingdoms of importance. This conjecture is supported by much similarity between the character and habits of the ancient Scythians, as known to us, and the qualities which the Mahrattas displayed in the days of their power—their aptitude for guerilla warfare and their genius for intrigue. On the other side of India another broad-headed people inhabit the plains of Bengal. They exhibit affinities with the Mongolian races that have overflowed the north-eastern frontier and have peopled the hills and valleys of Assam and Burma. The Bengalis are believed to be Mongolo-Dravidian in their origin, and to contain little, if any, Aryan blood. The Burmese are a Mongolian race.

There has been very little immigration by sea. On the west coast are small colonies of Jews and Arabs (known as Moplahs) which settled here, the former, perhaps, in the first, the latter in the tenth century, of our era. On this coast also Nestorian Christianity found a refuge from the persecution to which it was condemned in the west: it survives to this day in a Christian population of about half a million. More important in the material interests of the country was the immigration of the Parsis, who, driven from Persia by Mohammedan persecution in the eighth century of our era, settled in the vicinity of Bombay and have become the most enterprising—and the most public-spirited—of the merchants and manufacturers of that city.

Religious Differences

Racial distinctions are, however, less prominent than differences of religion, by which, in some cases accentuated, they may in other cases be concealed. Buddhism arose in India: its founder lived and preached in the neighbourhood of Patna. For eight centuries it contended successfully with Brahminism for the faith of the people, and it commanded numerous and powerful adherents up to the seventh century of our era. It was finally overpowered, and in India proper is now practically extinct. But it has maintained what was won by its missionaries in Tibet, Ceylon and Burma, and in the latter commands ten million adherents. Within the limits of India proper Hinduism has become the ruling cult, and indeed—comparatively small sects, such as the Parsis, apart—it is commonly assumed to be the faith of all who are not Mohammedans. This impression is incorrect. Hinduism has no pretensions to dogmatic rigidity : it is not so much a faith as a system of society ; and, indeed, can only be defined as an acceptance of Brahmin supremacy in all matters spiritual and ceremonial, and of the caste system which, under Brahmin ascendancy, fetters with ritual prejudice every action of man's life. But the hill tribes and the lowest classes of the plains population, so far from being ministered to by Brahmins, are treated by them as too degraded to be approachable. Those that need the services of a priesthood support special " black Brahmins" of their own. Moreover these people are, in greater or less measure, free from the food scruples that complicate Hindu life. Hinduism in matters of belief is the most tolerant of religions, and has gradually drawn within itself a host of tribal or local creeds. But it is intolerant in respect of ceremonial purity, and has not cast its net over classes who are so degraded as to eat what it pleases them. The border line is not precisely defined ; but these classes (which may conveniently be called the " coolie castes ") probably comprise at least fifty millions. They live in social degradation ; but the country would do badly without them. It looks to them for its supply of field and casual labour and for the working of its factories, mines and tea-gardens. Upon Indian coolie labour depend the sugar plantations of Mauritius, Natal, Fiji, and the West Indies; and without them the administration of Burma would have been well nigh impossible.

Moreover, we should exclude from the Hindu community sects which have formally seceded from its regulations, and having proselytized from various castes, have substituted new for ancient caste distinctions. The most important of these sects is that of the Sikhs, which numbers 3,014,466, mostly belonging to the Punjab. Two other movements of reform,—the Brahmo Samáj in Bengal and the Arya Samáj in the Punjab,—are represented respectively by 5,504 and 243,514 adherents.

Hindus, properly so-called, may be reckoned at 177 millions—about 56 per cent. of the population. But the name merely gives an appearance of unity to a most heterogeneous association of humanity, divided not only by rigid distinctions of caste but by wide differences of race, appearance, dress, language and ceremonial. It includes the light-complexioned Aryan of the north, the dark-featured Dravidian of the south, and even some pure Mongolian tribes whom Brahmin complaisance has adopted. Hindus speak at least twelve separate languages, distinct in vocabulary and script. More than a million of them know enough English to use it freely, and can accordingly combine for a common purpose.

The Mohammedans are a more closely knit society. Their religion is definite and dogmatic, and in India its solidarity has hardly been disturbed by schism. The mixture of Persian and Hindu (called Hindustani or Urdu) which is the *lingua franca* of Upper India, is understood throughout the country by all Mohammedans of any education. The Mohammedans number 66 millions, or 21 per cent. of the population. Their faith entered India from Central Asia, and their numbers should naturally decrease with increasing distance from the north-western frontier. With one important exception this is the case. In Sind and the Punjab Mohammedanism is professed by more than half of the population, in the United Provinces by a seventh, in Bombay by a tenth, and in Madras by only a fourteenth. The exception is in the eastern districts of Bengal, where (as amongst the Malays[1] further south, and about the same epoch) the creed spread rapidly through a population that had not been Hinduised and is now embraced by two-thirds of the inhabitants. The Mohammedans of Northern India generally profess to be descended from immigrants of Persian, Afghan or Moghal (Tartar) blood. In appearance they are easily distinguishable from Hindus. But this is due very largely to differences of dress and habit—beards as a rule are worn by Mohammedans but not by Hindus—and beyond doubt a very large proportion of the Mohammedan community is of purely Indian origin and is Mohammedan by conversion only. Conversion is still proceeding, and owing perhaps to a more liberal diet and less artificial marriage law, Mohammedans are increasing more rapidly than Hindus. During the last decade their numbers rose by nearly 7 per cent., whilst amongst Hindus (including for this purpose the coolie castes) the rate of increase was 5 per cent. only. Mohammedans and Hindus live side by side throughout the country; but the former are sharply distinguished by peculiarities of dress, and by their names, which are commonly scriptural (from both the Old and the New Testament) or doctrinal, such as were affected by the English Puritans.

There are 3,876,103 Christians, of whom 3,574,770 are of pure Indian, 101,675 of mixed European, and 199,776

[1] Between the Malays and the Mohammedans of Eastern Bengal there are some curious points of resemblance. Both races are largely aquatic in their habits, and were in the past addicted to piracy; both migrate far more readily than other Indian peoples.

of pure European descent. The latter are for the most part only temporarily resident in India: indeed, the British army of occupation contributes at least 80,000 of them. The Native Indian Christian population has more than doubled in the course of the last generation, and during the past ten years its number has increased by 34 per cent.

The arrival of the Parsis in India has already been mentioned. They number only 100,100, but they contribute to the industrial, commercial and public life of India in an infinitely greater measure than to its population. Their religion is that commonly known as Zoroastrianism, directly descended from that which was held by Cyrus, Xerxes and Naushirwan. It accounts for the contradictory tendencies of Nature, and of human action, by recognising an eternal struggle between the Spirit of Good and the Spirit of Evil: it venerates with scrupulous respect the natural elements; fire is indeed an object of worship, and to avoid polluting it, or the earth, in the disposal of corpses, the dead are exposed in "Towers of Silence" to be eaten by vultures.

Caste

It has been remarked that Hinduism has but little unifying force. Indeed the caste system which it has evolved is a means of isolating from one another groups of mankind. It illustrates very strikingly the extraordinary artificiality which human ideas can impose upon human society. A man is born into a caste and can never leave it. He can eat with no one but a caste-fellow, and the kinds of food he can eat are strictly limited by the distinctive scruples of his caste. His food must be cooked by a caste-fellow unless he employs a Brahmin, and there are hundreds of low castes whose members refuse even Brahmin cookery; nay more, cooked food other than sweetmeats is polluted for him by the touch—even by the shadow—of any one who is not a caste-fellow. He can take water from the hands of men of lower castes, but only of certain specified castes. These food *taboos* complicate daily life to an almost incredible degree and altogether prevent the growth of the good fellowship which with us is cemented at the dinner table. But they are not peculiar to the Hindus. We are told, in the story of Joseph, that it was " an abomination to the Egyptians " to eat with the Hebrews. Herodotus mentions that in his day there were similar objections to eating with Greeks. The peculiarity of the Hindu caste *taboo* is that it affects marriage as well as food. To marry outside the caste has been for Hindus as unthinkable as to us would be marriage with a sister. The result has been to divide the Hindus into a number of distinct breeds of mankind, as separate for all practical purposes as the species of the animal or vegetable kingdom. The first question that is asked of a stranger is : " To which breed (*zát*) do you belong ? " There are between two and three thousand castes in India, and there are so many kinds of Hindu humanity.

Each caste has a government of its own, its affairs being regulated by a committee (*pancháyet*), which can punish the disobedient by fine or excommunication. According to popular ideas most castes can be arranged one above the other, as on a list of precedence, which, it is interesting to note, is in very general accord with an anthropometric classification based upon measurements of the nose. Very low down the scale lie the un-Hinduised multitudes which we have grouped together as " coolies " : they have castes of their own, but are regarded as outcasts by those above them and live in the most amazing contempt. They inhabit separate quarters of the village ; they may not draw water from the village well ; their touch is polluting ; on the western coast they are even prohibited from approaching a high-caste man within a defined distance.

At the head of the scale stand the Brahmins, numbering fifteen and a half millions—a twentieth of the population. They constitute a hereditary priesthood and hold the monopoly of communicating between man and the gods. With the gods they live in close communion ; a Brahmin will set aside some portion of his meal for the god, and summon him to partake by blowing a little shell trumpet. Their ghostly privileges do not, however, prevent them from taking to secular employment which is literary or distinguished. They are *par excellence* the schoolmasters of the country. They enter the civil service of Government in large numbers, and in some districts hold the lion's share of appointments. They will serve in the army ; there are two Brahmin regiments. They hold much land, although they will not themselves cultivate it. One subdivision of the caste will touch the plough, but has consequently fallen greatly in esteem. A Brahmin, however poor, is held in reverence, and is commonly addressed as " Máhárâj " (Your Highness). To insult him is a crime ; to offer him violence a sacrilege. Under native rule he enjoyed the most liberal " benefit of clergy " ; and at the present time a Hindu jury can hardly be brought to convict him of a crime that is punishable with death.

In the earliest Sanskrit writings—the Vedas—the Brahmins are mentioned, but as appointed ministers not as hereditary priests. They appear, however, to have striven from very early days to form themselves into a separate in-breeding class :[1] their monopoly of spiritual or magical influence would obviously be fortified were it associated with scrupulous purity of blood. It would be further strengthened were the Aryan—or half-bred Aryan—community around them induced to group itself in

[1] A tendency towards the establishment of a family monopoly may be noticed to-day amongst the (married) Shinto priests of Japan.

similar isolated classes, since men would not feel jealous of Brahmin exclusiveness if they were privileged by a similar exclusiveness themselves. Brahmin influence and writings accordingly exalted purity of blood as well as ceremonial purity. For several centuries they were opposed by the antagonistic propaganda of Buddhism, in which the equality of mankind was a cardinal doctrine. But while Buddhism was still a popular creed—in the third century of our era—Brahmin views on the organisation of society were published in a remarkable Sanskrit work known as the *Institutes of Manu.* It recognises a long series of castes, headed by the Brahmins. Immediately below the Brahmins two castes—of military men (*Kshattriyas*[1]) and of business men (*Vaishyas*[1])—presumably including Aryan or semi-Aryan families of social repute, are permitted to share with the Brahmins the title of "twice-born" and the privilege of wearing a sacred thread. Of vastly inferior position are castes further down the scale. But the theory, while discouraging inter-marriages, did not absolutely prohibit them: cross-breeding is, indeed, elaborately discussed as a source of new caste complications. At this time and for five centuries later, Buddhism was still a force in the country. But with the triumph of Brahminism the people submitted to be unalterably classified on a system which limited their freedom but flattered their self-respect. Marriages have been limited within the caste for at least twelve centuries, and it has become possible often to tell a man's caste by his features. In other countries pride has been satisfied by sentiments of nationality, and society has tended to become increasingly compact. In India these sentiments did not exist, and the desire for particularity ruled unchecked. Communities that were united by tribal relationship, or by a similarity of

[1] With which the Rajputs and Banias of the present day identify themselves.

occupation, became castes. Many of the lowest Indian castes represent aboriginal tribes; a still larger number are linked to particular occupations. There is indeed a separate caste for almost every occupation or profession, although its members do not all follow the craft of their caste. Doctors, barbers, weavers, carpenters and blacksmiths may none of them intermarry. Vanity or self-esteem —the desire to be particularised—is the strongest of the passions that spring from self-consciousness. By it the Hindus have been reconciled to an artificiality of life which is without parallel in other countries.

How far are these crystallised conditions yielding to the solvent influence of the West? Food scruples are undoubtedly giving way. For many years, Hindus who, venturing upon a voyage to Europe, have there adopted Western habits of life, have submitted on their return to humiliating ceremonies of purification, and, abandoning china and glass, knives and forks, have reverted to Hindu manners and a vegetarian diet. But they are now much less ready to renounce comfort that has once been experienced, and have become sufficiently numerous to hold their own and to influence others. Educated Indians now commonly eat in European fashion and of European dishes —nay more, will sit at table with Europeans and eat with them. And amongst the lower classes the rules of diet are becoming more elastic, owing in great measure to the infractions that cannot be avoided during railway travel. Few scruples remain against biscuits, soda-water and tea. But the stronghold of caste is not in particularity of diet but in the limitation of cross marriage, and in this respect, if one looks below the surface, the marriage fields appear to be actually narrowing. New castes are even now arising; a subdivision of a caste will decide to enhance its social importance by prohibiting the re-marriage of its widows, by marrying its children in infancy, by abstaining from some article of food, or even by renouncing the cultivation of some particular crop. It forms itself into a caste and will no longer intermarry with its former caste-fellows. This is, however, in the lower levels of society. In the higher ranks there has also been manifest of recent years a reactionary spirit which displays bitter hostility to Western influences, and is willing to appeal to any superstition that may help to exclude them. But the vigilance of this spirit is evidence in itself of an inclination towards reform. Cases of caste inter-marriage, or of inter-marriage between Hindus and Mohammedans, are still of the very rarest occurrence. They are indeed illegal unless the parties formally abjure their religion. Even so one of the most prominent leaders of the Arya Samáj has recently ventured to marry out of caste, and there are men of influence who admire his temerity. A proposal so to modify the marriage law as to legalise mixed marriages without question of religion has lately received surprisingly strong support amongst the elected,—and independent,—members of the Viceroy's Legislative Council, and had the Government decided to accept the reform its decision would clearly not have been distasteful to the leaders of advanced opinion, although it might have been suspected by the masses and have been condemned as a scandal by reactionary orators. There have been revolts in the past against Brahmin restrictiveness. Within the last six centuries the brotherhood of mankind has been the standard of several popular movements. But the sectarians have generally ended by conforming to the system they condemned: they have formed themselves into a caste, or a series of castes. Such has been the fate of the Lingayets of Madras, of the disciples of the reformer Kabir, who, at the time Luther was urging the Protestant revolt in Europe, proclaimed in India that before God all men were equal. But the new movement is supported by something more substantial than feelings of philanthropy. A suspicion is forcing its way that in-and-in-breeding has cost India much vitality, and that if she desires to meet Europe on equal terms, she must widen the area within which marriage is permissible. This ambition touches the self-esteem of the upper classes, and may overpower the resisting force of religion or custom.

DIFFERENCES OF LANGUAGE

Such, then, is Indian society, minutely and antagonistically subdivided by differences not only of religion, but of breed. Across these differences lie others, of language and of dress, which, while smoothing in no way the more vital distinctions, give a uniform stamp to the people of a locality. Excluding the hill tribes, thirteen distinct languages are spoken, each with a distinct written character of its own. Eight of them are connected with Sanskrit—that is to say, Sanskrit grew as a classical development out of an early form of one of them. *Hindi* is the most widely spoken. It occupies the Indo-Gangetic plain, apart from its western and eastern extremities, and extends down the centre of the peninsula almost as far as Nagpur. It is used, with dialectic variations, by about 125 millions. Some of its dialects are of independent origin. But throughout this tract colloquial Hindustani is more or less understood. At the western end of the Indo-Gangetic plain, and in Sind, *Lahnda* is spoken by eight millions ; at its eastern end *Bengali*, with *Assamese* (akin to Bengali), by fifty-two millions. In the upper portion of the peninsula *Uriya*, on the north-eastern coast, is the language of eleven millions ; crossing westwards, *Mahratti*, *Gujarati* and *Rajasthâni* are spoken respectively by nineteen, eleven, and twelve millions. On their frontiers these eight languages shade insensibly one into the other in village speech ; but a knowledge of one of them would leave the others quite unintelligible. The area of the peninsula further south is divided between four languages which are not related to Sanskrit, *Telugu* (twenty-one millions) and *Tamil* (seventeen millions), towards the east, and *Kanarese* (eleven millions) and *Malayalim* (seven millions) on the west. Along the Afghan frontier—*Pushtu*—the language of Afghanistán, is spoken. It is akin to Persian. The language of Burma (spoken by eight millions) belongs to the Tibetan family. The Mohammedan community of Upper India use Hindustani, a form of Hindi that embellishes its vocabulary by borrowing from Persian. They write this language in the Arabic script. Elsewhere Mohammedans use the tongue of their locality in speaking and writing ; but by men of any education Hindustani is more or less understood.

Hill Tribes

We have to add to these varieties of race, caste, religion, and language, the numberless peculiarities of the hill tribes. In the hills of the peninsula and along the foot of the Himalayas they are gradually adopting Hindu ideas and converting the rules of a tribe into those of a caste. They represent the aboriginal element with which Hinduism has always been contending ; and they owe their survival in independence to the inaccessibility, unhealthiness or poverty of the lands they inhabit. There are probably ten millions who are still outside the pale, and it is amongst them that the efforts of Christian missionaries have been most conspicuously successful. To the hills of the north-eastern frontier Brahmin influence has never penetrated, and the tribes that inhabit them—of Tibeto-Burmese stock—illustrate the development of human society when unguided by formal religion or by priests. They have attained some measure of civilisation, being acquainted with weaving, iron-working and the cultivation of irrigated rice. But they have lived in a perpetual state of warfare, which so isolates tribe from

WARRIOR OF THE ASSAM HILLS ON THE WAR-PATH

tribe—and indeed village from village—that in one district seven distinct languages divide 150,000 people. British rule has been extended over a portion of this country; roads have been made; schools have been opened in which their children display much natural ability. But the tribesmen are still hardly reconciled to the abolition of head-hunting, which formerly gave colour and excitement to their lives. One tribe in these hills—the Khasis—of different origin, representing perhaps a *stratum* of humanity which extended over India before the Dravidians arrived, have preserved to modern days the practice of the Matriarchate. Property belongs to the women, and descent is reckoned through females, a man's future representative being his sister's son. The Khasis are of great natural intelligence, and, untainted by such cruelties as head-hunting, are rapidly adopting the Christian faith. Descent through the female line is also the rule in the far-distant community of the Náyars of Malabar. Polyandry is not extinct. Sanctioned by the example of a heroic family in the great Sanskrit epic of the Mahabhárata, it is still openly practised by some Himalayan tribes, and secretly, it is said, by the largest, and most typical of agricultural castes in the Punjab.

Unifying Forces

Speaking the same language and wearing the same costume, people, however much divided by racial or sectarian prejudice, can hardly resist an impression of unity; and in some parts of India these similarities have undoubtedly engendered such sympathy in feelings as may justly be described as a national sentiment. Throughout the large area in which Hindi is spoken the more catholic interests of a large and important Mohammedan population have counteracted any tendency of the Hindus to cohere. But the Bengalis on one side of this area and the Mahrattas on the other, each sharply distinguished by language and by dress, have undoubtedly developed national feelings and national characters. Amongst Mohammedans may also be noticed a certain uniformity of idea and aspiration. But in their case the feeling of unity is unassociated with any particular part of the Indian continent.

As yet very faintly overshadowing these distinctive interests is the consciousness of the national existence of the Indian people as a whole. This feeling owes its birth to the English language, which is used in political discussion throughout the country, and, to a much less extent, in the family life of the more advanced Hindus. It has undoubtedly concentrated the intelligence of the educated classes on to ideals for which they can work together. The illiterate multitude may be inclined to view with suspicion the advances of men whose opinions are in violent opposition to traditional ideas. And the Mohammedans, so far, have generally held aloof from the propaganda of advanced Hindu politicians. But the politicians claim to stand for the credit of India against those who belittle her capacities ; and their words evolve heat which may gradually weld fragments of different races, religion, and languages into something that approaches national solidarity.

CHAPTER VIII

MANNER OF LIFE

A EUROPEAN visiting India is struck by the poverty of the people and the contentedness with which they bear it; he is amazed to find that men will gladly take service for half-a-crown a week, finding themselves in everything, and he cannot but reflect upon the causes of this difference between East and West. It is due at bottom to a difference of outlook upon life: the ambition of the West is to acquire comfort and amusement, that of the East to acquire dignity and leisure. To the humblest servant his post gives some sense of rank, but very little reason for exertion. Europeans are not of course insensible to dignity; it is enhanced by display, and luxury is accordingly desired for its effects upon others as well as for the pleasure it intrinsically affords. In the East, where dignity is infinitely more precious, it can also be enhanced by expensive display, but the display takes the more primitive form of generosity to others, shown either by hospitably entertaining caste-fellows, or by maintaining a host of dependants. The larger is a man's household the greater is his repute. Accordingly families have been multiplied without check, the land has been subdivided down to subsistence level, and any surplus income from rents, profits or salaries is spent upon feeding others. Not a man rises in the world but a crowd of poor relations cling to his skirts, living in his house, feeding at his hands, and offering him in return their respectful salutations. Such a theory of life does not encourage industry. Cultivators of some castes are industrious, but, generally, slovenliness is apparent in the fields, and beyond question the people could increase their incomes very greatly indeed did they think it worth while to make greater exertions. After pay-day mill hands will absent themselves from work unless offered special enticements. Such savings as accrue are not invested at interest: they are converted into jewels or secretly hoarded. Mohammedans have, indeed, religious scruples against the taking of interest upon money. Contract with the West is no doubt producing an effect: a desire for comfort is certainly growing. Well-to-do men—Government officials and lawyers—are rapidly adopting European habits of living. Where opportunities are unfettered by the past, as, for instance, in the new Punjab canal colonies, the peasantry are displaying in houses and in dress a marked rise in the standard of comfort. A stronger desire for gain may in part be satisfied by an increase of energy, but it will inevitably be attended by a painful disturbance of existing conditions. It is difficult to improve agriculture and to increase the surplus available from the land, so long as the land is divided, uneconomically, into very small parcels. Moved by a commercial spirit, landlords have endeavoured to amalgamate holdings, to substitute hired for cottier labour, by ejecting their tenants. The immediate result is the misery and degradation of the tenants, and the process has been checked by tenancy legislation. The investment of money in industrial undertakings is increasing in popularity, and is less impeded than formerly by jealousy and distrust. But the dream of education and intelligence is still to secure service under the Government—however poorly paid—or at the least to engage in clerical as opposed to practical business. So is dignity best secured, as understood in the East—and, although less exclusively, —in the West also.

A generation ago a field labourer was almost satisfied with the Scriptural penny a day: he now expects twopence, and often something more. His wife's earnings will bring the family income up to about eighteen pence a week. The coarse grain which he eats is so exceedingly cheap that in grain, at English prices, the eighteen pence is equivalent to four shillings. He requires no firing for warmth and no warm clothes. The tobacco he smokes is exceedingly cheap,—often, indeed, grown in his own cottage garden. He pays no house rent. It is not usual to take house rent in Indian villages ; those who hold land occupy their houses rent free, and labourers are expected in lieu of rent to render some small occasional services to their landlord. His children gather wild vegetables, and catch some fish when the streams are in flood. So long as Nature is kind, he lives and multiplies, and can even afford to spend a good deal upon drink. His caste connexions secure him some sense of importance.

A social gulf divides the tenant from the coolie. But in the crowded districts of the Indo-Gangetic plain a tenant holding three or four acres of land, after paying his rent, will not enjoy more than double the coolie's income. Were his income fourfold the coolie's—amounting, that is to say, to about £16 a year—he would in popular estimation be quite well-to-do. This standard is generally attained in the less crowded districts, where holdings are larger and rents are lower. The rent paid for the holding usually ranges from an eighth to a quarter of the produce after deducting seed grain ; it is not included in the foregoing estimates of his income. Where competition for land is keen, and the crop is grown easily, without the use of manure or irrigation, landlords sometimes claim one-half of the produce. But power to enhance rents has very generally been limited by statute, and, indeed, in some provinces the State has charged itself with periodically determining the rents of a large proportion of the tenants. In the Madras and Bombay presidencies, in Burma and in Assam, cultivators hold direct from the State, paying much less than an economic rent. In fertile tracts, such as the delta of the Kistna river, they are exceedingly well-to-do, with incomes running up to £50 a year or even more, and displaying their prosperity by wearing gold bangles. But profitable holdings are commonly sublet. Throughout India there is a deplorable tendency for a cultivator, whose land pays him well, to sublet it at a rack-rent, and to live in leisure on the proceeds. He is secured in his tenant-right by the protection of the State. But his fields are in hands too poor to improve them.

The village communal servants are generally remunerated in kind, receiving from each cultivator so many sheaves of wheat or cakes of sugar. Those who work with their hands and are of inferior status—the village potter, barber and carpenter—make about as much as a small tenant; those of higher rank—the accountant and the priest—enjoy from £7 to £8 a year. It will be understood, of course, that these estimates of income apply throughout to men who represent large classes: in individual cases they may be considerably exceeded. In Upper India, at the head of village society stands the landlord, or the principal landlord, for, there being no rule of primogeniture, the proprietorship of the land is often subdivided amongst a large number of persons who individually are no better off than the general run of tenants. When the village belongs to a large estate and the landlord has his residence elsewhere, or where, as in Madras and Bombay, there is no landlord, a village headman is appointed from amongst the cultivators. Scarcely less important than the landlord or headman is the village money-lender, whose substantial house stands prominent amongst the cottages of the tenants. His income approaches a European standard, and would commonly exceed £200 a year.

Incomes are very small, and life ordinarily very frugal, but there is not a man who does not at times launch out into the most reckless extravagance. This is on occasions of family ceremonies, of marriages in particular, when he gains or loses repute amongst his neighbours and caste-fellows according as he is lavish or prudent in his expenditure. Such finery as can be commanded is displayed in a procession, and hosts of relatives and connections are invited to a heavy meal which is enlivened by music, and ends, if funds permit, in a display of fireworks. Of the expenditure upon marriages comparatively little goes in substantial presents to the young couple. But generally the father of the bride has to pay heavily for the bridegroom, and a large family of daughters is a ruinous responsibility. Bridegrooms are particularly expensive when they have passed the higher educational examinations: the rising marriage value of diplomas in engineering has been quoted as a satisfying, if remarkable proof of the growing popularity of technical instruction. Before an impending marriage prudence vanishes. Six months' income is spent without compunction: a man making three shillings a week will borrow three or four pounds. When holdings are large and rents low a tenant will frequently spend the equivalent of eight years' rent—or, say, £15—on a single marriage. Money is also prodigally wasted in litigation. The careful frugality of everyday life cannot resist the excitement of the law courts. It follows that such surplus as the land offers to its cultivators is gathered very largely by lawyers and money-lenders.

It is, then, not surprising that indebtedness should prevail—that it should be the normal condition of everyone to owe money. The money-lender grips village life as closely as the priest. It is traditional to be in his books; for in the days of Native rule, cultivators were generally expected to pay their land tax before their crops were harvested (to obviate the risk of their absconding with the proceeds), and they could only contrive to do this by borrowing. The rates of interest vary greatly in different parts of the country. A substantial cultivator can generally borrow cash at 15 per cent.; smaller men pay higher according to their circumstances, often as much as 37½ per cent. Coolies borrow freely at 75 per cent. When grain is borrowed, for sowing or subsistence, exorbitant interest is sanctioned by custom—25 per cent. for wheat and 50 per cent. for millet. Compound interest is charged and, with a run of three bad seasons, loans of these grains may be respectively doubled or trebled. But the money-lender must not be figured as altogether extortionate. Bad debts are numerous and he not uncommonly forgives them: indeed he will sometimes free a debtor for reasons that are sentimental, as, for instance, on condition that the debtor will discharge a vow for him by going on a pilgrimage or setting free a heifer. If he is more grasping than custom warrants, the dread of violence, or even of murder, is before him. But custom, it must be confessed, permits him to make very large profits.

The houses of an Indian village are generally clustered together, giving it the semblance of a little town. Each village community concentrated its inhabitants for defensive purposes. It was often at bitter feud with the villages that adjoined it; and in North-Western India it was constantly threatened by marauding immigrants, and very frequently protected itself by an earthen rampart. In Bengal a different custom prevails, and the cottages are scattered over the fields—not because there has been no occasion for defence but because the people have been conscious of their inability to defend themselves. In North-Western India the houses are generally flat-roofed—constructed of kneaded clay—after a fashion that was perhaps introduced from Central Asia. They stand close together, with no house gardens, and during the hot weather the village presents an appearance of sombre aridity that is hardly redeemed by the fine mango trees with which it is surrounded. Further east the roofs are gabled and tiled. In Bengal thatch is used ; the roofs are very highly gabled, with the ends of the roof-tree bent downwards towards the ground so as to offer as little resistance as possible to the violent winds that descend upon the country during April and May. In the peninsula gabled roofs are the rule : each house possesses a little garden of its own which gives an air of amenity to the village. Speaking broadly, in Upper India a house consists of a courtyard round which are disposed buildings for men, women and cattle, presenting to the roadway an expanse of blank wall. In eastern India and the peninsula village houses front the street through a yard or garden, and resemble more nearly the conventional cottage. In the towns, where land is valuable, yards are dispensed with, and the fashion of house construction approaches that of Europe. But the streets are overhung with projecting balconies, often elaborately carved, which frame picturesquely the vistas below them.

The Indian dietary is exceedingly simple. The rich often live on a few pence a day. The Mohammedans take meat—poultry or goat's flesh—when they can afford it ; but to the majority of good Hindus animal food is tabooed. In Northern India, and down the western side of the peninsula, unleavened cakes of wheat, barley or millet are the chief staple of diet ; with them is taken some pulse, which may be served either as a soft mash or split and parched. Some vegetables are added. In Bengal and the eastern region of the peninsula, where rice is the main crop, rice is the universal diet. Instead of pulse fish is eaten, the rivers offering an abundant supply. In these tracts Brahmins have a dispensation : fish is allowed them, and in some localities even ducks. But fowls are prohibited. The cow is associated throughout India with religious ideas, and to Hindus beef-eating is abhorrent. At certain Mohammedan festivals kine are sacrificed and their flesh eaten. But this provokes much bitterness of feeling between the two communities. Orthodoxy is shown by fanciful strictness in diet: by many castes onions are, for instance, rejected as impure, and one new-grown sect eschews lentils because their pink colour suggests blood. The hill tribes subsist on small millets, which they make into gruel; the relish is increased by a slight alcoholic fermentation produced by stale remnants which are always left in the cooking pot. But for several months in the year they support themselves very largely upon wild products, and it is amazing to find how much food the jungles will yield if explored by necessitous experience. The Indian people drink surprisingly little milk, but they do not condemn it as unclean or share the prejudice of the Mongolian tribes on the eastern frontier, who, although untroubled by many food scruples, rigidly taboo the products of the cow. An oily butter—made by boiling down cream—is, however, greatly relished throughout the country. By the upper classes, who generally take no alcohol, sugar is eaten with avidity, and the sweetmeat seller pervades every railway platform. To the coolie classes spirits are very attractive, and their growing prosperity is unhappily displayed in a growing expenditure on the purchase of drink. The distillation of spirits has been practised in India from the earliest time: rice, palm sap, and sugar provide materials for fermentation, and still more plentiful and inexpensive are the sugary flowers of the wild *mahua* tree (*Bassia latifolia*), which offer to the poorest an effective intoxicant. Distillation is easy, but it is as far as possible repressed; and, if the State licenses distillation and the vend of spirits, it restrains them severely by a heavy excise. Amongst the upper classes also a taste for alcohol, chiefly European spirits, is growing, a sign of the emancipating influence of Western example. Many drink openly; still more in secret. Tobacco is chewed and smoked by all classes, except orthodox Brahmins and the strictest sect of Mohammedans. Opium is eaten, generally in moderation, by high and low. The Sikhs are especially addicted to it, but its charms are most compelling amongst the people of Assam, where it appears to relieve the acute bowel diseases which are a peculiar scourge of this locality. In its case also the State limits consumption by raising the price; the actual cost of a pound of opium is between five and six shillings: it may not be sold in Assam for less than three times this amount. In China opium is smoked. In India it is eaten: to smoke it is disreputable, and it is confined (under severe restrictions) to a limited class of people in the towns. Other narcotics are obtained from the hemp plant. They also are very heavily taxed and the cultivation of the plant is prohibited except under licence. If it is vicious to deaden the self-consciousness it is a vice to take these drugs. They are Oriental substitutes for alcohol, and, like alcohol, they are very injurious if taken in excess. Their use is strange to us, and we therefore regard it with particular suspicion.

A Hindu sits down to meals with his caste-fellows, but not with his wife: she waits upon him and begins when he has finished. He dines with the precautions of a magic ceremony, sitting within a square marked off on the ground, significant of such isolated purity as is required for a sacrifice. Should the shadow of an alien fall upon this square it contaminates any cooked food that lies within its borders. These formalities may not be relaxed even upon a journey, and you may see cartmen halted upon the roadside, each cooking and eating within his own enclosure. The suspicions with which Hindus regard food have infected the Mohammedans also. A generation ago very few Mohammedans would use glass or crockery, or would sit down to table with Europeans.

11—(2134)

Amongst Mohammedans of education and position these prejudices are rapidly vanishing ; they are disappearing, but more slowly, amongst educated Hindus.

The typical and primitive Hindu costume consists of three unsewn sheets of cotton—the loin cloth (*dhoti*), the shawl, and the turban. The former is in substance a long kilt, the back lower edge of which is drawn forward between the legs and tucked in at the waist in front ; it is thus converted into the semblance of a pair of breeches. This simple dress is commonly worn by orthodox Brahmins throughout the country. Generally, however, the shawl has given place to the more convenient coat, which fashion now permits to be made in European style, single-breasted, fitted with buttons, and provided with pockets. But in its original form it is fastened by tapes, double-breasted, overlapping towards the right with Hindus and towards the left with Mohammedans. This curious distinction is universal. For Hindu women the typical garment is the *sári*, a cloth passed several times round the waist, with the loose end carried round over the head so as to form a hood. Underneath is worn a bodice. Brahmin women often wear the *dhoti*, and village women a petticoat in place of the *sári*. Mohammedans do not affect the loin cloth ; they wear trousers (*pyjámas*), which may be worn loose or almost skin-tight, and this article of Mohammedan dress has become fashionable for Hindu gentlemen of position. Mohammedan women wear either *pyjámas* or petticoats, according (speaking generally) as they belong to the upper or the lower classes. The great distinction between Northern and Southern India in the matter of dress is the fondness of the southerners for bright and varied colours : this appears to be a characteristic of the Dravidian races. A crowd in Madras is a very brilliant spectacle. In Upper India, and generally throughout the tracts using languages that are akin to Sanskrit, white is preferred, by the male sex at all events. On the north-west frontier, where Afghan fashions prevail, men wear very baggy trousers, and cover their heads with a large turban folded round a conical skull cap. Further east, in the Hindi-speaking area, the turbans are smaller, and are often discarded for a small rounded cap of muslin. Still further east—in Bengal—the turban disappears: Bengalis, Uriyas and Assamese go bare-headed, surprising though it may seem, under an Indian sun. As worn by them, the *dhoti* is very voluminous, generally of muslin, and a loose end hangs down in front. Across the peninsula, on its western side, coloured turbans are in vogue; amongst the Mahrattas they are of very large size and of "cart-wheel" shape. The Mahrattas are markedly old-fashioned in costume: all classes prefer the *dhoti* to *pyjámas*, and they yield but slowly to the fashion of wearing socks and patent-leather shoes, which finds much favour with educated young men, especially in Bengal. Throughout India the Mohammedans have of recent years adopted the fez as their distinctive head-dress—a homage paid by fashion to the Turks. The costumes of Burma are peculiar to the country. Silk, which comes into fashion in Assam, on the Burmese frontier, is here the most popular material of dress. In Assam it is of local production: the Burmese import it from China and Japan. Silk-clad, in delicate tints of yellow, green and pink, the Burmese people introduce a note of flowery brilliancy into the tropical scenery of their land. The women, like those of Japan, leave their heads uncovered, and rely for adornment upon careful hair-dressing and the wearing of flowers. They are dressed in a short jacket, and a waist-cloth drawn so tightly round the legs as to suggest comparison with a hobble-skirt. The costume of the men is a jacket, and a short loin-cloth: round their heads a coloured handkerchief is loosely twisted.

With us the family has become an institution for children; in India its ties endure throughout adult life. A Hindu seldom becomes independent of his father: he is a partner with his father in the family property, but his own earnings are merged in this property: he remits them to his father and receives his maintenance. On the death of the father the eldest brother takes his place. The typical Hindu family is a joint co-parcenership. But partition may be claimed, and is not infrequently claimed. Mohammedan families are less closely knit, but patriarchal authority is at least acknowledged. To a Hindu his son is of immense importance, since his welfare after death is regarded, vaguely but sincerely, as dependent upon the offering by the son of family sacrifices. To be sonless is the greatest of misfortunes. But relief may be obtained by the adoption of a child. Family affection is, as a rule, very strong, and a father is not ashamed of showing it in public. You may see him very often carrying a child and leading another on his way with his wife to a festival or market. There is little home discipline as we understand it. Children are rarely punished, and (in Bengal especially) fathers do not care to insist that their sons should keep celibate the years of their youth or even of their boyhood.

Women are popularly supposed to fare badly in India, and they certainly do not enjoy the freedom and respect which they have always been accorded by Teutonic races. On the subject of female frailty Brahmin moralists have been as severe as some of the early Christian fathers of the Mediterranean churches. Mohammedans, it has been alleged, deny woman a soul. Mohammedan girls are taught the Koran: but women have no definite place in the Mohammedan paradise, where the faithful are to associate with celestial *houris*. Human nature is, however, stronger than human imaginings, and, as a matter of fact, the mother of the family is surrounded, in the East as in the West, by a halo of respect, though the halo is diffused less by her own than by her husband's dignity. Polygamy is against her. It is in theory allowed to both Hindus and Mohammedans. But a second wife is expensive: domestic quarrels are troublesome; and of a hundred wives ninety-nine possess husbands to themselves. By their law Mohammedans are permitted four wives and as many concubines as they please: but it is only the rich who take advantage of this licence. At home women of the better classes are secluded in apartments of their own; abroad, they carefully conceal their faces. They know the outside world by hearsay only. But they regard these precautions as a distinction, and when a poor family rises in the world the women insist upon self-imprisonment. The strict seclusion of the *zenána* is, of course, beyond the means of the multitude; indeed, cultivators' wives often work in the fields, and coolie women are as active and as free as their husbands. It was no part of early Aryan Hinduism that women should be shut up. The women of the early Sanskrit epics shared life with the men, even choosing their own husbands; and some classes of Brahmins, the Mahrattas especially, allow their wives a measure of freedom. Complicated are more attractive than simple fashions, and the Hindus, who have infected the Mohammedans with prejudices about diet, have themselves been drawn into isolating their women. A wife whose prospect is limited to the home—whose functions are solely those associated with reproduction—can hardly amuse her husband in conversation, and to resort for entertainment to the houses of courtesans is as excusable as it appeared to the judgment of Socrates. Women of this class possess much influence, especially in Bengal, where they have identified themselves enthusiastically with the "national" movement in politics.

A Hindu wife may not be divorced. Mohammedan law admits of divorce upon very trifling grounds, but its practice is limited by a money penalty. On marriage a man settles a dowry upon his wife ; it may be only in name, but on her divorce it becomes actually payable.

Dignity which is reflected from the husband vanishes with his death, and the widow is a pitiful figure in Hindu society. Mohammedans permit her to re-marry ; not so Hindus, and the surest sign that a low caste is rising in the world is the withdrawal from its widows of all hopes for the future. It must be remembered that Hindus are married in infancy and that a large number of widows have hardly seen their husbands. There are over 300,000 widows under sixteen, and, incredible though it may appear, 18,000 widows are children under six. Frequent scandals are the inevitable result. Nor does it suffice that widowhood should be hopeless : it is also despised. With hair cut short, in mean attire, the widow lives as the servant of her late husband's family. In earlier days even life was denied her. Religion invited her to accompany her husband, and in a solemn service of devotion (or *suttee*) she ascended his funeral pyre and was burnt with him. Eighty years have passed since this form of human sacrifice was made criminal by the British Government. But in memory it is still regarded with favour, and now and again attempts are made to revive it. More than half a century ago the re-marriage of widows was expressly legalised, but public opinion did not endorse this reform in the law, and has scarcely been influenced by it. That widows should be permitted to re-marry is a favourite text for discourses on social reform, and some advanced Hindus have dared to prove their acceptance of it. But in Bengal, even now, a father who ventured to provide a husband for his little widowed daughter could not assure himself that the highest social position would protect him from discredit. In Western India and in the

Punjab, however, woman's right to enjoy her own life is distinctly growing in public sympathy. The bars of the *zenána* are being raised : women of the better class may be seen accompanying their husbands in public unveiled ; and in some places educated Indian ladies have succeeded in establishing clubs of their own, where they can meet at least one another on the badminton or tennis court, or even at the bridge table. In these aspirations they are immensely remote from their uncultured sisters. But new ideas, sprinkled upon the surface of society, may filter down into it.

In Burma there is the greatest possible contrast : women are as free as in the most liberal countries of Europe. They do not marry till they can feel the passion of love, and in many cases they select husbands for themselves. So far from being secluded from the world, they are the principal shopkeepers of the town, and throw themselves heart and soul into the buying and selling which is so universally gratifying to female desires. At liberty to display their costumes and possessions, and to compare them with those of their acquaintances, they naturally spend more upon themselves than Indian women do, and Burma is a much better market than India for imported goods. They are shrewd in business, and do not permit liveliness of temperament and freedom of manners to weaken the rules of prescribed morality. Marriage is a civil contract : divorce is permissible but rarely practised, and a woman, once married, is faithful to her husband. She relieves him of most of the troubles of life, and the Burmese men take their cares very easily.

In Burma life is pervaded by an air of gaiety ; in India it is regarded in a very serious spirit, by which even children are subdued. You will never see them romping at play, and their games are of the quietest description. They take no pleasure whatever in teasing animals, and birds and beasts of the household are extraordinarily tame. These are not so much petted as treated with the consideration that is due to members of the family: the cultivator appeals to his bullocks as "my brothers." To adults life offers few pleasures of the senses: eating is a monotonous experience of the plainest dishes: drinking, for the respectable, is limited to water: there are no attractions in sport or in physical exercises. Life may be happy when seasons are favourable: but it is not joyful. Fairs and festivals give some excitement to the women who can attend them, and caste ceremonies and entertainments to the men. They derive their pleasure rather from the gratification of a sense of dignity and importance than from the exercise of the functions of mind or body. It should be added, however, that English school games are rapidly gaining in popularity, and of evenings the parks of Bombay and Calcutta are as crowded with youths playing cricket, football or hockey, as are the public playgrounds of an English city.

CHAPTER IX

RELIGIOUS BELIEFS AND OBSERVANCES

FROM the day when man, self-consciously comparing himself with his surroundings, became aware of the existence of Good and Evil, he has variously ascribed these conflicting tendencies to mysterious influences in the objects around him, to the great forces of Nature, to entities or personalities independent of these forces, or to the contradictory impulses of his own soul; and he has sought in each case to win his way between them by magic, by propitiation, by faith and service, and by mysticism, charity and self-control. These different conceptions are associated in some measure with stages in the mental development of mankind. But one does not appear to have driven out another, and however transcendental be the heights which are scaled by a spiritual religion, you will find amongst the less intelligent of its votaries traces of superstitions that are a link between them and their remotest ancestors.

HINDUISM

The beliefs of the ancient Aryan invaders may be gathered from a collection of Sanskrit hymns and formulas (the Vedas), some of which are believed to have been composed over three thousand years ago. These tribesmen (to whom we are ourselves racially akin) reverenced and propitiated the great forces of Nature—the Sun, the Sky, and the Fire-flame. They were a pastoral people of simple habits, eating meat freely and by no means insensible to the charms of intoxicants. They do not appear to have been idolatrous or to have invested their divinities with human forms. But they believed in the persistence of the souls of their ancestors, and on occasions solemnly offered them food. This belief has come down through the centuries to the Hindus of to-day. Investing the unity of the family with a religious significance, it has profoundly affected the structure of society, binding it firmly to the patriarchal model, which by a similar belief was sanctified to the Romans, and is still the social ideal of China and Japan.

More varied and more complicated were the beliefs of the Dravidian races by whom the Aryan immigrants were surrounded. Gathered not in open pasture lands, but amidst hills and forests, their conceptions were deeply coloured by the idea of dread. These conceptions still subsist in their primitive — or "animistic" — form amongst the hill tribes of the peninsula. The material objects of man's environment are believed to possess wills of their own, and to have the power and the desire to oppose and thwart him. The power increases with the size or peculiarity of the object. Large trees, isolated rocks, are regarded with suspicion, and are propitiated by being daubed with vermilion; and similar respect has been accorded to railway locomotives when they first made their way into the hills of Central India. Each tribe takes as its *totem* a plant or an animal, and venerates it as its representative in the natural world. The lands of each village are overshadowed by local influences which will only yield to local knowledge: a tribe annexing the lands of others will maintain one of the original inhabitants as the village "medicine-man." These ideas grew less material; the influences of Nature were separated from natural objects and endowed with a distinct and more or less personal existence. The mysterious forces of the tree were ascribed to dryads that haunted it; from the branches of a large fig (banyan) tree are often suspended dozens of little saucers in which the dryads are fed with offerings of curds. A complicated system of polytheism developed, in which the gods were invested with forms akin to that of man, and were presented by idols to the eyes of their worshippers. And being respected rather from fear than from admiration, they were represented by idols which were generally exceedingly grotesque.

Confronted with these elaborations of magic and idolatry, the beliefs of the Aryans took a double course. To make a religion for the people they annexed wholesale the Dravidian conceptions, engrafting them on to their own system as well as might be. But, for the more intelligent, they were refined by philosophic speculation which followed much the same lines as in classical Greece. Hindu philosophy has been expressed in writings from centuries before Plato down to present times. The forces of Nature were unified into a supreme existence: this was conceived as the underlying material essence above which this world's existence floated as an unsubstantial and delusive show; or as a spirit which included the principle of animal life. Life when conceived as part of the eternal was obviously indestructible: the soul of man passed after death to another animal, and was again passed on in an endless series of transmigrations. Neither theory offered anything to human hopes or morality. But from these speculations were derived two practical religions—Buddhism and Jainism. Both arose at about the same period—five or six centuries before the commencement of our era. The founder of Buddhism, Gautama or Sakya Muni—called "Buddha," or "The Illumined"—was not of the Brahmin caste, and his doctrines protested against the authority of an exclusive priesthood. Refusing to discuss the existence of a God, he was convinced of the non-existence of a human soul: personality was no more than a passing combination of unstable qualities. Accepting, as he did, the doctrine of transmigration, he could not deny the continuity of life ; but life was merely the manifestation of desire—the expression and the result of sensual cravings. He invested transmigration with a moral significance. The transmigrating life ascended or descended the scale of existence—was transferred to an animal of high or low type,—according to the conduct of its last possessor. We suffered what we had deserved in previous existences. Man could ameliorate his future by controlling his thoughts and actions, by following the " eight-fold way " of morality. Nor was this all. To a cold philosophy unhappiness appeared to be the portion of mankind, resulting from pain and disappointment in the present, and from delusions in regard to the future. Relief might be obtained by a repression of desire, whether for woman's love, or for worldly goods or for life everlasting ; and those who could master their natural cravings might ascend into a condition of peaceful, passionless indifference, moved only by feelings of love for others,—nay, more, life's flame being unfed by the fuel of desire, they might win the greatest of boons in release from the perilous course of transmigration. So emotionless a creed can hardly have been attractive to the world at large : its rules appear to have been designed for the regulation rather of the ascetic than of the working life, and it expressed itself in the foundation of monasteries and nunneries. For upwards of twelve centuries Buddhism competed with Brahminism for popular respect; but we may conjecture that, like Buddhism and Shintoism in present-day Japan, the two creeds did not divide the people, but shared almost indiscriminately their alms and devotions,—in fact, that the priests of each cult were its only sectaries. Buddhism was adopted by Ceylon before the commencement of our era : it spread to China in the fourth century, and we owe to the narratives of two Chinese pilgrims such information as we possess of India during the fifth and seventh centuries. Indeed, to the speculations of Hindu

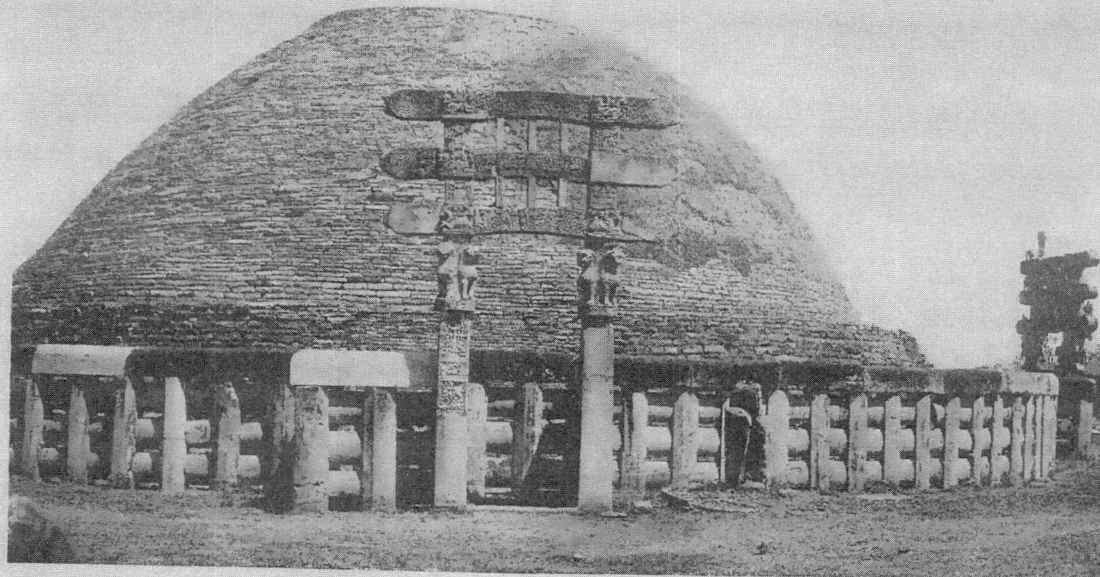

Hoffmann, Calcutta

BUDDHIST TOPE AT SANCHI IN CENTRAL INDIA (CIRC. 300 B.C.)

philosophy the religions of Eastern Asia are in such debt as Christianity must acknowledge to Greek meditations. Buddhism apart, we may detect Indian ideas in the Nature worship (Shintoism) of Japan. But the philosophical abstractions of Buddhistic teaching could not satisfy the masses, and its tenets were enlarged by the deification of its founder, and by the widening of the path which led to its promises. In India proper it was vanquished by Brahminism, and has been dead for the last ten centuries. In Burma it has held its ground for fourteen centuries, but divides its authority over the people with the capricious demons of a spirit world. Here the monastic system, indeed, survives : it is utilised as a temporary discipline, and to pass some years in the habit of a monk is a feature in the customary training of youth. The monasteries teach as well as discipline, and a knowledge of reading and writing is far more diffused in Burma than in any Indian province. Nor can the character of the people be unaffected by a religion which inculcates kindness to men and animals.

Jainism, rising alongside of Buddhism, is still professed in India by over a million persons. It did not drift so widely from Brahminism, maintaining caste, and respecting priesthood. It was as strict as Buddhism in its injunctions of morality ; but the object of self-denial was rather to win personal sanctity than deliverance from the "Wheel of Life," and its saints receive the honours that are due to Divinity. Transmigration was accepted with all its possibilities : Jains will not hurt the meanest insects. They shrink from the plough because it injures insects, and have found more lucrative pursuits in trade and money-lending.

We now revert to the development which Hinduism underwent to provide a faith that would appeal to the mass of the people. It strongly maintained the sanctity of the Brahmin and the obligations of caste. In other matters it was content to widen its embrace, and it cheerfully enlisted in its system every divinity or rite that was in possession of the ground. Gods are now recognised to exist by hundreds of thousands. Prominent in this multitude are the three divinities Brahma, Siva and Vishnu, which to the philosopher present metaphysical conceptions, and, to the crowd, personalities for their dread or admiration. Brahma represents creation; having created, the god is quiescent, and but few temples have been erected in his honour. Siva is the lord of birth and death: he typifies the changes which interrupt and carry on the continuity of life, and he figures, now as reveller, now as ascetic, the varied ranges of life's activity. Associated with him are the symbols of decay and of reproduction. He is most commonly represented by the *phallus* or *lingam*. You will find it everywhere, in the forecourt of his temples, set up in the open air under village trees, and enshrined in houses for family worship. A numerous sect in Southern India are called "Lingayets" from their habit of wearing it in miniature. Vishnu represents a more placid conception, which may perhaps be described as the Spirit of Man. In numerous incarnations he has appeared upon the earth—sometimes in animal form (a concession, perhaps, to totemistic ideas), but most notably in the persons of two heroes of the past—Ráma and Krishna—whose exploits are to-day the theme of the Indian story-teller. The former was a prince of Oudh, who by the deceit of his stepmother, was driven into exile, accompanied by Sita, his faithful wife. In his wanderings he undertook labours such as those of Hercules: his wife was carried off by a giant of Ceylon, but was rescued with the assistance of a troop of monkeys. The tale illustrates resignation, fortitude, and wifely fidelity. It is the theme of one of the two great Sanskrit epics; in the sixteenth century it was rendered into Hindu by Tulsi Das, a writer of extraordinary fire and skill, whose poem is still the favourite reading of millions, and is the foundation for dramas or pageants by which the incidents of the story are kept evergreen in popular remembrance. Tulsi Das moralises by the way to very high purpose, and his verses have been of incalculable value in raising the ideals of the Hindi-speaking peoples. The story of Krishna is of a different complexion. Miraculous incidents attending his childhood appeal to the sympathies of mothers and children. But he is associated rather with love than with holiness, and the ardours and successes of his amatory adventures give an erotic flavour to devotional transports. We find, then, this sexual leaning in the cults of both Siva and Vishnu ; but the latter is the more human of the two, and has given birth to some movements of purifying reform.

A conception which has exercised enormous influence is that of female divinities, or *saktis*. The chief of these is the consort of Siva, known as Durga, Káli, or the "Great Mother," whose idols illustrate in grotesque deformity the human passions of lust and cruelty. Her cult has prevailed in the atmosphere of Bengal. She is propitiated with bloody sacrifices ; to extremists among her votaries any sexual restraint is a denial of her authority, and she expresses, or has produced, a profound difference in morality between the inhabitants of the eastern and western plain. It is extraordinary beyond words that ideas of this description should be in the minds of the industrious clerks that throng the offices of Calcutta.

Without in any way denying the authority of others, a Hindu of position connects himself specially with one of these cults, and bears marks of pigment on his forehead to express his allegiance. They are drawn upright if for Vishnu, horizontally if for Siva, and are curved, with a dot, if for the goddess. But the incidents of life may be varied by the interposition of countless other gods ; indeed, there is a divinity for every phase of human activity, pleasure or suffering. For the worship of tradesmen there is a God of Wealth ; for scholars a Goddess of Learning. Craftsmen propitiate the tools of their craft : the clerk adores once a year his pen and inkpot. The divine is even seen in an epidemic of smallpox,[1] and vaccination has until recently been opposed as derogatory to the influence of the " Great Mother." But there are minds which rise above this tangle of beliefs. Men of culture and learning—Brahmins and others—will smile when they speak of popular theology. Their religious exercises are thought and study assisted by the daily reading of the Bhagavadgita,—a treatise composed in the fourth century, which emphasises, allegorically, the vanity of desire, and the enduring consequences of self-control in thought and action.

Hindu worship is individual, not congregational. The temple bell rings, a shell trumpet calls the god to attention, and the people gather to the altar with offerings of flowers. There are fewer men than women. Generally the cultivator takes his religion easily, and is less concerned with formal worship than with the magical rites that propitiate the seasons of sowing and harvest. Grace may be obtained in various ways—by adoring the image of the god, by circumambulating his shrine, by repeating, thousands of times over, the sacred names of Rama and Sita, by bathing in sacred waters, by pilgrimage and by asceticism. Pilgrimages are exceedingly popular, and since merit is not lost by using the train, they add very considerably to the earnings of Indian railways. There are shrines throughout the country—from the slopes of the Himalayas to the sea-coast at Cape Comorin—each annually attracting a crowd of visitants. Prominent in sanctity is the shrine of Jagannáth (a title of Siva) on the Orissa coast. Food taboos are for the occasion

[1] It is curious that in China, also, smallpox should be regarded as a mark of divine favour.

Hoffmann, Calcutta

RIVER-SIDE TEMPLES AT BENARES: ON THE GANGES

suspended and all may eat freely of the temple rice ; the god is drawn forth in his chariot, and, in days gone by, the most ecstatic of his devotees flung themselves to death beneath its wheels. Rivers are generally regarded with veneration : riverside towns are clustered thick with temples leading down by steps to the water's edge. Muttra on the Jumna and Benares on the Ganges are particularly holy, and during festival time people crowd into them by the hundred thousand to win by bathing a remission of sins. The meeting of two rivers is a place of sanctity. At the confluence of the Ganges and Jumna, near Allahabad, a bathing fair attracts on occasion half a million people ; the rivers are then low and their broad sandy beds are covered with a city of booths and shanties. The Ganges is apostrophised as " Mother " : its water is a precious libation and is carried by pilgrims from shrine to shrine. It is the dream of pious Hindus to die upon its banks, or at least to have their ashes thrown into its current. Still more remarkable is the worship of the cow : she animates one of the strongest feelings of modern Hinduism. Neglected, half-starved, though she may be on village pasture-grounds, to kill her or any of her tribe is an abominable sacrilege, exciting passions which set Hindus against Mohammedans, and are capable of setting Hindus against the British. This sentiment is, however, generally controlled by practical exigencies : Hindu cultivators will sell useless cattle to hide-merchants ; Hindu town-councillors will accept amongst their duties the supervision of slaughter-houses. But the sentiment remains—though it be kept in the background—and can easily be agitated into activity. The origin of this cult has baffled enquiry. No clue can be found in Vedic literature. The cow may have been a local totem which was adopted by the Brahmins to win popular favour. Even so does the Arya Samáj—a present-day revival of Vedic worship—side with popular prejudice in proclaiming it abominable to slaughter kine.

The ascetic life was practised in India before the time of Buddha, and the lapse of centuries has not clouded its esteem nor diminished its rigours. Ascetics are familiar figures in an Indian scene. Almost naked, sprinkled with ashes, and wearing long plaits of false hair, they wait for alms at the roadside, wander in groups from shrine to shrine, and congregate in large companies at bathing festivals. Some mortify their flesh with unsparing severity: they will hold up an arm until it withers in the socket, or habitually sleep on a bed of sharp prongs. More human, and more useful, are those who serve the community as spiritual directors (*gurus*), and illustrate the distinction between the prophet and the priest. It is the *guru* to whom the Hindu looks for the direction of his conscience; his Brahmin priest is concerned with ceremonies. Asceticism is not confined to the poor and unlettered; in its ranks you may find men of culture and education. It has generally become the profession of a lifetime, but there are men who have merely passed through the discipline and have returned to a secular career in the world.

Men vaguely believe in the transmigration of the soul. Yet they offer oblations to the souls of their ancestors, preserving a custom, however inconsistent, which has come down through the ages from Vedic times. At an annual festival each Hindu householder offers alms to the shades of the last seven of his ancestors, the offerings decreasing in size with the remoteness of the relationship. To die without a son is to interrupt this celebration, and is considered to be one of the worst of misfortunes. But if the prayers of his wife do not move the Goddess of Fecundity a man may preserve the continuity of his family by adopting a boy.

Ceremonies of mystic significance not only hallow the

HINDU ASCETIC

course of life but attend upon its most ordinary incidents. A journey is not undertaken—much less a marriage—until priests or astrologers have certified the auspices. From birth, when a Brahmin prepares a horoscope, till death, when a Brahmin arranges the pyre, nothing occurs but under Brahmin influence. A boy who belongs to the "twice-born" castes is solemnly invested with the "sacred thread." This is a loop of thick nine-stranded cotton string, made by Brahmins, which passes over the left shoulder and hangs across the body to the waist. The "re-birth" which it signifies was originally into ascetic discipline. It is never put off, and is a conspicuous badge of the privileged orders. Marriage is an elaborate ceremonial; in its course the boy and girl, hand in hand, take seven steps round a fire altar with skirts knotted together to symbolise their union. The little bride returns to her people to await maturity, which the law admits at twelve years, and the opinion of many classes even earlier. At death the body is cremated, burial being, however, granted to persons of extraordinary sanctity. The relatives will not touch the corpse, and it is borne to the pyre by low-caste hirelings. A shallow trench encircles the pyre, shutting it off from the mourners around it. The eldest son steps across the trench, applies a torch, and hastily retires from the contact. When the fire has burnt down, the ashes of the dead are collected to be thrown, if possible, into the waters of the Ganges.

There have from time to time been movements of reform, to simplify and spiritualise beliefs, and to substitute morality for ceremonial. Perhaps the broadest of them all sprung in the fifteenth century from the teachings of Kabir—a man, it is said, of the weaver caste,—who urged the unity of God, the brotherhood of man, and the possibility of communicating with the Divine by ecstatic meditation. He condemned alike the distinctions of caste and the Brahmin priesthood. Disciples flocked to him from both Hindus and Mohammedans, and he founded a sect which still includes numerous adherents. Moreover, his influence spread beyond the circle of his flock. His sayings are quoted as texts throughout Northern India, and his doctrines inspired the reformed religion of the Sikhs, who, beginning in the Punjab as a pietistic sect, grew into a powerful military confederacy. They also rejected caste and the Brahmin priesthood; proselytes could be admitted by adoption, and avowed their membership by some peculiarities of costume. Their tenets were recorded in a holy book (the *Granth*), which owes no small debt to the sayings of Kabir. The faith is now professed by three million persons, but under Brahmin influence many of them have receded from its original simplicity. In Bengal somewhat similar doctrines were preached by Chaitanya, who initiated the *sankirtan*, or service of song, which is the nearest approach among Hindus to congregational worship. The Brahmo Samáj is a theistic sect of more recent date. It owes much to Christian influence, and its adherents threw caste behind them, adopted European dress and manners of life, and freed their women-folk from the restraint of the *zenána*. Half a century ago it hoped to revivify Bengal, and made numerous converts amongst the educated classes. But it has lost much of its vitality, has become tainted with some Hindu prejudices and now counts but a few thousand adherents, divided, moreover, by dissent into three churches. The Arya Samáj is a still later movement of Hindu reform, and is a very active force in North-Western India. During the last ten years its adherents have quadrupled. Professedly its faith is that of the ancient Vedic hymns; but these compositions offer no support to the cult of the cow, which this sect has vigorously adopted. It receives converts from any caste but those lowest in esteem, and within its pale admits

Bourne and Shepherd, Calcutta

A HINDU FUNERAL: AT THE PYRE

of no caste distinctions. Like the Brahmo Samáj, it is practically interested in the education of women, and in the raising of the marriage age. It numbers 243,524 adherents, but its influence is much wider than these figures would imply. We may refer here to the great attraction which educated Hindus find in theosophy. Its conclusions adapt themselves readily to the speculations of Brahmin philosophy, and can be held by orthodox Hindus without derogation to their traditional beliefs.

CHRISTIANITY

Mention has been made in Chapter VII of the numerical strength of the Parsi and Christian communities, and an outline has been given of the Parsi tenets. Christian missionary endeavour may conveniently be assigned to three epochs: the Syrian, opened by the arrival of the Nestorians in the fourth or fifth century; the Portuguese, dating from the conquests made by that nation in the sixteenth century and glorified by the name of St. Francis Xavier; and that of comparatively modern times, which, commencing in the early part of the eighteenth century, has exhibited the solicitude of all branches of Western Christianity. A large Nestorian church grew up on the west coast; it still retains its ancient ritual, although, pressed by the Portuguese, it has, in part, confessed allegiance to the Church of Rome. The Portuguese missions also converted largely on the west coast, but were still more successful in the southern districts of Madras. During the past two centuries missions have spread throughout the country, sent by America and Australia as well as by Europe, and have presented to the people every leading development of Protestant thought, as well as the doctrines of the Roman Church. Of the native Indian Christians, 728,721 are of the Nestorian connection, 1,393,720 are Roman Catholics, and 1,386,798 belong to Protestantism in its various forms. Of these, 332,372 are included in the Church of England and 52,199 in the Salvation Army.

MOHAMMEDANISM

Eight hundred years have passed since Mohammedanism was introduced into India by invading armies. It had become the religion of the Afghans, Persians, and Tartars, who from the eleventh to the sixteenth century pressed across the passes of Afghanistan, and, coming to plunder, stayed to colonise. Aided by their prestige, the faith developed growing centres of its own—notably in Eastern Bengal—and at the present time it is gaining upon Hinduism steadily, if slowly. In the directness of its belief and the simplicity of its ceremonial, it is in the strongest possible contrast to the older religion. The first of its tenets is the Unity of God—a dogma which permits of no speculative refinements. Images, whether of men or animals, are prohibited, and Mohammedan architectural decoration is purely formal. No priesthood is recognised: its spiritual leaders are preachers, not priests. Beyond circumcision, no ceremonies are used of a sacramental type. Prayer is obligatory—for the individual, wherever he may be, at stated hours of the day, and congregational in the mosque on Fridays and festivals. The teachings of its founder—known doctrinely as the Prophet of God, but generally accorded still higher honours—are set forth in the Korán, which is held to have been dictated by divine inspiration. Fidelity and zeal will be rewarded in Paradise, not by joys which are spiritual and indefinite, but by gratifications which are appreciated by the sensual man. The future of women is less clearly indicated. Before the majesty of God all men are equal; Mohammedanism is essentially democratic, and the highest will acknowledge the lowest as his brother. From influences

MOHAMMEDANS AT PRAYER

that might soften rigidity of belief the Mohammedans are protected by special distinctions. They are marked off from the Hindus by differences of dress, and also by differences in their system of nomenclature. A man confesses his faith by the name he bears; indeed, Mohammedan names not uncommonly express a doctrine of religion or an attribute of divinity. Thus distinguished, and meeting one another in public worship, the Mohammedans never forget that they belong to a brotherhood apart; and they are isolated sharply from the Hindus around them.

Mohammedanism—or the faith of Islâm—is, like Christianity, derived from Judaism. The Korân has borrowed very freely from the Old Testament : the Jewish patriarchs and prophets are held in great respect, and their names, like that of the Prophet, are often given to children. Christian influences are also conspicuous. It may possibly be held that the teachings of Mohammed were a protest against the icons and metaphysics of Greek Christianity. But they were tinged by the Gospels, the outlines of which are generally known to all Mohammedans of education. Our Lord is held in very high reverence, and Jews are as much disliked as by many Christians.

Fenced round, though it be, from outside influences, the religion has been unable to withstand corrupting additions. Saints are accorded honours that are almost divine; by the uneducated they are undoubtedly worshipped. Their shrines are places of popular pilgrimage at which festivals are held, that, to all appearance, differ little from those of the Hindus. Indeed, Mohammedans and Hindus are both disposed to share in the pleasure of each other's amusements, and some Hindus will take part in the processions which enliven Mohammedan festivals. Converts from the lower castes of Hindus have formed a large proportion of the Mohammedan community. Their earlier impressions still linger with them; their faith is corrupted by local superstitions, and with ritual observances, which in effect confess the polytheism they have renounced.

The dogmatic simplicity of the faith of Islâm has not limited the ingenuity of schismatic reformers. In India the most prominent disagreement is that which separates the Sunni and the Shiah sects. They differ as to the authority of certain commentaries on the Korân ; but the question on which their feelings are most deeply divided is the legality of the Prophet's three immediate successors. Abu Bakr, Umar and Usman were elected by their followers, in disregard of the claims which Ali might advance as being the son-in-law and heir of Mohammed. Ali succeeded to the fourth vacancy ; but his son, Hussain, was killed by seceders who forgot the sanctity of the Prophet's blood. The Shiahs hold that Ali was Mohammed's first legal successor, and that Hussain died in the glory of martyrdom. His tomb is with them a place of pilgrimage ; and each year they celebrate his death by mourning processions. The sect has its headquarters in Persia, and may, indeed, be regarded as a Persian dissent from a religion of Arabs : its strongholds in India are the cities of Lucknow and Hyderabad. But, wherever there are Mohammedans, there are annual celebrations of the death of Hussain ; and models of his shrine —prettily constructed of paper and tinsel—are carried in procession, and are finally thrown into a river or pond. There is loud lamentation, but also music and dancing ; and Sunnis (as well as low-caste Hindus) ignore the meaning of the festival that they may share its excitements.

The Mohammedan marriage is a civil ceremony—a contract entered into before a notary. Divorce is recognised and needs little formality. But the husband is obliged to pay over the dowry, the settlement of which is part of the marriage contract. So safeguarded, marriages are in fact seldom annulled. The dead are not cremated, but are buried in the hopes of a personal resurrection.

India affords an interesting study to those who would search religious beliefs for the origin of so-called "national" characteristics. Two powerful religions exist side by side, professed by communities that are in great measure related by descent. Intellectually the Hindus have been by far the most progressive: they have eagerly pursued Western literature and science; class-rooms and examination rooms are crowded with their boys, and their foremost men attain a high European standard in knowledge and eloquence. To the Mohammedans, Western learning has been far less attractive; until recently they have indeed held back from acquiring it, and their ignorance of English has cost them dearly in the loss of appointments in the superior service of the Government. This difference may perhaps be ascribed to the effects of a speculative and of a dogmatic religion. Hinduism is tolerant of opinions—indeed, careless of belief—so long as there is due regard of ceremonial observances. Mohammedanism is the reverse—rigid in its doctrinal tenets, suspicious of anything which may tend to undermine them. This rigidity also affects its sentiments, and such feelings as loyalty, generosity and gratitude are accepted without question as laudable guides of conduct. To the Hindu mind it appears that motives, however excellent in themselves, may quite legitimately be analysed before they are actually followed. The obligation of a vow cannot be evaded. But, when unfettered in this way, the attachments of man may reasonably be guided by the calculations of his intellect.

Here then we seem able to trace differences of character to differences of religion. But this clue does not assist to account for the character of the Parsis. They are a peculiar people, distinguished by their commercial and industrial capacity; they have not only accepted but have assimilated Western standards. In their religion there appears nothing to foster these aptitudes. Their distinctive progressiveness must, apparently, be ascribed to their blood; and they have certainly taken care to preserve any racial peculiarities they may possess, for they admit no converts, and marry only amongst themselves. Why, then, do they differ so widely from their kinsmen who remained in Persia and were converted to Islám? An Indian environment has to them, apparently, been a developing force.

CHAPTER X

EDUCATION AND ITS EFFECTS

MANY and varied are the means of grace which religion has offered for the improvement of mankind: it is now fashionable to believe that education may be substituted for them all, and may even be trusted—so far go enthusiasts—to eradicate the strongest peculiarities of racial or local character. Yet it may, perhaps, be surmised, from the variety of the theories which educationalists discuss, that they are not quite satisfied with the practice of any of them. In India, English literature has been substituted for Oriental literature without in any way anglicising the ideas of the students; science has been tried in the place of literature in the hope that it would give accuracy to minds that are satisfied by indeterminate conceptions; book-work has been relieved by hand and eye-training and the cult of gymnastics; and at present great hopes are entertained of the withdrawal of students from the influences of their homes and their subjection to boarding-house—or hostel—discipline. This idea may be fruitful indeed, since it would modify very drastically the student's environment; and, beyond doubt, a change of circumstances affects character more deeply than does the amassing of knowledge. No amount of study will work such a regeneration in an English labourer or artisan as comes about after a short residence in Canada. And such alterations as have occurred in Indian ideas and habits are due very largely to the experience young Indians have gathered in Europe and America.

ENGLISH EDUCATION

India owes her introduction to English literature, not to the British Government, but to Christian missionaries.

In the early days of British rule the State found that it responded most closely to the wishes of the people by fostering Oriental studies in Sanskrit, Arabic and Persian. At the beginning of last century English schools were established in Calcutta, Bombay and Madras by missionary enterprise which will always be associated with the names of Martyn, Carey and Duff. These institutions proved useful to the Government in providing it with subordinate officials who could work in English; and official authority soon lost its suspicions and was ready to assist them. A generation later—in 1837—moved in great measure by the advocacy of Lord Macaulay (who was at the time a member of the Viceroy's Council), the Government of India decided to substitute English for Oriental studies as the instrument for higher education. This momentous conclusion had the effect of anglicising, not only high schools and colleges, but the official machinery of administration. It has led to the banishment of the vernaculars from public offices; and at the present day, in the more advanced provinces, you will hardly find a clerk—above the humblest position—who does not transact his duties in English.

For some years, however, the new learning was but moderately attractive. Its popularity amongst the Hindus dates from the establishment of examining universities which could attest the proficiency of students in various grades of learning by the grant of certificates, diplomas and degrees. Such universities were founded at Calcutta, Bombay and Madras in 1867; at Allahabad in 1870, and at Lahore in 1878. The examination hall offered an exciting method of achieving distinction. Moreover, the examinations were consecrated by the State as avenues to the public service, certificates of having matriculated, having passed the intermediate examination, or having graduated, being accepted as qualifying for different grades of Government employ.

And, since this employ has been in popular esteem superior to any other means of livelihood, to appear and to succeed at the university examinations has been the ambition of every youth of promise. Nor have the universities felt inclined to limit the numbers who try their fortune on paper: they have been supported almost wholly by examination fees, and the greater the number of candidates the larger has been their income. So stimulated, English education has become exceedingly popular amongst Hindu townspeople. Schools, above the most elementary grade, which teach in vernacular, attract few students unless English classes be added to them; and there is even a desire to use English as the medium of instruction for the infant classes of high schools.

There are now 3,590 [1] schools and 119 [1] colleges in which English is taught, respectively, to 590,000 and 21,500 students. The greater number of these institutions are managed not by the State or its departments, but by private committees or individuals; indeed, the State directly controls only one in six of the schools and one in five of the colleges. It is somewhat surprising that a Government of benevolent activities—which maintains hospitals, dispensaries, railways and irrigation canals—should have disembarrassed itself so largely of the business of education. Thirty years ago the policy was deliberately adopted of using private effort, so far as possible, in the establishment and maintenance of schools and colleges, and of fostering education rather by making grants-in-aid to such private ventures than by charging the State with the duties of public instruction. In reality at least two-thirds of the private institutions are dependent upon the State, in so far that they receive a grant-in-aid and could not make shift without it. They are most commonly in charge of committees of private

[1] Apart from institutions for purely technical instruction.

citizens, interested in education, or having boys to educate. Subscriptions are raised for the initial establishment of the school, but when once it has been started the income at the committee's disposal consists of little more than the Government grant and the fees collected from students. By this enlistment of private interests and private liberality, the teaching of English has without doubt been extended much more rapidly than would have been the case had its initiation rested with the State. And the utmost economy is secured, since committees have no desire to spend money upon what they consider to be unessentials, and feel no objection to paying teachers the lowest salaries they will accept. The buildings are squalid and overcrowded, and the teachers come and go, without influence over the students, and contented indeed to do no more than hear them repeat their lessons. Missionary schools and colleges are on a higher plane. And it should be observed that the State has become aware of the dangers attending the grant-in-aid system, and is now modifying its policy by accepting a larger responsibility for the direct provision of education in institutions of its own.

But, indeed, if the view be taken that the study of English should be ancillary to higher education, it is easy to criticise destructively the results that are obtained, whether in government or in private institutions. Assuming that the school course lasts over eight years, some 80,000 students should annually be fit to appear at the University matriculation examination, or at the School Final examination which has lately been instituted as an alternative. The number that actually appears is less than 24,000, of whom considerably more than half are rejected by the examiners. It is difficult for masters to teach and for students to learn in a strange language ; text-books that are not understood may be committed to memory, but memory will not serve an examinee unless he can use it selectively. Only 8,000 students proceed to the intermediate examination, and of these more than half fail to pass. For the degree again half those appearing are unsuccessful, and the number of degrees annually granted hardly exceeds 2,000. But, according to popular ideas, a knowledge of English is not merely a stepping-stone to high education: it is desirable in itself, however trifling it be. A small acquaintance with the language will secure a clerk a few rupees of additional pay; and youths who at school acquire a mere smattering will improve their knowledge vastly in after life—being greatly assisted by the reading of newspapers—so that you will not infrequently meet men who speak and write English with fluency, whose school record was of the very poorest. Of the popularity of English education there can be no doubt, and the Mohammedans, who at first held aloof, are now seeking it in rapidly increasing numbers. According to the last census, 1,300,000 Indians are literate in English. This may appear to be an insignificant proportion of the population. But it includes the majority of those who are qualified by their restlessness to disturb public opinion.

The spread of English has facilitated, and in some ways greatly improved, the work of Government. From amongst the graduates of the universities can be secured men who are intellectually capable of serving the State in responsible executive and judicial capacities; and those who at college have been less successful provide an ample supply of industrious and obedient clerks. Education may also claim to have raised the standard of official conduct; certain it is that Indian judges and magistrates have become very much more reliable than they were a generation ago, and while the development of an influential and critical Indian bar has no doubt contributed to this improvement, it has assuredly been fostered by the ideals that are presented by English literature. When, however, we come to enquire how far the new learning has generally modified Indian views or conduct, we are surprised to find how small has been the change, compared with that which Western knowledge has brought about in Japan within the space of a generation, or has effected within the small Parsi community. Indeed, it is possible to suspect that if British rule were withdrawn Western ideas would vanish with it. And if it be urged that these ideas are shallow-rooted because they have been planted by an alien government, it remains to be explained why they have not taken deeper hold in the Native States where Indian aspirations can follow their own course. Lessons may be the wheels of a nation's progress, but can hardly give the power that is needed to move the car. In themselves they are merely as machinery which is lifeless unless fired by a spirit of change. The most conspicuous effect of English education is indeed not moral or material, but political. In towns, throughout the country, a large class has sprung up, sufficiently acquainted with English to follow the words of journalists and advocates, the members of which feel united by the use of a common language, realise the possibility of an Indian nationality, and will eagerly adopt a patriotic ideal which involves no practical change in habits of mind or social usages. The Nationalist party, with its mission of criticising and frequently of condemning the British Government, owes its existence to the English language. It naturally advocates the spread of English education. The university senates have been its strongholds, and it bitterly resented the interference of the Government, some eight years ago, to reduce the size of these bodies; and, by providing that their members should possess educational knowledge or experience, to give them more of an educational and less of a political complexion.

Intellectually Indian colleges have produced notable

fruit: their foremost students can hold their own in European company; a Mahratta student has, indeed, been senior wrangler. But, whether because sentimentally attached to ancient ways, or lacking the vigour for change, or confused by a philosophical uncertainty of conviction, a Hindu student appears able to grasp a position intellectually and still to hold back from trusting his mind to it. The vague catholicity of his religion may perhaps have taught him that inconsistence is no ground for abandoning an opinion. This attitude is illustrated by common experience. An Englishman is constantly disconcerted by the extraordinary contradictions which he observes between the words and the actions of an educated Indian, who seems untouched by inconsistencies which to him appear scandalous. For upwards of half a century Indian youths have been studying a literature which sets liberty above conventionality, comfort above dignity, and exalts the romantic side of love: they give eager intellectual assent to these ideals, yet live their lives unchanged. Science, it might seem, would stiffen convictions and unify them; and the universities have offered the study of science, in English, as an alternative to the study of English literature. It has attracted students in considerable numbers, but they have generally shown no desire to utilise their knowledge, and are quite content if they can make use of it to secure a livelihood in literary employ.

From the moral point of view the results of education are not infrequently deplored by both teachers and parents. Home influences, it is asserted, have been subverted by the opinions of the class-room, and these have encouraged insubordination and made light of morality. Student life has, however, been irregular in many other countries. In India there has undoubtedly been a very abrupt change. Formerly the teacher was not merely the instructor but the spiritual director of his pupils, and was

13—(2134)

owed by them the extremest respect. In these days he may be a man of inferior caste; and in any case he considers himself paid simply to give assistance in secular studies. But, after all, the seeds of indiscipline are not only to be found in school class-rooms. Indian parents are notoriously indulgent, and the home is by no means a shrine before which impurity is abashed, or at least seeks to conceal itself. Too seldom is it held that youth should be celibate, or do Indian parents think on the lines that led to the establishment of English schools and colleges on a monastic basis. Indian youth is generally irregular, and indeed in Bengal numbers of students have been found to lodge in prostitutes' quarters. Self-control in this or any other direction has generally lacked the support of religious teaching. In religious matters the Government is severely neutral, and in its own schools and colleges instruction is limited to secular subjects. But private institutions are at liberty to teach what religion they please, although they are assisted by a State subvention; and the grant-in-aid system appeared to offer a means by which a secular government might encourage religious instruction. In this direction its success has been exceedingly limited. In missionary institutions the Bible is taught to non-Christian as well as to Christian students, and the former, who are generally in the vast majority, show no dislike to Scripture reading, and resent less bitterly than they did the conversion of one of their fellows to Christianity. An endeavour is made to influence the private life of the students, and it may perhaps be said, that in conduct and discipline youths brought up in missionary institutions compare favourably with others. In Mohammedan schools lessons are given in the tenets of religion, and the Korán is taught, with a commentary. The Anglo-Mohammedan College at Aligarh—the most successful Mohammedan college in the world—is on a definitely religious basis, and its students bear an excellent reputation for truthfulness and courage. But in Hindu institutions, which are the vast majority, the instruction is purely secular : the tenets of modern Hinduism would be difficult to teach, and could hardly be associated with lessons in morality. In the Hindu College at Benares self-control is inculcated upon grounds that are drawn from Hindu philosophy. Schemes are now on foot for the establishment of two "denominational" universities—one for Hindus and the other for Mohammedans,—and they have received a large measure of popular support. The examinations which such universities would provide for their degrees would test the acquaintance of students with religious subjects. The existing universities concern themselves only with secular knowledge.

The educational policy of the State is now exhibiting some important developments. The opinion has gained ground that universities should be more numerous, of smaller size, and should concern themselves with teaching, as well as with examining : further, that the Educational department should set a more conspicuous standard to private institutions by maintaining more colleges and schools of its own. It is also recognised more clearly that habits of good conduct can most effectually be instilled if students are removed from outside influences—those of their own homes included—by being lodged under supervision in hostels or boarding-houses. These are being energetically provided both by the State and by some missionary associations. From this new departure educational hopes draw much encouragement. And probably with reason, for, living his life in a scholastic atmosphere, a youth may not only acquire enduring habits of self-control, but may assimilate new ideas more effectively than when they are in daily conflict with the old-fashioned prejudices of his home. Educational policy is, in fact, reverting to the monastic system. This was, of course, as highly reputed in India as in Europe, and a college which has lately been established by the Arya Samáj is organised very completely upon a monastic basis, the students being altogether secluded from outside influence during the period of their college course.

It is an obvious criticism of British educational policy that it annually throws upon the country thousands of ill-educated and discontented young men who despise manual labour but are intellectually unfit for any position above a petty clerkship. The great majority of those who work for examinations fail to pass them ; indeed, failure is so general that to have tried unsuccessfully has come to be accepted as an educational qualification. Much unhappiness must result from this wastage. And those who succeed in the examination room purchase their success at the cost of their mental contentment. In the course of their education they have learnt to respect ideals which are so incompatible with their customs as not to be adopted in practice without a forfeiture of their most intimate relationships. The natural result is an instability and petulance of judgment. Irritated by a feeling of hopelessness, they will at times violently condemn the European standards which at heart they approve, and will fling themselves into movements of violent reaction. This is only to be expected. Ferments disturb the material upon which they act, and social changes are necessarily accompanied by restlessness and unhappiness. Unemployment is a further source of discontent. Government service can no longer absorb all those who are qualified for it : the pursuit of medicine, engineering or commerce has, so far, offered little, and the only openings are afforded by teaching, journalism or the law. These professions are now crowded. But whatever be the complications English education has introduced, it was obviously impossible to withhold it. And we must remember that it has produced men of high culture and ability who have by their service under the Government conspicuously increased its efficiency, and have brought about within the last generation an astonishing rise in the standard of official conduct. It has further created an Indian bar of great strength and intelligence, which, if unfortunately encouraging the litigious tendencies of the people, has done much to improve the administration of justice.

The Indian Press

English education has been the ferment from which has sprung an active and influential Indian press. Newspapers, in English and in vernacular, are published in hundreds for Indian readers. Judged by a European standard, the issues of most of them are exceedingly small. But in few countries does a single newspaper serve so many people : it is read aloud, passed from hand to hand, and we may probably assume that in this way it influences ten times as many persons as the copies it issues. A dispassionate judgment of the Indian press cannot be very favourable. A large number of papers display much ability. Several of those published in English are written with the mordant incisiveness of an accomplished journalist : the vernacular papers more often affect a rhetorical style, which makes a stronger appeal to popular feeling. As a rule they are against the Government, and indeed it is hardly possible to suppose that the press of a country which is under alien control should not display all the freedom it possesses in attacking the authorities. But unqualified condemnation has been merited by the practice of blackmailing individuals who are afraid of being pilloried; and also by the readiness of newspaper proprietors to add to their income by the publication of advertisements of a most disreputable description. Until six years ago the most advanced of

Indian journalists seldom permitted themselves openly to express sedition: the prestige of the Government was great, and when reform was advocated it was only from the Government that they could hope to obtain it. The authorities, although not infrequently irritated by fault-finding that was unjust, sustained it with apparent indifference. But of recent years the Indian journalist has found a more sympathetic ear for his complaints in a section of the Liberal members of the British Parliament. And his position and his courage have been greatly strengthened by the practical results that have followed his invectives, by the feeling that he has become able actively to influence the course of government. The immediate result of this increase of power has been an outbreak of very seditious writing, in which not only has British rule been violently attacked, but assassination has been advocated, covertly or openly, as a laudable means of bringing it to an end. So flagrant was the evil that the British Liberal party, with all its traditions, could no longer support in India the freedom of the press, and in 1909 approved the passing of a repressive measure in the Viceroy's Legislative Council. The Act gave power to the Executive to demand security from the editor of a newly-established paper, or from the editor of an established paper which published matter that appeared to the Government to be seditious; and the security might be forfeited and the printing press confiscated if sedition was thereafter published. From the executive order of forfeiture or confiscation an appeal lay to the High Court. It is generally admitted that these regulations had a moderating effect. But peace came from weariness: the public grew tired of restless quarrelling with authority, and thankfully hailed the gracious sympathy of the King-Emperor, and the pronouncements made by him in *durbar* at Delhi, as enabling them to abandon the conflict without "loss of face."

Technical Education

Turning now from literary education to practical or technical instruction we have a much narrower prospect to survey. It was, of course, impossible to administer the Government medical, veterinary and engineering departments without the assistance of an Indian staff, and the State found it necessary, many years ago, to establish special colleges for the teaching of these professions. There are at present four medical and four veterinary colleges, attended, respectively, by 1,500 and 500 students, and five engineering colleges attended by 1,200 students. The great majority of their graduates enter Government service. The Indian public has in fact no great demand for them. In the large towns private medical practitioners command a fair practice, but a considerable proportion of the most successful are pensioners who have completed their service under the State. Outside the presidency towns a veterinary surgeon could find no private practice that would support him in decency. Engineers are, of course, needed in large numbers on the railways, in cotton and jute factories, and in the mining districts. But men who have graduated at a college are of little use until they have undergone a practical training, and Indian youths are not attracted by the conditions under which young men learn engineering in Europe, serving a long apprenticeship, for the advantages of which they are expected to pay a premium. There are five agricultural colleges. In Western India the sons of well-to-do landholders are beginning to take advantage of a training which will help them to farm more profitably, but elsewhere the students take up agriculture merely to obtain Government service in the land-revenue and agricultural departments. Law colleges are far more attractive. There are twenty-four with 2,800 students. Legal advice and assistance are in great demand, and outside Government service, the bar is the only profession which offers a dignified career, in which ability can command generally a competence and sometimes a fortune. It should be added that technical classes below the college standard are in more request. Medical schools for the training of hospital assistants include 3,600 students, handicraft schools 8,200 students, commercial schools 1,400 students, and art schools 1,600 students. The teaching they impart is in great measure elementary, but their increasing popularity is a hopeful sign.

Foreign Educational Influences

A survey of Indian higher education, however rapid, must not entirely overlook the effect upon the country of the increasing resort of Indian students to foreign lands. Young men studying in a strange country acquire, consciously or unconsciously, from their surroundings even more than from their studies; and on their return to India they view the ideas and habits of their countrymen in a critical spirit which no class-room teaching could have imparted to them. The number of young Indians who are studying abroad is larger than is generally supposed. There are believed to be some 1,700 in the United Kingdom: many at the Universities of Oxford, Cambridge, and Edinburgh, very many more in London. In far fewer, but in considerable numbers, they are attending lectures or working in factories on the continent of Europe and in America. Japan is less popular than it was a few years ago, when the Indian Nationalist party hoped for great things from the sympathy of an Asiatic but progressive country. Originally Indian students were attracted to England by the hopes of passing the examinations that admit to the Indian Civil Service, the Indian Medical Service, or the English bar. In the two former few succeed; but Indian barristers are becoming exceedingly numerous—indeed on occasions the number of Indians who are called approaches a third of the total. There is now, moreover, an increasing desire amongst Indian gentlemen of means that their sons should complete their education in England; and there is a growing conviction amongst Indians of intelligence that for the industrial development of their country it is necessary that young men should learn on the spot the methods that have succeeded in more progressive societies. An association has been established for the financing of youths who desire to study manufacturing processes abroad, and numerous scholarships are awarded by the Government for this purpose. The success of the movement depends upon the readiness of Indian capitalists to embark upon new industries and to employ these trained men. Until within the last few years Indians who returned from Europe or America with technical experience could make use of it only as a claim for appointment to government service. But there is now undoubtedly a more practical desire for industrial development. It will easily be understood that the influence of European town life upon young Indians may be degrading as well as instructional, and not a few of them purchase their experience by the sacrifice of all mental and moral ballast. This danger has been recognised, and a special agency has been established in London for the guidance of those who will accept assistance from the hands of the State.

Vernacular and Primary Education

So strong is the persuasion that education should consist in the study of English that, speaking generally, it is only primary schools that limit their scope to the teaching of the vernaculars. There are special Hindu schools for the study of Sanskrit. But they are not numerous nor flourishing. The Mohammedans have for long time past maintained schools of their own, in which children commence by committing chapters of the Korán to memory, and then pass, through the vernacular, to the study of Persian or Arabic. But English classes are gradually being added to them, and they will soon differ only in their Mohammedan atmosphere from the secular schools that prepare for the university examinations. An English education is, however, obviously not for the multitude : it is too expensive, and it costs too many years of life. If the masses are to be educated it must be in the vernacular and within the limits of the primary standard.

In Burma schools have commonly been maintained by Buddhist monasteries, and from early times elementary knowledge has been generally diffused. But in India proper at the commencement of British rule any general acquaintance with reading, writing, and arithmetic was confined to three classes of the community—the Brahmins, the traders, and those belonging to the " writer " caste, who competed with the Brahmins for clerical service under the Government. Their sons were taught, in great measure, at home. There were Brahmin schools, in which the students were rather the disciples than the pupils of their teacher. And, as already mentioned, there were special schools for the Mohammedans. But they affected but a very small proportion of the population. Within the last half century, the British Government has called into existence a very large organisation for the teaching of the elements of knowledge in vernacular. It embraces over 120,000 schools in towns and villages, attended by over five million pupils, of whom, however, about a quarter are in infant classes. Only one-seventh of the pupils are girls. Humiliation of caste are not recognised in this system : it is for the low as well as for the high castes, but much practical difficulty has been experienced in giving effect to this revolutionary principle. The pupils are generally expected to pay a small fee—two or three pence a month. But exceptions are freely given, and the free list includes quite a quarter of the pupils.

The Indian finances have never provided an amount that was adequate for the support of this organisation: the school accommodation has generally been cramped and squalid, and the teachers very imperfectly trained and underpaid. But the popularity of the instruction has depended more upon the habits of the community than upon the expenditure of the State. In Bengal, Bombay and Madras parents are not disinclined to send their sons to school, and in these provinces, of the boys of school-going age, almost a third are under instruction. In Burma the proportion is about a quarter, but this does not include all the children who are learning to read and write in monastery schools. In the United Provinces and the Punjab it hardly reaches a fifth. It is a curious reflection that these should be the provinces in which the admixture of Aryan blood is largest. Little more than half a century has passed since the Punjab was annexed; this may partly explain its backwardness, and its schools are certainly now gaining popularity. The indifference to education of the people of the United Provinces is difficult to explain; it is noticeable amongst the Hindi-speaking people of the adjacent districts of Bengal and the United Provinces, so that it cannot be ascribed to peculiar indifference on the part of the provincial authorities.

If we include the adult population in our review we find that in the whole of India only 16,938,815 males and 1,600,763 females are able to read and write. The percentages of these numbers on the male and female populations are, respectively, 10·5 and 1·0. Elementary education is most widely diffused in Burma where 37 per cent. *of the male population* was classed at the census as literate.

In India proper it is most general in Madras with a literate percentage of 13; the percentage is 12 in Bombay, 11 in Bengal, and only 7 in the United Provinces and the Punjab. But these figures refer to the male population only; if females are included, the percentages will fall, almost, by a half.

In respect to primary, as in respect to higher, schools the policy of the Government has been divided between two theories of maintenance—that they should be supported by public funds, and that they should be left to private enterprise assisted by a grant-in-aid. Different provinces have inclined some to one and some to the other of these theories, and it is possible to compare the results. The latter undoubtedly conduces to the multiplication of schools and of pupils, but it is much less efficient than the former in its educational results, and of the thousands of schools which have sprung up under this system in the districts of Bengal a large proportion scarcely lead their pupils beyond the alphabet. Generally, indeed, village schools can be given little credit if they are judged by the proportion of pupils that successfully complete the primary standard. On the salaries they receive the schoolmasters cannot be expected to be capable or diligent. The emoluments of proportionately few reach £12 per annum, and there are thousands who cannot reckon upon half this amount. Special classes have been provided for the training of village schoolmasters, but the period of training cannot be adequate if any attempt be made to pass through the course the large numbers who are awaiting it. With so poor a teaching staff a strong inspecting staff was doubly necessary. But here again lack of funds has denied what was required for efficiency. Village schools give clever boys some opportunity: a provision of scholarships enables them to carry on their studies in English schools. But, so far, primary education has not made the peasant class less conservative in their ideas, more ready to adopt improved farming processes, or less ready to waste money upon marriage festivities. The educational value of elementary knowledge may easily be overrated. But an extending acquaintance with reading, writing and arithmetic is undoubtedly enabling them to deal on better terms with landlords, merchants and money-lenders who may desire to exploit them, and is helping them to share more equitably in the produce of their fields.

Inspection apart, the expenditure upon *primary vernacular* education from public funds, whether imperial, provincial or local, has not exceeded £800,000 a year. This is brought up to £1·3 million by school fees (£300,000) and subscriptions (£200,000). Improvements which are needed to secure a reasonable minimum of efficiency in teaching the existing number of pupils would involve an additional expenditure of at least £300,000. As was announced at the Delhi *durbar*, the educational budget has been increased by this amount, but primary schools will not secure the whole of it. Moreover, it is becoming very clear that a very substantial increase must be made in the scope as well as in the efficiency of primary education. The Indian Nationalist party maintains very strongly that primary education in India should be free and compulsory according to the modern doctrines of Western countries, and also of Japan. They claim in their favour that the principle has actually been accepted by two of the Indian Native States: but an examination of the results is not convincing, and it may be urged that even in England compulsory education has not altogether fulfilled expectations, so large a proportion of the pupils (for one thing) forgetting on leaving school what they have learnt there. Great difficulties are in the way of its general adoption in India. To give elementary schooling to *all boys alone* would probably entail an additional expenditure of at least

£4 millions a year, equal approximately to the loss which the Indian exchequer will sustain from the impending relinquishment of the trade in opium with China. Moreover it is likely that legal compulsion would be actively resented in those parts of India where the inhabitants are weakest in education but strongest in character. At the same time it is difficult to hold that the Indian people should not enjoy the educational opportunities that progressive nations have held necessary for themselves, and the Government has undertaken to develop primary instruction very largely indeed.

Female Education

In India, as elsewhere, women gather round the ark of time-honoured prejudice, which indeed can hardly be attacked unless they are tempted from their allegiance. If a change is desired in social ideas and habits, endeavour must be made to win their sympathies, and in India these so far have remained almost unassailed. Society offers no fundamental objection to the schooling of a youth till he reaches manhood, but a respectable girl must not leave the house when she has attained marriageable age, and hence must abandon her studies before she is twelve. Zenána missions apart, there are no governesses for home education. The number of girls at school is only 4 per cent. of those of school-going age, and quite one-third of them are in the infant stage. Less than 15,000 girls are reading above the primary standard; there are only 2,500 in high schools and 317 in colleges. Generally, there is no desire whatever to have girls taught. And there is a special difficulty in the provision of teachers. There are thousands of young widows to whom the prospect of learning and of teaching would give interest to a future which is now a blank. But a widow is no more emancipated than a wife, and, according to current opinion, would forfeit all respectability by facing the world in independence. Indians do not favour what the Japanese have accepted—the co-education of boys and girls up to the age of twelve. Female education is then deplorably backward. Indeed only in Burma has it given any colour to society, and here less than a tenth of the girls are at school. In India men who wish for female sympathy upon public questions must seek it from the women of the town.

But there are signs of an advance. Girls' high schools and colleges, established by missionary societies are beginning to draw pupils from a wider circle than Christian or Anglicised families. The Parsis have for many years recognised the claims of their girls to a good education, and a measure of freedom in life ; the emancipation of woman is almost a doctrinal tenet of the Brahmo Samáj community in Bengal, and its ladies are prominent in Calcutta society. Even in the most orthodox Bengali families it has become the fashion to provide some home tuition for the daughters, who, if altogether unlettered, have some difficulty in getting married. The Mahrattas, in Western India, have never insisted very particularly upon the strict seclusion of their women-folk, and are now, it seems, inclining to the idea that their girls might at least attend school till they are married, even if their marriage be postponed till the age of fifteen or sixteen. The raising of the marriage age is certainly the first practical step to reform, and this question has been taken up with particular zeal by the Arya Samáj revival in the Punjab, which has included female education in its propaganda, and has accomplished much in the establishment of girls' schools. Members of this sect will even permit their young wives to attend school. Movement seems then to be in the air. And it will be quickened very greatly should, as is not improbable, woman's education be associated with feelings of patriotism—if to educate his daughters be accepted as incumbent upon a father who considers his self-respect bound up with the progress of his country. Many of the Nationalist leaders are convinced that for the advancement of India the women must step forward as well as the men ; there are heart-searchings upon this question, and they may gradually undermine existing prejudices. If reform is coming, the State will do well to advance to meet it, and to avoid the shadow of a reproach that it was inappreciative of the importance of woman's interests.

Educational Expenditure

The expenditure upon education, in all its branches, that is met from public funds—imperial, provincial and local—has been mounting rapidly, and now exceeds £2·5 millions a year, somewhat more than an eighth of the expenditure upon the army. Further very substantial increases to the educational budget have recently been announced in Parliament.

CHAPTER XI

EUROPEANS IN INDIA

SPEAKING generally, Europeans can live in India only as birds of passage, and, preserving their characteristics, are hardly better able to settle down and breed in the country than are the snipe and duck which, during the cool months of the year, resort to Indian feeding-grounds. The climate is injurious to the European temperament. Children may be born in India without detriment; if sent to Europe before sexual maturity approaches they show no sign of degeneration. But if they remain in India until and after this critical period in their lives, they appear to lose their energy of mind and body. Their nature may not change so completely as to bring on sexual maturity at as early an age as with Indian children, but they begin to experience sexual feelings earlier than is habitual with their race. This fact is strikingly significant, since it indicates the effect of the Indian climate upon physical constitution, and assists us to believe the common opinion that the climate also affects very prejudicially the European character. European influence can then make for itself in India no established, enduring centre: military occupation cannot be strengthened by colonies. There is, indeed, one place which has seemed to some observers to be capable of European colonisation—the Vale of Kashmir. This lies amidst the Himalayas, 5,000 feet above the sea-level. But the suitability of Kashmir for the breeding of Europeans has never been demonstrated; and, since the whole of the arable area is occupied for cultivation, foreigners could obtain room only by forcibly dispossessing the people of the land. Some doubt may be felt as to the precise cause which renders an Indian environment so injurious to Europeans. The sun's rays are felt more than in many tropical countries. The heat may at times be equalled in Australia or North America, but never over such long periods. And India is saturated with malaria, the effect of which on the human constitution is exceedingly enervating. Be the cause what it may, India enfeebles white races that cling to her breasts.

The number of Europeans who make a passing home in India appears, indeed, to be surprisingly small. There are some 60,000 Dutch in the island of Java, a considerable number of whom have permanently settled there. If we exclude the British military forces, and the persons that are attached to them, there are hardly double this number of Europeans living in the wide territory of India. Of these the Government officials and their families may be estimated[1] to form an eighth. The non-official Europeans who are temporarily resident in the country in the pursuit of commerce, planting, or other professions, do not probably much exceed 50,000. The remainder are families, generally in poor circumstances, that are domiciled in the country, and do not differ very markedly in their conditions from the better class of the Eurasian, or, as it is now styled, the "Anglo-Indian" community. This community includes over 100,000 persons, but within it have been classed a large number of families whose only connection with Europe is a small admixture of Portuguese blood.

In the interests of the Indian people, perhaps the most important class of Europeans in the country are the

[1] The census figures which have as yet been published do not classify the European population according to the occupations of its members, and it is thus impossible to determine the proportions in which this population is supported by Government service, and by each of the various occupations in which non-officials are engaged.

80,000 white troops, that form a third of the Indian Army. Not only does this force repress the internal dissensions which antipathies and jealousies are ready to provoke : it dams back the torrent of invasion which for thirty centuries at least has poured across the mountain frontiers. If Central Asia is less prolific of men than in former days, Afghanistán and Nepál are well stocked with warriors, who are, as yet, untouched by the material arguments that have rendered war distasteful to the nations of Europe. The hopes of the most ardent of Indian patriots are overshadowed by visions of these tribesmen ; and the demands of the Nationalist party seldom aspire to the evacuation of their country by the British garrison. In the next place come, we suppose, the European officials by whose agency the Indian Government maintains order, administers justice, and gives effect to its multifarious designs for improving the production of the country and the condition of its people. The effect upon India of European government officials, military and civil, will however be described in subsequent chapters, and we are here concerned with the relations which have existed between the Indian people and Europeans who have resorted to India, not in the service of the Government, but in non-official capacities.

Europeans came to India primarily for trade. They represented the influence and capital of powerful companies which aspired to enhance their profits by maintaining a monopoly, and viewed with the extremest jealousy any of their fellow-countrymen who attempted to share in the Indian trade outside their charter. Such private traders, from time to time, fitted out ships and arrived in Indian ports. They were regarded as interlopers, and not infrequently were deported by force. In those days England was not a democratic country, but the pretensions of the East India Company to exclude all but its shareholders from the Indian trade could not fail to arouse the bitterest hostility. The original company was forced to open its arms to a rival syndicate; but the widened corporation was not less strict in its opposition to private adventurers, and it was not until 1833 that the Indian trading ports were made free to all who wished to do business in them, and that Europeans were permitted to find their way, uncontrolled, into the country districts. India is now, of course, open to all who wish to enter the country, without regard to nationality. The French, Dutch, Danes, and Portuguese, who in former days competed with the British for Indian commerce, have hardly attempted to regain in private business the position they lost in those forceful days. With the Germans it is different: they have resorted in considerable numbers to Calcutta, Bombay and Rangoon, and play an important part in the mercantile life of these cities. These German colonies are sufficiently numerous to maintain clubs of their own.

There is a singular contrast between the mercantile history of Calcutta and of Bombay,—the ports by which India transacts more than three-fourths of her oversea traffic. In Calcutta the Native Indian trading community has generally been content to deal with other countries through the agency of European firms; and, although Indian merchants are gradually entering into direct relations with importing and exporting houses in Europe, nine-tenths of the trade passes through the hands of the European colony in Calcutta. In Bombay the mercantile genius of the Parsis has for many years past aimed at an independent position; Indian merchants of other classes have followed suit, and at the present time European firms in Bombay have the handling of no large proportion of the traffic—probably not of more than a fifth. The British merchants of Calcutta have been assisted in retaining their position by the profits that have accrued to them from other sources—from the financing of planting enterprises for the production of silk, indigo and tea that are carried on by Europeans in districts of the interior. The hinter-land of Bombay is unsuitable for the cultivation of these products, and its agriculture has never attracted European capital. Both cities have become centres of large manufacturing industries; the environs of Bombay bristle with the chimneys of cotton-mills; the banks of the river Hoogly at Calcutta are lined with jute-mills. In both places the pioneer mills were erected with European capital and were managed by Europeans. The jute-mills of Calcutta are still for the most part in European hands. But a very large proportion of the capital represented by the cotton-mills of Bombay has been subscribed by Indians, and very many of the mills are controlled by Indian managers. To Karáchi Europeans have been attracted by the large export trade in wheat, and to Rangoon by the export trade in rice, and also by the financing and management of rice and timber mills. In Calcutta, Bombay, Karáchi, Rangoon and Madras a considerable number of retail shops are in European hands. Up-country, there is a mercantile settlement of Europeans at Cawnpore, which is a large collecting and distributing emporium, and has also developed an important group of factories. In a less degree this is also the case at Delhi.

While industrial undertakings are no longer exclusively financed by European capital they still draw most of their support from it. The total private capital invested in India through joint-stock companies is estimated at £157 millions; two-thirds of this has been subscribed in England in gold, and is owned by companies which have their headquarters in London. Of the balance that was subscribed in India, a very large proportion was remitted from the United Kingdom for investment, and is controlled by European directors in Calcutta and Bombay. The activities of the English companies are chiefly engrossed by railways (£37·8 millions), tea-planting (£15·6 millions), and jute-mills (£2·8 millions). The Indian companies have found cotton-mills the most attractive investment. These employ £12 millions, and mills of other descriptions £5·5 millions: next in importance come trading and shipping ventures (£8 millions), mining (£5·6 millions), banking, loans and insurance (£5·3 millions), and planting, whether of tea, coffee, silk or indigo (£2·5 millions).

To certain districts of the interior Europeans have been attracted in considerable numbers by the planting industry. So long ago as 1780 the East India Company perceived that the exports of indigo and silk could only be increased if it actively intervened to promote their cultivation, and it embarked upon schemes for this purpose. Its up-country agents made no attempt themselves to grow either the indigo plant or the mulberry, but they established factories for the extraction of indigo dye, and silk-reeling filatures; and they encouraged the cultivators to grow the raw material by offering them advances. By 1833 the commercial objects of the Company had become incompatible with its administrative responsibilities, and it was prohibited by Parliament from engaging itself in trade or industry. Its investments in the indigo and silk businesses passed into private hands. Planters in some cases purchased estates, so as to obtain the powers of control which are enjoyed by a landlord; but very generally they were content to deal with the tenants of Indian landlords in the vicinity of their factories, binding them to their interests by becoming their creditors. A large number of Europeans settled in Eastern Bengal, which was at that time an important centre of indigo production. But the system on which they worked involved the control of other men's tenants by means of money obligations, and was very distasteful to the landlords of those tenants. Moreover, it easily lent itself to oppressive measures of interference; and in 1860 a widespread agitation arose against the indigo planters which ended in their abandoning Eastern Bengal. In Western Bengal (Bihár), where the people were less resentful of interference, and numbers of Indian landlords themselves engaged in the business and sympathised with it, European indigo planters found a more congenial field. Prices were high, profits were large, and for a generation the indigo planter of Bihár was a dominating and picturesque figure in society, representing the sporting tastes, open-air life, and generous hospitality which Thackeray has associated with the planter squires of Virginia and the Carolinas. Indigo-planting has now fallen upon evil days. It is threatened with extinction, not by the jealousies of Indian landlords, but by the discoveries of German chemists. Under the competition of artificial indigo the price of the natural product has fallen by more than a half, and during the last twenty years the exports of indigo from Calcutta have declined in value from £500,000 to £150,000. Attempts are being made to utilise the planters' connections and goodwill for the production of sugar. But Bihár cannot grow the sugar-cane in the luxuriance which it attains in Mauritius and the West Indies, and the results have, so far, not been altogether promising.

The history of Indian silk has also been one of decline. Filatures under European control were established in the districts of North-Eastern Bengal, where the mulberry can be cultivated successfully as a field crop. Some Frenchmen, as might be expected, were attracted by this venture. But the industry did not fulfil its early promises. In Bengal, as elsewhere, the silkworms have suffered grievously from disease; and the Government has been at pains to introduce to the ryots Pasteur's method of discovering and rejecting diseased eggs by means of microscopical examination. But a defect less easily remedied has been the poor quality of Bengal silk. The silk moth is in Bengal possessed of strong reproductive vitality, passing through three or four generations,—and yielding three or four "flushes" of silk cocoons,—in each season. But the silk it produces is harsh and brittle. Many filatures have been closed, and the value of the raw silk annually exported does not exceed £400,000.

Tea planting, on the other hand, has extended and prospered. The exports of Indian tea are worth £8 millions a year, and if an adequate supply of labour can be maintained, the industry should have a widening future before it, since there are large possibilities of increased consumption, especially in Russia and the United States. The tea tree grows wild on the hills that occupy the frontier between Assam, Burma and China, and it was in ignorance of this fact that seventy years ago experiments were initiated by the State for the introduction of the Chinese plant into India. Plantations were established at various points along the outer Himalayas; they produced tea of good quality, but only yielded heavily on the eastern, ranges—in Sikkim, near the hill station of Darjeeling, where a moist climate is perennially maintained by sea-winds from the Bay of Bengal. On the discovery of the indigenous Indian plant its seed—and seed obtained by hybridising it with the Chinese plant—was substituted with great advantage for Chinese seed. Plantations opened in the Duárs at the foot of the Sikkim Himalayas proved that the tea plant would flourish in the Indian plains; its leaves might not possess the flavour which they developed at a higher altitude, but on the other hand, its yield was considerably heavier. But it is in the two valleys of Assam that tea gardens have reached their most striking development. Rows of flat-topped tea bushes here cover the face of the country, and the production

Bourne and Shepherd, Calcutta

TEA GARDEN : ASSAM

of tea has dwarfed into insignificance all other branches of agricultural industry.

The system on which tea is cultivated differs radically from that which was followed in the production of indigo and silk. It is grown upon land which belongs to the planter,—which has been purchased and reclaimed by him from waste,—and the plants are tended by labourers (coolies) who are in his service. There are then no such occasions for friction between tea planters and their Indian neighbours as disturbed the course of the indigo industry. But there are very great difficulties in obtaining the labour that is required. Waste land that is suitable for tea-growing is only to be found in localities that are thinly populated, and labour is generally not procurable locally, and must be hired from a distance. Where, as is the case with the tea gardens situated at the foot of the Sikkim Himalayas, the recruiting grounds are within a distance of two or three hundred miles, the labourers are hired and imported by petty contractors, who are also responsible as gangmen for their control and supervision on the gardens. But the tea gardens of Assam are far more remote; between them and the districts from which they draw their labour there stretches a distance of five or six hundred miles, and until recent years there was no railway communication, and labourers could only be imported by river. In these circumstances it was necessary to employ special agencies, not only for recruiting coolies but for transporting them, and these agencies have been mostly in the hands of Europeans, who hired the labourers and passed them on to the gardens. Substantial inducements were required to persuade coolies to migrate so far from their homes; the expenses of transport were considerable, and a special law has given the planter some security against the absconding of his coolies before they had done some substantial work for him. It has authorised him to engage them upon an indentured basis—that is to say, to take engagements from them to serve for an initial period of three years, and on the expiry of these engagements to renew them, if the coolie consents, for further two-year periods. These engagements could be enforced by a magistrate. The opening up of Assam by railways has lessened the need of this artificial arrangement; the engagement of labour upon ordinary conditions is extending and the special law will shortly be withdrawn. But the effect of this system has been to equip each tea garden in Assam with a large force of imported labourers, who live and work under the direct control of the European garden manager. He is responsible in this province not merely for directing the cultivation and manufacture of tea, but for regulating the lives of many hundreds of families who are housed upon his estate, and look to him not merely for their wages, but for their social and domestic comfort. The Government has prescribed a minimum wage, and has laid down rules to secure proper housing, sanitation and medical attendance. But the well-being of this large coolie population, exceeding half a million in number, depends in the main upon the interest that is taken in them by the European garden manager. Amidst the many hundreds of managers that are employed there must be some who are unworthy, and scandals have not been unknown. But there is no question whatever that in material circumstances—in food, dress and belongings—the coolies are infinitely better off than they were as the dregs of the crowded population from which they were drawn, and that the capital and energy which Europeans have devoted to the growth of tea have incidentally brought some measure of prosperity to hundreds of thousands who in their original homes were generally underfed, and suffered miserably under stress of famine.

In the early days of the tea industry the planters usually owned their gardens. There has been a great change in this respect. The gardens have now passed very generally into the hands of companies, whose agents reside in Calcutta, and the planters are for the most part salaried employés of the companies. Their remuneration is on a moderate scale: their responsibilities are heavy, and during some months of the year their duties are very exacting. But their open-air life has its advantages; each group of gardens has its polo-ground, and their society is cemented by the training which they undergo as volunteers. The tea planters of Assam maintain two regiments of Light Horse, and sent a detachment to the South African war, which served with distinction. It may be said that Assam presents the nearest approach to an English colony that exists in India. But the members of this colony all have before their eyes an eventual return to their home country.

Coffee planting is of much less importance. It is practically confined to the south-west corner of the peninsula, where the sea-winds, falling upon the hills of Coorg and Travancore, do not permit the air to lose its moisture. Coffee, like tea, is grown by hired labourers on plantations that have been laid out by European capital. Its production in India has suffered severely from attacks of the fungoid disease which would have ruined the planting industry of the neighbouring island of Ceylon had not the planters courageously determined to root up their coffee bushes and substitute tea for them. Indian coffee can hardly withstand the competition of coffee from Brazil. Twenty years ago the exports amounted in value to a million sterling annually. They have now fallen to half this value.

In India, as in Africa, there is an outcrop of gold-bearing quartz, situated, relatively to the size of each continent, at about the same distance from its southern extremity. It occurs in the neighbourhood of Kolár, on the plateau of Mysore, and here a European mining settlement has grown up which reproduces in miniature the features of the African Rand. The attention of prospectors was attracted by disused surface workings, and some thirty-five years ago capital was invested in reopening and deepening them. The first ventures were disappointing, but in 1881, upon the discovery of the Champion reef, it became evident that the shareholders were in possession of an exceedingly valuable property. There are now eleven companies on the ground in whose service are five hundred European and four hundred Anglo-Indian employés. Some of the companies are exceedingly prosperous, paying far more than 100 per cent. upon their actual capital outlay. Electrical power is obtained from falls on the River Cauvery, and although it is transmitted a distance of ninety miles, its cost is very moderate (about £18 per horse power), so that gold can be extracted in paying quantities from low-grade quartz, which could not otherwise be crushed at a profit. The mines annually produce about 600,000 ounces of gold. They are situated in the Native State of Mysore, and the relations between the mining community and the State officials have always been exceedingly harmonious.

The mining of mica and of manganese affords little scope for European supervision and control. Indians share in financing and managing the large coal-mining industry of Bengal, but a considerable number of the largest mines belong to British companies, and the large profits that have accrued have added very materially to the prosperity of European mercantile houses in Calcutta, and have afforded scope for the employment of a large staff of Europeans in the mining districts. A number of Europeans and Americans are employed in exploiting the oil-fields of Burma.

The great mass of the staff employed upon Indian

railways is, of course, Indian. In the higher grades of subordinate service domiciled Europeans and Anglo-Indians are very numerous; indeed, for these communities the railways have provided by far the most extensive and popular means of livelihood. But a very considerable number of Europeans have been imported, under contract, for employment as platelayers, fitters, and engine-drivers. Twenty years ago it was uncommon to find any but a European as engine-driver on either passenger or goods trains. More confidence is now felt in Anglo-Indian and Indian drivers, and there is a tendency to restrict the engagement of Europeans, since their terms of employment, including as they do a passage out and home, are naturally more expensive than those with which residents are satisfied.

To a European possessed of ability, but not of capital, the law has offered by far the most tempting avenue to wealth in India. A conflict in the law courts moves the pride, or the gambling instincts, of an Indian with a force that is almost irresistible; as the price of victory he will not grudge the savings of a lifetime, or hesitate to incur debt that will never leave him a free man. The Indian law courts are organised on a generous scale that contrasts surprisingly with the poverty of the country. The most lucrative practices are ordinarily of course afforded by the civil side of the High Courts; and it is round the High Courts, in the provincial capitals, that the British bar is most in evidence. But criminal proceedings are often exceedingly profitable to counsel, especially when they are urged by the rivalry of neighbouring landlords, and barristers of reputation can frequently add very greatly to their incomes by taking up cases in magisterial courts. Numerically British barristers may not appear of much importance, and of recent years they have had against them the competition of Indian barristers who annually qualify in large numbers for the Indian practice by being called to the English bar. But the influence of the European bar upon the legislative and judicial procedure of the country has been enormous. In the Viceroy's Council the legal portfolio has always been held by a barrister, and a large proportion of the High Court judges are barristers, selected for appointment generally in England but sometimes in India. With this support in official circles the profession has been able effectively to suggest elaborations in law and procedure which go beyond the needs of an Oriental country, and to oblige the courts to treat counsel with a deference which sometimes protracts inexcusably the course of litigation.

The five most prominent daily newspapers in India are in the hands of a European editorial staff. They appeal primarily to the official and non-official European community, but they have succeeded in attracting a large Indian *clientèle.* For their news and for their articles they rely very greatly upon the assistance of certain of their subscribers ; they may lack the piquancy of modern journalism, but they are generally well-informed, well-written and reasonable in their views. Their attitude, as a rule, is in support of the Government, and differs widely from that of their early predecessors. Until half a century ago the British editors who were the pioneers of journalism in India not infrequently attacked the Government with the most venomous hostility ; and up to 1822 the Government occasionally exercised the power of summarily deporting its bitterest critics from the country. This power was relinquished by Lord William Bentinck, whose concession is not infrequently apostrophised as giving freedom to the Indian press. As a matter of fact, it only affected European journalists.

We have not yet referred to a class of Europeans;

living dispersedly about the country, whose labours, many will think, surpass those of all other classes in value to the Indian people. These are the missionaries. The Europeans who come to India to seek a livelihood or a fortune are generally drawn from the British Isles. Amongst the mercantile community Germans, as has already been stated, are an element of some importance, but generally European mercantile, industrial and professional communities are of English, Scottish, or Irish nationality. Missionary endeavour is more cosmopolitan. Amongst Roman Catholics you will find, for instance, French and Bavarians; and missionaries of the Reformed churches who come from homes in the United Kingdom share the field with Germans, Americans, Canadians, Australians and New Zealanders. The Americans are particularly prominent; they labour amongst the most uncivilised of the hill-tribes, they maintain large schools and colleges in towns, and it seems that they may ascribe some special influence over their pupils to the fact that they do not belong to the governing race whilst sharing the enlightened views upon which it prides itself.

It would be out of place in this account to attempt to appraise the spiritual results of missionary endeavours. But it may be mentioned that the Indian Christian churches now include three and a half million pure-bred Indian adherents—apart from those who from their mixed parentage have inherited a predilection for European beliefs. During the last two decades the Indian Christian community has increased in numbers respectively by 31 and 34 per cent—rates which together represent an increase sevenfold that of the general population—and it is evident that Christianity is gaining ground with some rapidity. Of the native Indian Christian population one-fifth traces its origin to Nestorian, two-fifths to Roman Catholic, and two-fifths to Reformed or Protestant missions ; during the past ten years these three communities have increased their numbers, respectively, by 27, by 24, and by 69 per cent. Amongst Reformed churches the Anglican is the largest, with 332,372 adherents ; but, relatively to other churches, it has been losing ground, having increased within the ten years by 8 per cent. only, whereas all other Reformed denominations, taken together, have more than doubled their numbers. The Baptists now approach the Anglicans in the size of their community : but extension has been most rapid in he Presbyterian (283 per cent.), the Congregationalist (257 per cent.), and the Salvation Army (177 per cent.) communities. The material benefits of missionary endeavours are to be seen very clearly in localities where Christianity has been offered to classes that have remained outside the pale of Brahminism—hill tribes, for instance, and the lower *strata* of the coolie population. Not only have conversions been numerous : they have been accompanied by a marked rise in the standard of comfort, and in the self-respect of the proselytes ; and amongst the hill tribes of eastern India, and the outcasts of some Madras districts, Christians are sharply distinguished from the non-Christians around them by a greater appreciation of neatness and cleanliness, and also, in some cases, by increased intelligence and industry. Amongst the higher and better educated classes, whose interests have naturally always attracted a very large share of missionary enthusiasm, evangelization has been less successful ; and the influence of Christianity has accomplished less material change. The slowness with which the Anglican church is extending may doubtless be ascribed to the fact that it has interested itself specially with these classes of the community. But it is urged, and with justice, that in these circles success must not be measured by formal conversion, and that to missionary teaching and influence should be ascribed some measure of the advance in morality, and in the character of aspirations, that have been manifested by the educated classes during the two last generations. Missionaries can certainly claim to have played a most important part in introducing English education into India; the first English schools that were established in Calcutta, Bombay and Madras, over a century ago, were founded by missionaries; and the usefulness of their *alumni* in the public service contributed very materially to the adoption of English by the State as the basis of higher instruction throughout the country. A large number of schools and colleges are now in missionary hands. The vast majority of their pupils are, it is true, not Christians. But they all of them acquire some knowledge of the Christian Scriptures. And of recent years efforts have been directed towards securing closer sympathy between teacher and pupils by the establishment of missionary boarding-houses, where youths, attending secular schools, reside under the influence and control of a Christian house master. These endeavours to promote the welfare of Indians, without exclusive regard to their proselytising effect, have kindled a spirit of sympathy which has gradually softened the antagonism towards Christianity that remains so evident in China. Conversions no longer arouse the bitterness that attended them a generation ago. Indeed, the tolerance with which Christianity is regarded is so marked as to appear to some earnest missionaries as to be a source of discouragement. When there is no zeal to excite opposition, it will also, they fear, be lacking to stimulate conversion. But, judging from the figures of the last twenty years, Christianity is spreading with accessions of rapidity.

PART III
THE GOVERNMENT

CHAPTER XII

HISTORICAL SKETCH OF INDIAN GOVERNMENTS

In days of antiquity nations that had settled down to peaceful industry lived in constant danger from pastoral tribes, who, covetous of their luxury while despising their civilisation, were accustomed to forays by a nomadic life and were fierce with the strength of an animal diet. A civilised conqueror is proud of his acquisitions: nomads contemptuously destroy what they subjugate. In our own times a horde of pastoral (*Baggára*) Arabs has depopulated the Soudan and threatened the existence of Egypt: and, since the commencement of our era, nomadic forces, whether Tartar or Teuton, have uprooted,—in Europe and in Asia,—every civilisation then existing except those of China and Japan.

Beyond the mountain barrier of India is a most effective nursery of nomadic habits. The Tartars of Central Asia are compelled by the climate to be incessantly moving: during the drought of summer they must seek pasture northwards,—in the region of Siberia: during the winter they are driven southwards by the snow. Fired by tales of Babylon, of Nineveh and of Constantinople they could move westwards without much hardship were they not repelled by an opposing army: to the east China lay open to them and they overran it, but were unable to destroy a civilisation that could take refuge behind the walls of a multitude of fortified cities. Southwards, India tempted them across the Afghan mountains.

The passes were difficult, but the prize was attractive; and, divided amongst petty kingdoms and unprotected by walls, the Hindus could offer no effective resistance. Accordingly, for centuries Northern India has been invaded by hordes of immigrants. Sometimes the invaders were too few to flood the country and merely infused new habits and ideas. But at other times they came in a devastating torrent, annihilating the past and sterilising the future, until the conquerors had developed a civilisation of their own.

There has been immigration across the north-eastern frontier also. The tribes that inhabit the hill country that stretches between India and China and runs down into the Burmese peninsula, are generally of Tartar, or Mongol, descent, and have poured into their present homes across the steppes of Tibet. They have also poured into the plains, and amongst the population of Bengal there is evidence of a considerable admixture of Mongolian blood. In early days the sea coasts of India were secured from attack by ignorance of navigation: since the sixteenth century this defence has failed her, and British rule is the survivor of many powers that have landed on her shores.

Beyond the limits of their country the Indians have spread further than history records or is generally realised. In the temple architecture of Java and Cambodia there are indisputable signs of Indian influence, and, hard by Java, the island of Bali is inhabited by people whose society is organised on the Indian caste system. There were Indian colonies on the confines of China—far north of the Himalayas,—and in their gipsy population the countries of Europe shelter tribes that have straggled from Indian homes. But worn down during many centuries by the tread of hostile invaders, Indians lost all impulse for adventure, and believed that religion forbade them to cross the sea. British rule has given play to the fecundity of the people, and emigration has recommenced. Coolies leave the country in thousands for employment in Ceylon and the Malay peninsula, and, in lesser numbers, for the sugar plantations of British colonies throughout the world.

The relations that have existed between the invaders and the natives have depended very greatly upon the religion of the new-comers. So long as they were polytheists, after the first clash of arms, they accommodated themselves easily to the habits of the country,[1] and merged themselves in its indigenous population. The extension of the Roman empire was solidified by a similar intermixture; and a Greek kingdom, founded on the borders of India by the successors of Alexander the Great, became, to all appearances, quite Indianised. But when the invaders were Mohammedan there was no such combination. They maintained themselves as a class apart, and the Hindus and Mohammedans of India, as with an emulsion of oil and water, are mingled together but do not mix. Similar has been the case with Christian invaders. A polytheist views without repulsion the divinities of an alien race: indeed it may interest him to prove that they are the same as his own under different titles. To a revealed faith all other religions are anathema: it views its own tenets with a passionate not with a philosophical devotion: it condemns all others and would convert those who hold them—an attitude which must provoke antipathy. From a social standpoint Indian history may then conveniently be divided into three epochs, according as those who pressed in upon the country were polytheistic, Mohammedan or Christian.

[1] The last of the Tartar invaders of China—the Manchus—endeavoured, for political reasons, to keep themselves distinct from the Chinese by some differences of costume. But the two races have intermarried freely, and the Manchus have adopted to the full Chinese culture, language, and habits—have even worn the queue.

THE ARYAN INVADERS

(I) The Epoch of Polytheistic Invaders

The first invasion of which any record exists, was that of the, so-called, " Aryan " tribes, who came through Persia but belonged to the European family of nations. They entered India in several waves of immigration, the earliest of which occurred more than 1,500 years before the birth of Christ. They possessed a collection of hymns and religious formularies, which incidentally throw much light upon their habits. They were a pastoral people, of simple tastes, with religious ideas and ceremonies,—and a family and tribal organisation—resembling very closely those of the early Greeks and Romans. In parts of Rajputána they established separate settlements, but generally they took wives of the country and merged themselves in the population of the northern plain. But although their racial effect was limited, the influence of their thought extended throughout the length and breadth of the country. India owes to them two heritages of vast importance which have come down through the changes of thirty centuries, —Sanskrit literature and the Brahmin priesthood. Sanskrit literature is of vast extent, and in thought and expression deserves to be compared with the classical writings of Greece and Rome. It embraces every activity of human thought—in religion, grammar, poetry, mathematics and philosophy,—but it concerns itself little with observation, and leaves history absolutely untouched. For our knowledge of the history of the Hindu period we have to trust to inscriptions, coins and the records of outside observers. The effect of Brahminism has already been discussed. For a period Buddhism competed with it. But for centuries it has been, and it remains, the dominant fact in Hindu society.

In 326 B.C. India was invaded by Alexander the Great. He remained in the Punjab eighteen months. But he left no traces behind him, and his victories merely ruffled the surface of the country. The notes which certain of his generals took the trouble to record, testify admiringly to the prosperity of the people, and the courage and chivalry of their leaders. We obtain more detailed information from the diary of a Greek envoy—Megasthenes—who a few years later was accredited by the Seleucid king of Syria to the court of Chandragupta, the king of Patna. This ruler was the founder of the Mauriya dynasty, which adopted Buddhism, and at one time drew under its sceptre the greater part of India. The cultivated intelligence of Megasthenes found nothing to condemn in Oriental administration. He praises it whole-heartedly. Public affairs were committed to special departments of State, one of which was specially charged with irrigation. The people were contented and prosperous. Their capital was large; but it was defended only by a palisade. The State's regard for its subjects was so didactic that it might have been inspired by the Chinese. Chandragupta's grandson, Asoka,—the greatest of the dynasty,—published far and wide throughout the country some excellent moral maxims by engraving them upon pillars, or upon rocky cliffs that overlooked highways. But the dynasty endured only for a century. We next learn, from Chinese historians, and from coins, of invading hordes of Scythians that swarmed into the country during the early centuries of the Christian era. They established kingdoms, and ruled over peoples which, to judge from their coins, must have attained a high degree of civilisation. Indeed these invaders appear to have brought with them some appreciation of Greek culture, and for four centuries coins that were issued in the Punjab and Western India actually bore inscriptions in Greek. In the fourth century of our era Brahminism asserted itself in a dynasty—the Gupta—which, like the Mauriya, had its capital at Patna and extended its authority far and wide. We obtain a glimpse of it from the diary of a Chinese Buddhist pilgrim (Fa Hian) who in A.D. 420 came to India on foot to visit places that were sanctified by the founder of his religion. The country was peaceful and prosperous: Fa Hian was struck by the mildness of the government and the leniency with which it inflicted punishment. But the dynasty did not outlast a century and a half. Immigration from Central Asia recommenced, and 230 years later we learn from the notes of a second Chinese pilgrim—Hiouen Tsang—of the rule of a king named Harsha, who appears to have been of Tartar origin, and held his court at no great distance from the modern city of Cawnpore. Harsha adopted the Buddhist faith, and treated Hiouen Tsang as an honoured adviser. The Chinaman is thus hardly an unprejudiced witness: but it is clear from him that the general conditions were those of prosperity although cultivation had receded since the time of Buddha. The people rendered to the king a share of the produce which is computed as a sixth. Punishment had become more severe than under the Gupta dynasty, and we read of the infliction of death sentences upon Brahmin conspirators. At the present day a jury of Hindus can hardly bring themselves to convict a Brahmin on a capital charge. But this dynasty was even shorter lived than its predecessors that are known to us. It was ended by a flying incursion of Chinese, and Northern India relapsed into its Dark Ages—into a welter of confusion that lasted almost until the coming of the Mohammedans in the eleventh century. During this period, with a curious similarity to conditions in Europe, the country was harassed by the jealousies and ambitions of rival baronies, established by leaders of Rajput clans. The coins that are forthcoming are few and of the roughest workmanship. It seems probable that during these troubles the caste system hardened itself within the lines which have since so strictly limited intermarriage.

In peninsular India historical materials are even scantier. Two centuries before the beginning of our era the country was ruled by the Andhra dynasty in the north, and the Pallava dynasty in the south, and they apparently lasted, respectively, for six and eight centuries. From the image of a ship on some Andhra coins we may conjecture that the rulers of this dynasty favoured sea commerce; and it is evident from the references of Pliny that in his time (*circ.* 30 A.D.) there was an active trade between the Mediterranean and Southern India. It has left abundant vestiges in Roman coins. Of the kingdoms that rose and fell between the disappearance of these dynasties and the Mohammedan conquest, our knowledge hardly goes beyond the names that are borne by coins and inscriptions.

From Brahminical treatises, from the memoirs of Megasthenes and the Chinese pilgrims, and from traces which survive (especially in localities that never came under Mohammedan rule) we are able to depict the structure of Hindu government and society. The country was divided between rulers (rájas) whose powers were in theory despotic, but in practice were limited by the authority of the Brahmin priesthood. Hallowed by all the influences of religion, they could rely upon the unquestioning obedience of their subjects: absolute submission to the Rája was a duty inculcated and acknowledged. But religion insisted no less strongly on the duty of the Rája to protect and cherish his people, and to decide upon their petitions with even-handed justice. Revolt was rare, but war was not uncommon, for the kingdoms were generally small and there were many rivals for jealousy to set at strife. The warrior caste of Rajputs was then of great importance. The Government was supported by a share of the produce which might extend to a fourth, but seems generally to have been a sixth—the share that was rendered to their landlords by the tenants of classical Attica. The dues received by the State were mainly expended by it in payment for services, and were in this way returned directly to the people. Indeed this process was often simplified by the exaction of service in lieu of produce, each section of the community being bound to furnish so many men for so many days for the construction of public works, or the cultivation of the Rája's demesnes. In two localities the rendering of services (a *corvée*) in place of tribute continued down to the days of British occupation. Caste and tribal distinctions apart, the ráj (kingdom) was the larger unit of society : the smaller unit was the village. The country was divided into villages, each containing a certain area of land,—in densely populated localities often less than a square mile. The houses of the inhabitants were grouped together, so as to resemble a miniature town, and were not uncommonly surrounded by an earthen rampart. This might suffice as a safeguard in village warfare, but could hardly withstand the fierceness of Tartar assault. The village lands might be held by a number of cultivators—of various castes—each of whom had his separate holding : or they might be held jointly by the members of a brotherhood, who either divided the produce in accordance with the fractional shares to which they were entitled, or occupied fields in quittance of such claims. The former type probably indicates settlement by colonisation : the latter settlement by conquest. But on whichever of these systems the village lands were occupied, the village society was so organised as to give every inhabitant a fixed position in a community of interdependent individuals. For the performance of general services there was a staff of village servants—the village priest, accountant, barber, washerman, carpenter and watchman—who were remunerated by definite shares of produce. Labourers were similarly supported by a customary share. The affairs of a community were managed by an elected headman, or by elders, who also represented it in its dealings with the State. It is obvious that this organisation rested entirely upon the recognition of custom as a final authority. And to this day custom, throughout rural India, weighs infinitely heavier than experience or common sense. As an expedient for ensuring the continuity of human society the Indian village deserves our admiration. Armies might devastate its fields, or plunder its houses : but, so long as they spared some of its inhabitants, the organisation would restore itself when they had passed away. And within its boundaries competition was fettered by custom and could exercise none of its disintegrating powers.

(II) The Epoch of Mohammedan Invaders

A few years after the death of the Prophet (A.D. 632) a band of his Arab followers invaded and subjugated the province of Sind. But their influence did not spread, and they did not long retain the forcefulness of their individuality. It was not till four centuries later—in the eleventh century—that Mohammedanism was implanted in India by the armies of Tartar generals which entered the country by their customary route—across the Afghan border. For nearly two centuries (A.D. 1000 to A.D. 1192) Northern India was constantly invaded and plundered by the troops of Mohammedan kingdoms that had been established in Afghanistán, or in the country beyond it. One king—Mahmud of Ghazni—led no less than fifteen expeditions ; and, since the object was to secure not authority but riches, no limits were set to the cruelty and rapacity of his soldiers. In A.D. 1192 the invaders were confronted by a Hindu confederacy : they were victorious and decided to annex. Northern India was partitioned into a number of Mohammedan principalities, which with kaleidoscopic changes shared the domination of the country until the establishment of the Moghal empire four and a half centuries later.

Hoffmann, Calcutta

RUINS OF EARLY MOHAMMEDAN MOSQUE, BUILT OVER HINDU TEMPLE : AT DELHI

One of these kingdoms, which fixed its capital at Delhi, outgrew the others, and at times successfully asserted its superiority over almost all of its Mohammedan rivals. In A.D. 1292 a king of Delhi—Ala-ud-din—carried his victorious arms to the extreme south of the peninsula, and erected a mosque on the cape which looks out towards Ceylon. But the effect of this expedition was transient, and, a few years later (A.D. 1336), a Hindu kingdom arose on the Tungabhadra river which for two centuries safeguarded Southern India from the zeal of the invaders. Its policy was guided by Brahmin advice, and it stood for the last hope of orthodox Hinduism. Its capital—Vijáyanagar—attained a size and importance which excited the lively astonishment of European travellers. In A.D. 1398 the pretensions of Delhi to general supremacy were shattered by a bloody Tartar incursion led by Timur the Lame, and new Mohammedan kingdoms were rapidly founded by generals or governors who were sufficiently strong to assert their independence. No less than fifteen separate Mohammedan kingdoms divided at various times the sovereignty of Northern India and of the upper portion of the peninsula,—founding capitals which to this day attest their past magnificence by splendid buildings and by handicrafts that supplied the luxury of a court. The north-eastern corner of the peninsula was secured from invasion by the hills and forests that encircled it; and Vijáyanagar still guarded the line of the Tungabhadra. But in A.D. 1556 this last stronghold of the Hindus fell before a Mohammedan combination; and nothing now remains of the city but a deserted wilderness of ruins amidst the jungles which fringe the river's banks.

The Mohammedan States of this period were essentially military kingdoms and represented the success of adventurous talent. Some of their rulers were indeed of servile origin. Rulers and dynasties changed with extraordinary frequency. Aliens by race they remained alienated from the Hindus by the exclusiveness of their religion. Sympathy in these circumstances could hardly be expected, and there is much to show that the government was generally cruel and tyrannical. In the prosecution of never-ceasing wars, for the upkeep of brilliant courts, and for the construction of splendid monuments, money was required : the ancient Hindu system, under which taxes were rendered in grain or in labour, would not serve these purposes : it was broken up : the land revenue was made payable in silver, and in amounts which were enhanced until they left the cultivators but the merest pittance. According to an oft-quoted dictum of a Mohammedan lawyer, a cultivator had no right to expect more from his land than food for himself and his family, and seed grain for the following year : the rest of his produce he owed to the State. This was tantamount to an assertion of State ownership, and so impoverished did the people become under the exactions of the Government that there remained in them no spirit for resistance or even for complaint. As by Imperial Rome, so by these Mohammedan dynasties, it was realised, consciously or unconsciously, that political discontent is starved by poverty, and that a subject people may be taxed into apathy if not into contentment. Architects will not consider that they wasted their revenues. They found India singularly lacking in public buildings. They introduced from Byzantine Asia the dome, the pointed arch, the minaret, and the simplicity of outline which became characteristic of Saracenic architecture ; and they erected palaces, tombs and mosques that are amongst the finest monuments of the world. The Hindu workmen whom they employed were permitted in some cases to graft upon Saracenic outlines details that were conceived in the more ornate spirit of Hindu art : they embellished the arch with curves or scollops, or

Hoffmann, Calcutta

MOHAMMEDAN ARCHITECTURE AT ITS BEST: THE TOMB OF HUMAYUN AT DELHI

substituted for it the rectangular, flat-topped portal, with decorated brackets and pendants, in which Hindu architecture has applied to masonry a design that was originally carved in wood-work. The mosques at Jaunpore and Ahmedabad are brilliant examples of this composite style, in which Mohammedan and Hindu ideas blended with a freedom which social habits, less plastic than masonry, would not accord them.

During the sixteenth and seventeenth centuries these independent Mohammedan kingdoms were gradually absorbed into the Moghal empire, which after the fall of Vijáyanagar could extend its authority to the extreme south of the peninsula and bring all India under the sceptre of a single monarch. The Moghals were of a tribe closely akin to the Turks. The founder of the ruling dynasty—Bábar—a man of rare capacity, spoke a dialect of Turkish. He was descended, through Timur the Lame, from the family of Ghenjhiz Khan, another branch of which had, three centuries earlier, founded a Moghal empire at Pekin, and under Khubla Khan attained a power and magnificence which amazed the traveller Marco Polo. Bábar was born in the faith of Islám which had been embraced by the western branch of the family. But he and his immediate descendants exhibited an elasticity of religious opinion, and an appreciation of the luxuries and arts of life, which were curiously out of accord with the severe simplicity of orthodox believers. Akbar, the second emperor, and in some ways the most distinguished, allied himself with the Hindus by marriage connections, and attempted to found an eclectic religion of his own. To him and to his son and grandson—Jehángir and Shah Jehán—the world owes the splendid buildings at Delhi, Lahore and Agra, in which Mohammedan architecture attained the highest level of constructional art. Akbar developed the combination of Saracenic and Hindu elements, which is illustrated so brilliantly by the buildings of his palace at Fatehpur Sikri.[1] Under Jehángir and Shah Jehán Hindu influence gave way to Persian, and there was a reversion towards greater simplicity of outline. But flat surfaces were richly decorated with enamelled tiles or mosaics, exhibiting not merely the orthodox black-letter embroidery of texts from the Korán, but floral designs in Italian style, introduced by artists from Southern Europe. Jehángir is best known by the enamelled mosque at Lahore. Under Shah Jehán, in the palaces at Delhi and Agra, the great mosque at Delhi, and above all in the Táj Mahál at Agra, Moghal architecture reached its climax. It immediately decayed. Aurangzeb—known as the "Great Moghal"—who succeeded Shah Jehán in A.D. 1658, had no artistic sympathies. Religious orthodoxy fired his zeal, and military conquest his ambition. Twenty years of his reign were spent under canvas with his armies in the peninsula. He extended the empire of the Moghals to Cape Comorin, and brought home to the Hindus by special taxation that they were not only a conquered but a subject people. But he witnessed the awakening of Hindu forces which, a generation after his death, wore down to a shadow the authority of his successors. The Mohammedan empire covered more territory than it could control, and sank before the attacks of the Mahrattas on one side and of the Sikhs on the other.

The glories of the Moghal empire reached the ears of Europe, and attracted a number of European visitors. The British Government of King James I was indeed represented at the court of Jehángir by a special envoy, Sir Thomas Roe. We have then numerous accounts of the conditions of those days. They all dilate upon the magnificent extravagance of the court, the splendour of the public buildings, the efficiency of the police and the misery of the people. The assessment of the land revenue was systematised by Akbar: but its amount was enhanced

[1] In the neighbourhood of Agra.

Hoffmann, Calcutta

ECLECTIC STYLE OF AKBAR: HOUSE IN HIS PALACE AT FATEHPUR SIKRI

to meet the expenditure of the State until it left but the merest of pittances to the cultivators. And its collection was very generally farmed out to contractors who were compelled by their obligations to deal strictly with the people, and were not prevented by the State from squeezing them dry. The land revenue which Akbar collected from the districts of the United Provinces was actually larger in cash amount than that which is now received by the British Government. Prices were very low, and measured in grain it was two and a half times larger. At that time the canals which now irrigate two million acres in these Provinces had not been constructed, and the only means of transport was by cart or pack bullock.

The term "Mahratta" is loosely employed to cover the Mahratti-speaking population, of various races and castes, that inhabit the north-western area of the peninsula : in stricter use it denotes one caste of this population which claims relationship with the warrior (Rajput) caste of Hindu society, and, ordinarily engaged in agriculture or in cattle-breeding, readily forsook these pursuits for warlike enterprises. Men of this Mahratta caste rose to positions of importance in the armies of the Mohammedan kingdoms of the Deccan, and one of them was the father of Sivaji, the national hero of the Mahrattas. For many years Sivaji opposed with guerilla tactics the armaments of Aurangzeb, and finally established himself as rája of a territory which included the strong hill fortress of Raigarh. His descendants were not gifted with his talents ; but they could rely upon the assistance of a most resourceful and intelligent body of men, the Chitpáwan Brahmins, whose home was on the sea coast hard by. In appearance and in character these people exhibit a strong individuality : in their light grey eyes they differ startlingly from the typical Indian, and their features display little Aryan affinity and bear out a legend which implies that their forefathers entered India by sea.

Their representative, with the title of "Peshwa," at first advised, and later on superseded the degenerate Mahratta princes; and under Brahmin administration Mahratta armies, between A.D. 1720 and 1760, conquered the whole of the northern area of the peninsula, and made raiding expeditions into the Indo-Gangetic plain. The Moghal empire had been racked by a new invasion from Central Asia—headed by Nádir Shah, a military adventurer who suddenly sprang from the decadence of Persia. He occupied Delhi for six months, and retired with the plunder of its royal palaces. To withstand the Mahrattas was now hopeless, and from A.D. 1750 the Moghal emperor accepted their dictation. In A.D. 1761 a Mohammedan champion arose: an Afghan prince who had encroached upon the Punjab, broke up the Mahrattas in a defeat which shattered the influence of their Brahmin leaders. But this only enabled their most capable generals to assert their independence, and, at Baroda, Gwalior, Indore and Nagpur, to found military kingdoms which upheld Mahratta dominion and prestige. After no long interval they were to meet a stronger force in the British armies.

On behalf of the Mahrattas it cannot be claimed that they attempted to administer the provinces that they subjugated. The first use of their conquests was to extort a heavy tribute from a wasted country. In the kingdoms that they founded, their concern with their subjects was limited to the taxes that could be wrung from them: crime was left unchecked, and the country was pervaded by troops of adventurers who practised brigandage as their means of livelihood. It is hardly possible to conceive conditions that were more miserable for the poor than those which lay, a century ago, on the advancing track of British generals.

The domination of the Sikhs was of very different origin. It arose from a religious movement which in the fifteenth century offered the Hindus a simpler creed—

Bourne and Shepherd, Calcutta

MOHAMMEDAN ARCHITECTURE IN DECADENCE: GATEWAY AT LUCKNOW

a compromise between their own and that of Islám, tinged, moreover, it may appear, by Nestorian Christianity. It preached the Unity of God, the brotherhood of man, the love of God for man and communion with God by religious ecstacy, and it rejected caste and the Brahmin priesthood. Outside the Punjab these protestant doctrines won but few declared converts, although some of their teachers have influenced for good a very large section of Hindu society. In the Punjab they became the ground-work of a separate sect, whose adherents—known as *Sikhs*, or " disciples "—were recruited originally from all castes of the population and were united by their reverence for a sacred book. Cruelly persecuted by the Mohammedans they were transformed from a pietistic into a warlike confederacy, which ousted Mohammedan rule from the Punjab and, under Ranjit Singh, developed remarkable military vitality. But the power of the Sikhs did not endure half a century. In 1848 it yielded to the British on the hard fought field of Gujrát.

(III) The Epoch of Christian Invaders

Aryan and Tartar came for plunder but stayed to colonise, and contributed their blood towards the formation of Indian nationalities. To the European, on the other hand, India might offer her trade, but intimacy was denied by her climate, and the links which have bound the East to the West have been surface ties only. Four centuries ago, when Portuguese ships first anchored off the coast of Malabar, their commanders saw visions of colonies as well as of commerce, and for a hundred years the Portuguese strove to make a home in the Indian tropics. There sprang from them a considerable half-breed population which is still much in evidence on the western coast. But the European ancestors of this community could not endure the climate, and, deserted by them, its members have sunk into a position of neglected inferiority. They bear Portuguese names and are Roman Catholic in religion, but they exhibit in their complexion no trace of European descent. Less unfortunate, perhaps, but not less disappointing, has been the fate of the considerable half-breed community which has been brought into existence by the British in India. Their fathers also left the country: they were favoured by no political patronage; and, if they have maintained themselves in a higher status than the half-breed Portuguese, their ambitions seldom rise above employ as clerks and mechanics. An effort is now being made by British subscribers to provide them with special educational opportunities: they require them by their habits, but have hardly obtained them from the unswerving impartiality of the Indian Government.

Portuguese dominion fell, harassed by adventurers from other European countries and confronted by the growing power of the Mahrattas. Its records are blotted by much bigotry and cruelty: but they are illuminated by the virtues of Albuquerque, the piety of St. Francis Xavier, and are sufficiently heroic to have inspired the Lusiad of Camoens. To Indian ports came ships from England, France, Holland, Denmark, and Germany, the traders of each nationality in bitter rivalry with those of others, and not less bitterly opposed to any countrymen of their own who endeavoured to share their profits in the Indian trade. For centuries this trade had ministered to the luxury of Europe, where cotton and silk fabrics were precious curiosities, spices could not be grown, and no efforts could discover gold, pearls, and precious stones. Indeed from time immemorial the markets of the East had influenced the course of Mediterranean politics: Damascus and Alexandria, Genoa and Venice flourished or declined as they gained or lost commercial touch with them. The conquests of the Turks in the fifteenth century closed all direct trade routes between Europe and

Asia ; and the ships of the West were compelled to find a way, after many hazards, round the south of Africa.

The various competitors for the Indian trade were outdistanced by the merchants of England and France. These were antagonised, not only by the national jealousies of trade but by the wars that in Europe embittered their countries, and their mercantile rivalries grew into armed conflict in which from time to time their Governments took a hand. It was the French, under Dupleix, that first sought to outbalance their opponents by enlisting assistance from Indian allies : they intervened in the quarrels of Indian princes and were rewarded by concessions for the victories they had brought. So they secured the first large slice of Indian territory that fell under the rule of the contending parties—the east coast districts north of Madras—and could at one time call military aid from half of the peninsula. These schemes were, however, shattered by the victories of Clive at Arcot (1751), of Colonel Forde at Condore (1755) and of Sir Eyre Coote at Wandiwash (1760). The British also could strengthen their forces by Indian alliances and obtain territorial concessions around their warehouses and factories. The east coast districts passed to them from the French. France spared little attention for her sons in India ; and of themselves the talents of Lally and Bussy could not stem the tide of British success. French influence was overwhelmed, and could only retain three trading settlements.

During this conflict the British had established themselves at Bombay, Madras and Calcutta in such residential concessions as are now held by Europeans from the Government of China. They had become trained to war and could regard India as a field for military as well as commercial enterprise. In the Punjab the influence of the Sikhs was rising : in Rajputána long-lineaged princes and barons of the Rajput race, assisted by their courage and by the deserts that surrounded them, hardly maintained their independence against Mahratta aggression : along the hill ranges of the peninsula there were petty kingdoms that preserved the feudal system of Hindu days. For the rest the country was shared between the Mohammedans and the Mahrattas. At Delhi the Moghal empire survived in name : Oudh and Bengal in the north, Hyderabad in the centre of the country, and Arcot in the south were governed, practically in independence, by viceroys of this empire ; in Mysore, still further south, a Mohammedan kingdom had been established by the enterprise and courage of a soldier of fortune named Haidar Ali. But all India was overshadowed by the influence of the five Mahratta States whose capitals were at Poona, Nagpore, Baroda, Indore, and Gwalior. Of these eleven powers two, one Mohammedan at Hyderabad, the other Mahratta at Baroda, remained in almost unbroken alliance with the British. The others were gradually overcome. The Mohammedan ruler of Bengal invited reprisals by his attack upon the trading settlement of Calcutta and the cruelty, deliberate or unthinking, of the Black Hole. His power was annihilated by Clive on the field of Plassy (1757), and seven years later the victory of Buxar subjected to British influence the Moghal empire and the viceroyalty of Oudh. But for nearly a generation these successes were used to obtain, not territory, but money ; and it was not until the end of the eighteenth century approached, that Bengal was effectively taken under British rule. The sovereignty of the eastern portion of the United Provinces was ceded by the viceroy of Oudh in 1801. Two years later the British and the Mahrattas, after some years of alternating wars and alliances, put their rivalry to a final arbitrament. At Laswari Lord Lake defeated the army of Sindhia, stiffened though it was by French mercenaries ; and at Argaum and Assaye Colonel Wellesley (later the Duke of

Wellington) broke up a confederacy of the other Mahratta powers. From Sindhia's principality the western portion of the United Provinces was then annexed, and the province of Orissa from the territories of the confederacy: moreover, no longer fearing the Mahrattas, the princes of Rajputána accepted the protection of British authority. Meanwhile territory had been acquired in Madras by the annexation of Arcot and by the capture of Seringapatam from Tippu Sultan, the son of Haidar Ali. In 1817 war again broke out with the Mahrattas, and after the decisive victory of Mahidpur, by annexation from the territory of the Peshwa, the Bombay presidency stretched itself to nearly its present size. It was, then, during the first seventeen years of the nineteenth century,—under the viceroyalties of the Marquess of Wellesley and the Marquess of Hastings,—that the Bombay and Madras presidencies were constituted much as they are at present, and that the Indian Government established its position as suzerain of the Indian feudatory chiefships. The Punjab was not annexed until 1849, after bloody conflicts with the Sikhs on several battle fields. The Mutiny apart, this was the last of Britain's military enterprises on the plains of India. But during the viceroyalty of Lord Dalhousie (1848–1856) a large accession of territory was secured (Sattára in Bombay, Jhánsi in the United Provinces and Nagpur in the Central Provinces) by the escheat of States whose rájas had died without issue; and the province of Oudh was taken over on the ground that it was hopelessly misgoverned by its Mohammedan ruler. British dominion in Burma was secured by three wars—in 1822, 1852, and 1885.

The armies that won the earlier of these campaigns were for the most part composed of Indian soldiery. Indeed on occasions British troops constituted but a sixth of their strength, or even less. Under conditions of never-ceasing war, military service had become a profession that was untouched by feelings of nationality or patriotism, and Indians would enlist without scruple to fight under British leadership against other Indians. The British troops, by whose side they stood in full confidence of victory, were well-seasoned, long-service soldiers, specially enlisted for Indian employ, they and their officers sometimes stained with vices that would horrify the respectability of the present day, but animated by the desperate courage of the buccaneer. They plundered, they drank, they died of disease with dreadful rapidity: but they fought with uncalculating bravery, degraded in their hearts beyond measure should they turn their backs to an Oriental foe. But their numbers were few: their discipline could not withstand the amenities of peace; and the mutiny of their Indian comrades was a natural and inevitable consequence. The proportion of British troops in the Indian army is now maintained at a third, and they retain in their hands practically the whole of the artillery.

Until 1858 the general control of Indian administration was actually or nominally possessed by an association that was in its origin commercial—the East India Company: it was under the direction of this Company that British officers conquered and consolidated an empire for their home-land. Under the increasing interference of the British Parliament it stood at least as the figure-head of India down to the time of the Sepoy Mutiny. In that cataclysm it lost the last vestige of its authority, and the control of the Indian government was assumed by the British Parliament as an important, if exotic, function of its own. Twenty years later an Imperial title was drawn from India for the British Crown.

The coast districts of Madras gave the British their first experiences in administering an extensive area of Indian territory. But Bengal was the training ground upon which the mercantile employés of the East India

Company exercised themselves in the art of government, and developed into administrative and judicial services. At first they trusted very largely to their Indian subordinates : nor did they rise very far above the corrupted morals of those that surrounded them. Honesty was enforced by the strictness of Warren Hastings and Lord Cornwallis, and was assisted by the grant of liberal salaries. Knowledge came with experience, and lines were laid down that enabled the Indian Government, with the assistance of numerous military officers, to provide for the administration of the wide territories that were taken over during the sixty years that preceded the Mutiny. It was only to be expected that these lines should generally follow those that had been adopted by preceding governments. The Mahrattas had been content to maintain the administrative system of the Mohammedans in the provinces which they had acquired from them : they even preserved the Persian phraseology which was in use for official purposes. Accordingly British administration, whether it supplanted Mahratta or Mohammedan authority, was elaborated under Mohammedan influence, and preserves to this day some of the leading features of Mohammedan rule. Such, for instance, was the "district" system. The country was subdivided into districts of about the size and population of a large English county, over each of which was set an officer who represented the central authority in every branch of its activity except that of deciding upon civil disputes. He resembled in some ways a French *préfet*. He was head of the police and also chief criminal magistrate, the functions of detecting and of punishing crime being combined in a single department of public safety. He was also responsible for the collection of revenue. These functions still remain to his British successors. Other activities of the Government of to-day can only be efficiently controlled from a single provincial or imperial centre: the administration of railways, canals, post offices, schools and forests, for instance, is each entrusted to a separate department, whose officials are not under the orders of the District Officer of the locality in which they may be employed. But, even so, it is usual to consult the District Officer upon any changes that may affect the public welfare, treating him not only as a governor but as a representative of the people. This system of control has for many years appeared well suited to public needs and conducive to contentment, although it may certainly be charged with having sapped the independence of the village communal authorities. But village institutions have lost vitality, not merely because around them there has been the centralised authority of the District Officer, but because they have been overshadowed by the influence of the contractors whom we found and confirmed in possession of engagements for the collection of the land revenue. In one important respect executive authority has been surrendered into the hands of the people. It was to be expected that Englishmen, familiar with government by elected committees, would endeavour to introduce town councils into India. The tentative efforts that had been made to this end were consolidated and expanded in 1884, during the viceroyalty of Lord Ripon, when British India, rural as well as urban, was endowed with a very complete organisation of committees for the management of local and municipal affairs. They are constituted very largely on an elective basis, and, if they have frequently displayed imcompetence and dishonesty, they may be encouraged by the thought that self-governing bodies in the United Kingdom cannot pride themselves on being quite free from these defects. Their influence has extended beyond the scope of their duties. They have stimulated Indians of energy and intelligence to desire wider influence in the decision of questions that concern larger matters than local affairs.

CHAPTER XIII

BRITISH PROVINCES AND NATIVE STATES

IN some respects the map of India may be likened to an ancient tessellated pavement, the greater part of which has been destroyed, and has been replaced by slabs of uncoloured stone-work. The *tesseræ* represent the Native States: the plain stone-filling the territories that have come under British administration. If we omit Afghanistán, Nepál and Bhután, the relations of which to the British Government are of a special character, India covers an area of 1,773,168 square miles and contains a population of 315,132,537. Nearly two-fifths of this area (675,267 square miles) lies outside the dominion of British law and the jurisdiction of British law courts, being included in Native[1] States, which, subject to the suzerainty of the King-Emperor, are ruled by Indian chiefs and princes. The population of these States is 70,864,995. This does not greatly exceed a fifth of the total population of India; and it is, then, evident that generally the States occupy less fertile country than is included in British provinces. In the Gangetic plain there are but few relics of Native rule; and the sea coast is almost wholly British, except in Kathiawár, where there are no harbours of importance.

The Native States of India link modern administration with the Oriental methods of the past. But many of the most prominent of them are of quite recent origin, having been acquired by dynasties which sprang out of the

[1] Defined by the Interpretation Act of 1889 as: "The territories of any Native prince, or chief, under the suzerainty of Her Majesty, exercised through the Government of India, or through a Governor, or other officer, subordinate to the Government of India."

confusion that attended the dismemberment of the Moghal empire. Thus the premier prince of India—the Nizám of Hyderabad—governing a territory of 82,698 square miles with a population of over 13 millions—is descended from a viceroy of the Moghal emperor, who in the eighteenth century became sufficiently strong to declare his independence. At this period the Moghal empire was shrinking before the active depredations of the Mahrattas; and the important States of Gwalior, Indore, Baroda and Kolhapur represent the spoils which Mahratta leaders were able to retain. The Mohammedans also had their leaders—energetic soldiers of fortune, who as the emperor's authority declined carved out principalities for themselves. Such was the origin of the Mohammedan States of Bháwalpur, Bhopal, and Rampur: the small State of Tonk was conceded, on the authority of a British general, to a successful Mohammedan leader of banditti. In the Punjab Mohammedan rule was destroyed by the Sikhs, and the States of Patiála, Jind, Kapurthala and Nábha are survivals of Sikh conquests. Two States—Bhartpur and Dholpur—in the vicinity of Delhi consist of territory that was seized [1] from the Moghals by leaders of the Játs, a vigorous people of Northern India, believed to be of Scythian origin, who have contributed largely to the religious brotherhood of the Sikhs. Mysore was restored to its present Hindu dynasty by the British from the conquered dominions of Tippu Sultán. The large State of Kashmir was created by them to requite the founder of the present dynasty for assistance rendered during the Sikh war of 1848.

These States, which include most of those whose names are best known in England, have, like British India, been built up from the ruins of the Moghal empire. But there are others which can carry their annals further back into the past, and may claim to have survived from

[1] Or that was taken in exchange for territory so seized.

the days of Hindu supremacy. They have generally owed the continuity of their existence to the inaccessibility or the poverty of their territories, which did not tempt the cupidity of the emperor at Delhi, and left him satisfied with an acknowledgment of his suzerain power. Perhaps the most interesting principalities of this class are those held by chiefs of the Rajput clans which represent the purest Aryan blood in India. They inhabit the sandy country, on the margin of the Punjab desert, that has derived from them the title of Rajputána. Some of these dynasties may justly pride themselves upon their antiquity. The Maharája of Udaipur (or Mewar) can definitely trace his family back for six centuries, and if assisted by legend, for almost double this period. Other leading States of Rajputána are Jaipur, Alwar, Jodhpur (Marwar) and Bikanir. Touching Rajputána on the south-west, another group of Rajput States occupies the greater part of the peninsula of Kathiawár. The principal of them are Idar, Cutch, Gondal, Nawanagar, and Bhaunagar. Eastwards from Rajputána some Rajput dynasties have maintained themselves in the hilly country which divides the Indo-Gangetic plain from the peninsula. The most considerable are Orchha and Panna of the Bundela and Riwa of the Baghel clan. Along this line of marches, and in the mountainous country which extends down from it into the peninsula, numbers of petty chiefships which claim Rajput descent were left in semi-independence during the Moghal period and have been admitted to a ruling status by the British Government. In many cases their territories are no larger or more important than those of private landholders on their borders, and their claims to be recognised as separate centres of government were exceedingly slender. But the British Government has generally been liberal in its judgment upon claims to independence. In Central India and the Bombay presidency there are hundreds of little States—fragments of eighteenth century loot—which are indeed rather properties than chiefships, and have no such resources as are required for however modest a government. And their territories are commonly broken up into small parcels which are intermixed with British villages, so that their independent administration offers peculiar difficulties. Passing through Hyderabad and Mysore to the extreme south of the peninsula we find two considerable States—Travancore and Cochin—held by Hindu dynasties who claim Rajput affinities, and have preserved some of the most archaic features of Hindu policy.

On the Western frontier are two Mohammedan States of importance, administered by rulers of the Balúchi race. One of them—Khairpur—was permitted by the British to retain its independence after the conquest of Sind. The other—the large State of Kelát—occupies a position of much strategic importance, and was drawn into the British nexus by our wars with Afghanistan. There is a group of hill States on the slopes of the Himalayas north of Delhi, and another group in the mountainous country of Eastern Bengal, Assam, and Burma. These eastern States are inhabited by people and ruled by chiefs whose racial affinities are with the Tibeto-Burman stock. Manipur, lying between Assam and Burma, attained notoriety twenty years ago by a revolt in which the Chief Commissioner of Assam and some of his officers were treacherously murdered. For this the dynasty merited the confiscation of its territory. But the Government was content to transfer the rulership to another branch of the family. In Burma there are a large number of chiefships. But the authority of their chiefs is rather derived from the British Government then exercised in independence, and they can hardly be described as lying beyond the pale of British India.

Apart from those in Burma there are in all 620 Native

Indian States: but at least two-thirds of them are politically of very small account. Indeed not a few of them are so exceedingly small as to afford their chiefs little scope for independent administration. The authority of each ruling chief is linked to that of the British Government by the delegation of a British officer, entitled a "political agent," who acts as intermediary between him and the suzerain power. For groups of small States a single political agent is employed; and in some cases the functions of this officer are performed by the Commissioner, or the District Officer, of an adjacent British division or district. The States may be thrown into three classes according to the authority from which the political agent takes his instructions. In the case of 461 States this is the Government of the province whose territory the State adjoins. Six States—including Nepál in this connection—are in direct relation, through their political agents or "residents," with the Government of India: 154 are also in relation with the Government of India, but through an Agent to the Governor-General, who is in general control of a group of political agencies.

Afghanistán, Nepál, and Bhután, lie within the sphere of British influence and can have no direct relations with foreign powers. But with their internal affairs the British Government does not at all concern itself. The Amir of Afghanistán owes his position to arrangements that were made by the British on their occupation of the country in 1880. He is assisted by an annual subsidy, but no British officer resides at his court. There is a British resident in Nepál, but not in Bhután. In neither of these two States may Europeans be employed without the sanction of the Government of India. Europeans may not enter either Afghanistán, Nepál, or Bhután without permits from the State authority. These three States, then, occupy a somewhat peculiar position, owing not so much to their intrinsic importance as to the history of their connection with the British Government. Of the other States thirty-nine may be selected as distinguished by their antiquity or their resources: their circumstances are indicated by the figures shown on the two following pages.

The relations of the British Government with the Native States—that is to say, the extent to which the British Government and the States co-operate in the interests of the Empire and their peoples—have gradually developed out of the changing conditions of the past century. With many of their rulers treaties have been made, or agreements exchanged, which contain more or less precise stipulations. But their terms have related to the exigencies of the moment: these exigencies have changed, and fresh constructions have slowly been read into written obligations. After the assumption of the Indian Government by the Crown, *sanads* (or charters) were very generally distributed. But they were mainly concerned with the right to adopt heirs in default of descendants. The matters in which the British Government uses its suzerain powers have gradually been settled under the pressure of circumstances. Accordingly they vary immensely in the case of different States. The Nizám of Hyderabad has unlimited powers of inflicting punishment upon his subjects: he has a coinage of his own: his public services are organised upon such a system as obtains in British India. At the other end of the scale are petty chiefs whose resources do not admit of the entertainment of regular official establishments. They are judges as well as rulers, and their decisions in matters of importance require to be confirmed by the political agent. In settling the usage to be followed with each State the most meticulous regard has been paid to actual circumstances and past precedent, and there has resulted a body of customary observances which may be the despair of those who endeavour to compile it, or to

State.	Area.	Population.	Approximate Revenue. £	Military Force.	In Political relations with—
	sq. miles				
(1) Mohammedan States.					
Hyderabad	82,698	13,374,676	2,700,000	24,035 (incl. 17,500 Irregulars and 806 Imperial Service)	Govt. of India, direct
Kelât	71,593	335,227	60,000	690	do. through Agent to Governor-General for Baluchistán.
Bháwalpur	15,000	780,641	180,000	1,199 (incl. 604 Imp. Serv.)	Govt. of the Punjab.
Bhopál	6,889	751,500[1]	200,000	2,144 (incl. 400 Imp. Serv.)	Govt. of India through A.G.-G. for Central India.
Khairpur	6,050	223,788	100,000	377	Govt. of Bombay.
Junagarh	3,284	434,800[1]	200,000	161 (incl. 99 Imp. Serv.)	do.
Palanpur	3,177	244,800[1]	53,000	601	do.
Rampur	899	531,217	240,000	2,581 (incl. 317 Imp. Serv.)	Govt. of United Provinces.
(2) Mahratta States.					
Baroda	8,099	2,032,798	900,000	8,755 (incl. 3,800 Irregulars)	Govt. of India, direct.
Gwalior	25,041	3,050,000[1]	1,200,000	19,081 (incl. 5,613 Irregulars and 4,370 Imp. Serv.)	do. through A.G.-G. for Central India.
Indore	9,500	935,700[1]	600,000	1,958 (incl. 200 Imp. Serv.)	do. do.
Kolhapur	2,855	833,441	360,000	710	Govt. of Bombay.
(3) Sikh States.					
Patiala	5,412	1,407,659	430,000	3,429 (incl. 1,800 Imp. Serv.	Govt. of the Punjab.
Jind	1,259	271,728	110,000	1,460 (incl. 600 Imp. Serv.)	do.
Kapurthala	630	268,133	100,000	855 (incl. 500 Imp. Serv.)	do.
Nábha	928	248,887	100,000	760 (incl. 500 Imp. Serv.)	do.
(4) Ját States.					
Bhartpur	1,982	558,785	265,000	3,220 (incl. 1,020 Imp. Serv.)	Govt. of India, through A.G.-G. for Rajputána.
Dholpur	1,155	263,188	80,000	1,216 (incl. 630 Irregulars)	do. do.

[1] Estimated: precise figures for the Census of 1911 not available.

State.	Area.	Population.	Approximate Revenue. £	Military Force.	In Political relations with—
	sq. miles				
(5) Rajput States of Rajputána.					
Udaipur (or Mewar) ..	12,691	1,293,776	200,000	6,015 (incl. 3,466 Irregulars)	Govt. of India, through A.G.-G. for Rajputána.
Jaipur	15,579	2,636,649	460,000	17 382 (incl. 722 Imp. Serv.) and 10,000 Irregulars)	do. do.
Jodhpur (or Marwar) ..	34,963	2,057,553	420,000	4,464 (incl.1,210Imp.Serv.)	do. do.
Alwar	3,141	791,688	225,000	2302 (incl.1,600 Imp.Serv.)	do. do.
Bikanir	23,311	700,983	170,000	1,418 (incl. 500 Imp. Serv.)	do. do.
Kotah	5,684	544,879[1]	246,000	7,913 (incl 6,065 Irregulars)	do. do.
(6) Rajput States of Kathiawár.					
Idar	1,900	180,300[1]	48,000	——	Govt. of Bombay.
Cutch	7,616	513,429	155,000	5,107 (incl.4,000 Irregulars)	do. do.
Gondal	1,024	174,200[1]	145,000	203 Irregulars	do. do.
Nawanagar	3,791	360,300[1]	230,000	356 (incl. 145 Imp. Serv.)	do. do.
Bhaunagar	2,860	441,500[1]	220,000	592 (incl. 256 Imp. Serv.)	do. do.
(7) Other Rajput States of Northern India.					
Kashmir	80,900	3,158,126	900,000	6,283 (incl.3,370 Imp.Serv.	Govt. of India, direct.
Orchha	2,080	337,700[1]	400,000	1,350	do. through A.G.-G. for Central India.
Panna	2,492	202,600[1]	400,000	192	do. do.
Riwa	13,000	1,513,200[1]	200,000	1,714	do. do.
(8) States of Southern India.					
Mysore	29,444	5,806,193	1,400,000	2,886 (incl. 536 Imp. Serv.)	Govt. of India, direct.
Travancore	7,091	3,428,975	760,000	1,542 (of which 1,442 officered from British Army)	Govt. of Madras.
Cochin	1,362	918,110	500,000	325	do.
(9) States of Eastern India.					
Kuch Bihar	1,307	252,952	180,000	156	Govt. of India.
Hill Tipperah	4,086	229,613	53,000	330	Govt. of Bengal.
Manipur	8,456	346,222	30,000	——	Chief Commissioner of Assam

[1] Estimated : precise figures for the Census of 1911 not available

generalise from it, but has had the admirable effect of converting suspicion—and even hostility—into warm feelings of regard towards the British Crown. For of the general loyalty of the Indian princes there can be no question: they are amongst the strongest supports of the British Empire in India.

At the time when the East India Company was struggling to maintain its concessions it was a matter of first importance to secure that Native princes should not combine to oppose it; and the treaties that were negotiated at the commencement of the last century had for their principal object the isolation of the States from which attacks might be apprehended. At the present day States may maintain no direct political relations with one another. Taught by the prowess of French soldiers of fortune, who disciplined the armies of Sindhia and others, the Company also insisted that no Europeans were to be taken into service without express permission. This condition also still subsists. It was a further object to obtain military assistance, and, when it was discovered that the untrained forces of their allies were of little service, stipulations were made binding the more important States to provide subsidiary forces which were, as a matter of fact, organised and commanded by British officers, but were paid by the State, either by subsidies in cash, or by concessions of territory. These forces have gradually been amalgamated with the regular army: the last[1] of them which maintained its separate identity was the Hyderabad Contingent, and this was merged into the Indian Army in 1904. It will be understood that these subsidiary forces have always been distinct from the troops which the large Native States have maintained—and still maintain—under their own authority. These number about 93,000, but are

[1] If we except a survival of little military importance in Travancore.

of no great military value. They are indeed very largely employed on police duties, and when paraded in public, are of interest rather as picturesque survivals of mediæval India than as a possible source of military complications. In some States the troopers are still clad in chain mail: elsewhere you may find men dressed in uniforms that are copies of those worn by British soldiers in the days of Clive. From early days the British Government has imposed some limits upon the strength of these forces, and has provided against the construction of fortresses or arsenals. And, except in the case of Kashmir, which, bordering upon Central Asia, has special frontier responsibilities, Native States may only recruit from amongst their own subjects. It is a recognised obligation upon Indian princes that in a time of stress they should assist the Empire with all their resources. This obligation is generally a source of pride, and during the last quarter century twenty-seven States have voluntarily converted a portion of their military forces into corps of "Imperial Service troops," which, drilled and disciplined with some European assistance, could take their place with credit by the side of regular troops.

Until the viceroyalty of the Marquess of Hastings (1814 to 1823) the British rarely interfered to protect States from the aggression of more powerful neighbours unless it was politically of importance to maintain them intact: responsibility was not accepted for the general preservation of peace throughout the country. This Viceroy took a wider view of British duties, and to his intervention the States of Rajputána owed relief from the Mahrattas, and the multitudes of small States in Central India and Bombay are indebted for their existence. In later years the Sikh States of the Punjab were saved by the British from being engulfed in the dominions of Ranjit Singh. But ideas still fell short of a broader conception of British responsibilities, such as would warrant interference in order to protect the subjects of a Native State from gross oppression by their ruler. If we view the administration of British India as it stood two generations ago—during the first half of the nineteenth century—we shall find it falling very far short of present day standards: but practices that shock humanity, such as *suttee* and punishment by mutilation, had been stopped, and strict endeavours were made to repress the capricious exercise of official authority. Across the borders of British India—in the Native States—cruelty was still uncondemned: the ruler viewed his State as his domain, and constantly showed by his actions that he regarded the lives and property of his subjects as at his disposal. The most flagrant oppression was of common occurrence. The British Government might warn; but it did not actively interfere, and the only effective remedy which presented itself was to depose the ruler and annex his territory. So was Oudh annexed in 1856. The contrast in administration between British India and Native territory was so striking in those days that Lord Dalhousie might well conceive that he was acting for the people, when, on failure of direct heirs to the succession, he also incorporated Sattára, Jhánsi, and Nagpur in British dominions.

The point of view changed when Parliament intervened and assumed, under the Crown, direct responsibility for the government of the country. Misgovernment might necessitate the deposition of a ruler, but this measure need not involve the confiscation of his State. Indian princes were assured that, if direct heirs failed them, they might preserve the continuity of their dynasties by adopting sons. Charters (*sanads*) to this effort were issued to them; but the Viceroy—Lord Canning—formally declared that their grant would "not debar the Government from stepping in to set right such serious abuses as may threaten any part of the country with anarchy and disturbance, and from assuming temporary charge of a Native State where there shall be sufficient reason to do so." Since this declaration of policy it has been found necessary to depose Native princes: Baroda and Manipur offer well-known instances. But their States were preserved and were handed over to other representatives of the ruling families. If a proof be required that British policy is no longer actuated by any desire for annexation, one has recently been afforded by the grant to the Maharajá of Benares of the ruling *status* in respect to some British Indian territory which his family has for many years past held on proprietary tenure. It is obvious that by guaranteeing Native rulers against the rebellion of their subjects the British Government becomes responsible for securing their subjects against such gross oppression as would lead to rebellion. Nor can it witness with indifference the cruel mistreatment of individuals, which, however common under Oriental governments, creates a scandal in these modern days. So also with inhuman practices, and religious persecution: it is compelled by the public conscience to intervene. And it cannot permit the trade of the country to be strangled by the transit duties which would offer to Native rulers a convenient means of increasing their revenues,—or to be confused by a multitude of different currencies such as would come into existence did States, which are in close connection with British India, exercise an unlimited power of opening mints.[1]

Circumstances have, in fact, forced the British Government into the position of an arbiter not only between one State and another, but between the rulers of States and their subjects. Its interference is limited by the conditions of particular cases and is not defined in its extent

[1] Less than a dozen of the principal States now regularly mint coins of their own.

by general rules. It holds the prerogative of settling successions, and, although it would very rarely pass over the accepted heir, it could do so were he quite unfit for the position of ruler. During the minority of a rája it steps in as guardian, and obtains an opportunity of introducing reforms: the importance of preserving them is impressed upon him when he comes of age, and sometimes—as in the case of Mysore—they are safeguarded by express stipulations. The Government concerns itself anxiously with the education of young princes: a special college is provided for them and their relations, managed on the lines of an English public school. In some cases their fathers prefer to send them to England for their education, setting a fashion which is not unlikely to spread. A ruler who wishes for advice has the political agent at hand. But this officer is not obliged to withhold his suggestions until they are asked for. He may draw attention to matters in which the State compares very unfavourably with British India or with other States. A natural feeling of emulation often suffices to interest the rája in reforms: there is another inducement in the honours, titles, and decorations which are in the Government's hands for bestowal, and are greatly coveted. The addition of some guns to a chief's salute has not infrequently been more efficacious in the improvement of his administration than the most earnest exhortations. But progress can hardly be continuous when it entirely depends upon the passing tempers of an absolute ruler, and pains have been taken to convince Indian princes of the advantage of delegating some part of their functions to subordinate officials whose position can be regularised as in a government service. From early Hindu times the rája has customarily been assisted by a council: the term "durbar," which is commonly used to express the State authority, signifies the ruler acting with this council. But councillors that are hereditary, or that are dependent for their position upon the pleasure of the prince, can hardly aspire to check his caprice. Generally in the larger States public services have been organised on the model of those employed in British India, and the trial of cases has been committed to a separate judicial department. Where resources do not suffice for so ambitious a development, the rulers have been encouraged to appoint ministers—or *diwáns*—of proved experience, Indian officials having sometimes been lent for this purpose from the administrative services of British provinces.

On these lines very remarkable improvements have been effected in the government of Native States: many of them, indeed, approximate to British provinces in the efficiency of their administration, and need occasion to the Supreme Government very little solicitude. It is true that the distinction between public expenditure and the privy purse of the ruler is still imperfectly recognised, and that Indian princes generally consider that the revenues of their States may be drawn upon without question to meet their personal extravagance. But to those whose experience of Native States can go back a generation their present condition shows astonishing progress. It may indeed be a question whether in some ways too much has not been attempted, whether the picturesque directness of Oriental methods has not been sacrificed too freely to the mechanical uniformity of modern standards of government—at the cost, here and there, of some friction with the chiefs.

There are cases in which the Government of India exercises direct jurisdiction within Native States, based not upon legislation, but upon the prerogative of the Crown. Lands that are occupied by trunk lines of railway, or by cantonments, are treated as if in British India, their inhabitants being amenable to British law courts. There is a similar personal jurisdiction over

Hoffmann, Calcutta

A RÁJA IN DARBAR

Europeans and Americans who may be residing in Native territory.

The responsibilities of the British Government have been lightened very greatly by the growth of a feeling amongst the princes of India that their *status* is not one of mere subordination—that they can claim the dignity of co-operating with the Supreme Government in the interests of the Empire. We have already referred to the special troops which are maintained by twenty-seven of the leading States for *imperial* service. They include, altogether, nearly 20,000 men, comprising 15 squadrons of cavalry, a camel corps, 14 battalions of infantry, 2 corps of sappers, 7 transport corps and 3 transport escorts. Their organisation and drill is supervised by a few British officers whose services are lent for the purpose. But they are under the direct command of the ruler of the State. Imperial Service troops, led in one case by their prince in person, have taken part with credit in military operations on the Afghan frontier, in China and in Somaliland. Several Indian princes hold commissions in the British Army. Nor has the British Government failed to show a similar spirit of helpfulness. It has lent officers of its own to assist Indian chiefs in assessing their land revenue : in co-operation with the chiefs, it has suppressed organised bands of criminals which, if followed up on one side of the frontier only, would have taken refuge on the other. It demands the extradition of fugitive offenders : but, subject to certain safeguards, it grants similar extradition upon the warrants received from Native tribunals. In times of famine it has lent [1] to Native States on a generous scale, and has remitted large sums which they were unable to repay without much difficulty. It has assisted some States to develop small railway systems of their own. And, recently, to secure those of Central India a fair share

[1] During the famine of 1900–01 these loans amounted to £2,000,000.

of the profits from the opium trade, it has undertaken to remit to them a portion of the dues that are levied at the seaports on opium that is exported. It protects such of their subjects as travel abroad, or settle in foreign countries, issuing passports to them and taking them under its consular jurisdiction. Indeed, when the interests of the inhabitants of Native States are concerned, it hardly distinguishes between them and British subjects, not rigidly denying them official employment in British India and permitting them to compete for admission to the Indian Civil Service.

Candidly reviewed, the past has had its disappointments. Too often Indian princes have belied the promises of their youth and have been unable to withstand the enervating influence of their domestic surroundings. It has been asserted that they have been repressed into inaction by the Government's officious interference. There is no foundation for this excuse. The Government has thankfully respected the responsibilities of princes who have shown zeal and initiative. And it must be remembered that in governing his territory an Indian prince can obtain greater and more varied interests than are offered by the control of an estate to an English landholder.

British Provinces

We now turn to the provinces into which British India is subdivided. In separate chapters will be reviewed the principles and methods which regulate their administration in its various departments, and here it will suffice to enumerate them, and to offer some explanatory observations on the general character of the tracts and of the people that inhabit them.

We may first dispose of four small territories which can hardly be dignified with the title of province. The

Andaman [1] and Nicobar Islands in the Bay of Bengal are only of importance as a penal settlement: they are administered by a Chief Commissioner under the Government of India. Amidst the large area which is under political control in Baluchistán are four [2] British districts of which Quetta is the chief. Ajmer [3] and Merwara form a small *enclave* in Rajputána. These tracts are administered, respectively, by the Chief Political Officers (styled Agents to the Governor-General) in Baluchistán and Rajputána. Coorg [4] is a district on the borders of Mysore which, when annexed in 1834, was not handed over to the Madras presidency, but was placed under the control of the British Resident in Mysore. Ten British provinces remain. Some indication of their general circumstances is given by the statistics on the following page.

The three smallest of these provinces are technically under the direct control of the Government of India, which administers them through an officer bearing the title of Chief Commissioner. In practice, however, a Chief Commissioner is hardly more closely controlled than a Lieutenant-Governor, save in respect to matters of patronage—that is to say, in the selection of officers for the higher appointments. The differences in historical development between a Governor and a Lieutenant-Governor will be indicated in Chapter XIV. Formerly only Governors were assisted by Executive Councils. But such a Council has recently been established in the new Lieutenant-Governorship of Bihar, Chota Nagpur, and Orissa. Some account of the origin and constitution of the Provincial Legislative Councils will be given in Chapter XV.

	Area: *Square Miles.*	Population.
[1] Andamans and Nicobars	3,143	26,459
[2] British Baluchistán	2,711	501,395
[3] Ajmer and Merwara	46,656	414,412
[4] Coorg	1,383	174,976

Province.	Area.	Population.	Approximate Revenue.	Executive Head.	Composition of Legislative Council.
	sq. miles		£		
North-West Frontier Province ..	13,183	2,196,933	1	Chief Commissioner	No Council
Punjab	97,394	19,974,956	2,607,500	Lieutenant-Governor	27 members, of whom 15 must be non-officials, including 5 elected.
United Provinces	106,890	47,182,044	3,992,000	Lieutenant-Governor[3]	49 members, of whom 27 must be non-officials, including 20 elected.
Bihar, Chota Nagpur, and Orissa ..	84,395	34,485,634	1,792,300	Lieutenant-Governor with three Members of Council.	Composition not yet definitely settled.
Bengal	77,252	45,217,527	3,775,700	Governor, with three Members of Council	[2] 51 members, of whom 32 must be non-officials, including 26 elected.
Assam	52,958	6,713,635	812,000	Chief Commissioner	No Council : one is shortly to be established.
Burma	172,566	12,115,217	3,252,400	Lieutenant-Governor	18 members, of whom 10 must be non-officials, including 1 elected.
Madras	141,807	41,405,404	4,288,500	Governor, with three Members of Council	48 members, of whom 27 must be non-officials, including 19 elected.
Bombay	122,962	19,672,642	4,775,600	do.	48 members, of whom 29 must be non-officials, including 21 elected.
Central Provinces	99,803	13,916,308	1,629,700	Chief Commissioner	No Council : one is shortly to be established.

[1] The finances of this province have not been settled upon a separate footing from those of the Government of India.
[2] The constitution of the Bengal Council may be modified now that the boundaries of the province have been changed.
[3] An Executive Council will shortly (it is announced) be established in the United Provinces.

The North-West Frontier Province, on the Afghan tribal border, includes only five British districts, amongst which, however, is the important district of Peshâwar. The town of this name is the provincial capital. The most serious responsibilities of the Chief Commissioner concern the mountainous border land across the frontier, which is inhabited by turbulent tribes whose control may at any time raise political questions with Afghanistân. Until 1901 this province formed part of the Punjab. It was constituted in order that frontier politics might receive more continuous attention, and might come more closely under the watch of the Government of India. The population of the province is almost wholly Mohammedan. The people generally speak Pushtu, a language that is connected with Persian.

The Punjab[1] covers the plain which is watered by the upper reaches of the Indus and by the four large affluents that unite with the Indus shortly before their waters reach the southern border of the province. At one point it runs up into the Himalayas. But generally its surface is flat and well cultivated. Its capital is at Lahore; other towns of note are Multan, Amritsar, and Amballa. The rainfall is scanty and precarious, and nowhere else in India are irrigation works of such importance, or have shown such astonishing results. In the population Mohammedans predominate, but not very greatly. The Jats are its most distinctive people, sturdy men of much independence of character. A large proportion of them have been converted to Islâm, and from the ranks of those who remained Hindu was formed, for the most part, the protestant denomination of the Sikhs. The Punjab came under British rule half a century later than the older provinces, and from the educational point of view its people are backward. But there are signs of more rapid progress than are visible in the United

[1] Literally meaning "Five Rivers."

Provinces to the east. On the western border the language is Lehnda: going eastwards this shades into Punjábi, and this again into a dialect of Hindi. These are all in origin akin to Sanskrit. The Punjab is of great political importance, since it is the best recruiting ground in British territory for the Indian army.

The United Provinces include the tracts which may most properly bear the name of Hindustán. Until 1877 they were divided between two governments—that of the Lieutenant-Governor of the North-West Provinces, and that of the Chief Commissioner of Oudh. In that year the two provinces were amalgamated, the capital of each—Allahabad and Lucknow—being the residence of the Lieutenant-Governor during part of the year. Large towns are more numerous than in any other part of India: from amongst them may be mentioned Meerut, Barielly, Agra, Cawnpore, and Benares. Two districts run up into the Himalayas: in one of them is situated the summer headquarters of Naini-Tál. But generally the area is flat, densely populated, and closely cultivated. The rainfall is more assured than in the Punjab and irrigation is less generally practised. But it is vital to the existence of the western and central districts. About a quarter of the population is Mohammedan. The inhabitants are markedly conservative, and these provinces remained almost unaffected by the unrest which disturbed India so greatly during the years 1906 to 1911. The people speak Hindi in various dialects. With an admixture of Persian, Hindi is known as Urdu, and is used in this form in better class society.

The province of Bihár, Chota Nagpur, and Orissa, has recently been formed by the excision of these three territories from the province of Bengal. Bihár is an extension of the plain of Hindustán: its conditions are similar to those of the eastern districts of the United Provinces, and its people speak Hindi. Orissa includes the low-lying rice lands on the littoral of the Bay of Bengal. Its language is Uriya,—connected with Bengali, and related to Sanskrit. Chota Nagpur, lying between these regions, forms part of the hilly area of peninsular India. It is inhabited very largely by people of aboriginal descent: but Hindi may be regarded as the prevailing language. There is a Mohammedan colony of importance in Patna, the headquarters town of the province; but throughout the province Hindu interests vastly predominate.

Bengal has lately been reconstituted. Shorn of Bihár, Chota Nagpur, and Orissa, but extended eastwards by the abolition of the province of Eastern Bengal and Assam, it includes a homogeneous stretch of flat, densely populated rice country, throughout which the Bengali language is spoken. Hindus predominate towards the west: Mohammedans towards the east: in the province as a whole Mohammedans outnumber Hindus by about two millions. Calcutta is the provincial headquarters, and Darjeeling the hill station; but the Government will annually spend some weeks at Dacca in Eastern Bengal. The Bengali Hindus are intellectually exceedingly alert: they accept, however, without revulsion usually conservative social prejudices. The Mohammedans date their origin, by conversion, from the fourteenth century. They have held aloof from English schools, and have been, politically, quite eclipsed by the Hindus. But they have more enterprise than many other Indian communities: they are realising the advantages of learning English and may not improbably become a force in the State.

The little province of Assam includes the valleys of the Brahmaputra and Surma rivers, and a mass of hills which runs out into the plain between them. The headquarters—Shillong—is in these hills. The Surma valley is as densely populated as Bengal and the people speak Bengali. The Brahmaputra valley contains much waste land and offers more to emigrants than any other part of India. Its language is Assamese, akin to Bengali. In both valleys the tea-planting industry is of very great importance, and its interests have markedly affected the lines upon which the province is administered. The Chief Commissioner is in political control of the hill tribes which inhabit the wild country that stretches towards Tibet, and towards the areas that have been under Chinese influence. They are generally of Tibeto-Burman race, and are minutely subdivided by differences of language.

Burma is, geographically, distinct from India, from which it is separated by hills that no railway has crossed. Its greater portion is mountainous and sparsely populated. But it includes the valleys of the Irrawaddy and Salween rivers, with deltas of very remarkable fertility. The people are of Tibeto-Burman (or Mongoloid) affinities : they are for the most part Buddhist, and speak a language of their own. They exhibit more variety of tastes than the people of India, owing probably to the fact that their women are not secluded. The headquarters of Government are at the seaport of Rangoon : there is a summer station—Maymyo—in the hills beyond Mandalay.

The Madras presidency covers a straggling and irregular area of most heterogeneous character. The north-eastern districts contain a considerable Uriya population. To the south of them stretches a level tract in which Telugu is spoken. Further south, again, the language is Tamil, which changes to Kanarese and to Malayalim at the south-western corner. The coast districts are devoted to rice, which is grown very largely with the assistance of irrigation. The inland districts of the Telugu country lie on the peninsular black soil, or basaltic, plateau : their rainfall is precarious and their staple crop is large millet. Going southwards, the rock formation changes from basaltic to crystalline: small millets share the land with rice, and there is much irrigated garden cultivation. At the extreme south a stretch of level country bears good cotton. The Telugus, Tamils, Malayalims, and Kanarese are of the race called Dravidian. They profess Hinduism. A small admixture of Mohammedans recalls the days of Mohammedan dominion under Haidar Ali of Mysore and the Nawáb of Arcot. There is very little Aryan blood in Madras, to connect the people with Aryan traditions. Yet the influence of Brahmins is extraordinarily great; and education, although more widely diffused than in most other parts of India, has made but little impression upon social prejudices. Madras is the capital town of the province. There is a summer headquarters at Ootacamund in the Nilgiri Hills.

The Bombay presidency also includes tracts and peoples of great diversity. On the sea coast, at the extreme south, there are Kanarese: to the north we enter the Mahratta country which lies for the most part in the basaltic area of the peninsula where the rainfall is precarious and the main crops are millet and cotton. Below the hills which overlook the sea there is a narrow strip of rice country. Further north there is the tract known as Guzerát—at a low elevation, flat, and generally productive, but liable to catastrophic failures of rainfall. Finally there is the detached province of Sind, which is quite distinct from the rest of the province and has its closest affinities with the Punjab. Different languages are spoken in these four localities. The people of this province are undoubtedly the most progressive in India. It may be that they have more independence of character: authority certainly sits very lightly upon a Mahratta. It may be that popular ideas have been leavened by the emancipated energy of the Parsis, who are a very influential element in the community. But, whatever be the reason, it was in the Bombay presidency that the extreme formalities of caste rules were first disregarded; and at the present time it is here that relaxations have become most general in weightier prejudices. The headquarters of the government are at Bombay and Poona: there is a small hill-station at Mahableshwar on a plateau of the coast range. Among the towns Ahmedabad in Guzerât, and Karachi, the port of Sind, deserve special mention. For administrative purposes Aden has been attached to the Government of Bombay.

The Central Provinces include the Satpura range of hills, which are the dividing line between Northern and Southern India, and the districts that lie on either side of them. To the north they are watered by the Narbada, running into the Arabian Sea: to the south by rivers that flow towards the Bay of Bengal. North of the hill peaks the language is Hindi; south of them it is Mahratti towards the west, eastwards a peculiar dialect of Hindi. The agricultural conditions are exceedingly diverse: in the Narbada valley, wheat is the staple; in the Mahratta country, millet and cotton are most noticeable: to the south-east, the people depend upon rice. The headquarters of the province are at Nagpur: there is a small hill-station—Pachmarhi—in the Satpura hills, distinguished by charmingly picturesque scenery. Jabalpur, in the north of the province, is a large military cantonment and a town of growing importance.

A small *enclave* is now being carved out of the Punjab which, containing Delhi—the new Imperial capital,—will be under the direct administration of the Government of India. This shifting of the centre of government involves a sharp break in British traditions. Calcutta has been the capital of India for 140 years—from the time of Warren Hastings: it has also been the headquarters of the provincial government of Bengal since this government was established 60 years ago. It is no doubt inconvenient that the Government of India should be in specially intimate communication with any one provincial government: with however little reason, the other provincial governments will suspect that those who are in close touch with the supreme authority receive an undue share of its attention. It is also undesirable that the Government of India should be disproportionately impressed with the political ambitions of the Bengalis: they are but one of many intelligent races in India. The Federal Governments of the United States, of Canada, and of Australia have all established capitals of their own; and the Government of India has thus good precedent for separating itself apart. But Calcutta is the centre of non-official European life in India: at Delhi the Viceroy will be remote from its influence: the concerns which will lie nearest to him will be those of the Native princes of India. And the fact remains that the Government of India continues to share its summer capital, at Simla, with the provincial government of the Punjab.

CHAPTER XIV

THE EXECUTIVE GOVERNMENT

OTHER nations have acquired foreign dominion by the calculating or rapacious policies of their governments; but Britain owes her world-wide empire to the forceful—sometimes unscrupulous—activities of her sons. Their success has sometimes alarmed her: the annexation of Bengal in 1773 was followed by the deliberate pronouncement of Parliament that "to pursue schemes of conquest, and extension of dominion in India, are measures repugnant to the wish, the honour, and the policy of the nation." But she has generally supported them in difficulties; and if sometimes she has thwarted, disowned and even impeached them, she has rarely scrupled to avail herself of the advantages which they have obtained. Adventurous spirits may conveniently be financed and directed by a syndicate of capitalists, and until the time of the Mutiny India was governed by such a Chartered Company as is now developing the resources of Rhodesia. The British Parliament viewed its success with suspicion, and not infrequently intervened to limit its authority. In 1784 it established a State Board of Control, empowered to watch and guide the action of the Company's Directors, and in particular to deal with all correspondence of a secret or confidential character, which was not laid before the general body of Directors but disposed of by "a committee of secrecy" in consultation with the Board of Control. The principal member of the Board of Control was one of the Secretaries of State, the historical predecessor in office of the Secretary of State for India. But before the public the Directors still figured as the rulers of India, and they continued to make all appointments to the civil and military services—enjoying a patronage which they exercised with much honesty of purpose.

The Home Government

After the shock of the Indian Mutiny the British Parliament determined itself to assume the direction of Indian affairs. By a law passed in 1858 the supreme authority over India was vested in the Crown, acting through a special Secretary of State, whose pay was provided from the Indian revenues. The traditions of the Board of Directors were preserved by the establishment of an advisory Council, consisting, at present, of thirteen members, of whom nine must have had at least ten years' Indian experience in administration, law or commerce. Two of the existing members are Indians. The Secretary of State may, if he pleases, act in independence of his advisers, except in regard to matters, mainly affecting finance, which under the law must be disposed of by a majority of votes in Council. The Council has no right to see papers of a secret or confidential character. But it deals with a vast number of references upon matters of minor importance, for the consideration of which the members are grouped into seven departmental committees. The extent of the Secretary of State's control has depended upon his character and upon the strength of the Parliamentary majority behind him; and, so long as he can count upon the support of his party, a man of ideas and of masterful inclinations can, in fact, wield despotic authority. Under Queen Victoria's proclamation of 1858 it is the function of the Governor-General "to administer the Government in Our name, and generally to act in Our name and on Our behalf, subject to such orders and regulations as he shall from time to time receive through one of Our Principal Secretaries of State," and this definition of the relation of the Governor-General to the Secretary of State was confirmed by legislation in

Parliament. Pushed to its full legal limit the authority of the Secretary of State might deprive the Governor-General of all initiative and command. The extent of his interference is left to be regulated by considerations of expediency. In deciding upon these considerations the Secretary of State is supported by Parliament: the Governor-General may disagree; but he cannot appeal. Parliament, for all practical purposes, has come to be the House of Commons, and it may be then stated that the supreme control of Indian affairs is vested in a British politician who may never have visited,—and as a matter of fact has seldom visited—India, but may exercise despotic authority so long as he can command the approval of a majority in the House of Commons. The deliberations of the Secretary of State and of his Council are assisted by a secretariat and clerical establishment that are organised on a generous scale. The India office in London costs £600,000 a year, the whole of which is charged to the Indian revenues. To the cost of the Colonial office the Dominions and Colonies have not been expected to contribute.

The Government of India

Until, with the annexation of Bengal, the commercial undertakings of the East India Company were dwarfed by its administrative responsibilities, its interests in India were managed by councils of merchants at Calcutta, Bombay, and Madras, each under a president of its own, and acting quite independently of the others. Parliamentary legislation, commencing in 1773, established at each of these centres a governor, assisted by an executive council of three members, and declared the supremacy of the Calcutta, or Bengal, governorship, whose chief was given the title of Governor-General. From the time when the control of Indian affairs was transferred from the Company to the Crown he has also been styled "Viceroy." The strength of the Viceroy's Executive Council has gradually been increased until it now includes seven members, at least three of whom must have had ten years' Indian experience. One of the memberships—that for law and legislation—is now held by an Indian gentleman. Business is distributed amongst the Members of Council: each of them holds a separate portfolio, with general authority to pass orders himself on the papers set before him. But it is the duty of the Secretaries to the Government of India to submit to the Viceroy all cases of importance, and the Viceroy may, if he pleases, reserve any case for discussion, or for consideration in Council. Military affairs are dealt with by the Commander-in-Chief who is *ex officio* a Member of Council. He is, therefore, War Minister as well as Commander-in-Chief, with responsibilities that he may at times find it difficult to support. Up till 1906 military authority was shared between him and a Member of Council for the Military Department: but in that year the latter membership was abolished. The other six Members of Council hold charge, respectively, of (1) Home Affairs; (2) Revenue, Agriculture and Public Works; (3) Commerce and Industry; (4) Education and Sanitation; (5) Finance and (6) Law and Legislation. Railway affairs are committed to a Railway Board, which corresponds with the Government of India through the department of Commerce and Industry. Foreign Affairs—that is to say, matters concerning the Native Indian States and external politics—are retained by the Viceroy in his own hands.

If the Governor-General can command the support of the Secretary of State he is in theory as powerful as an Oriental despot. He has statutory powers of overruling his Executive Council, and also of vetoing any legislation of which he may disapprove: he may even legislate on his own sole authority, subject to the limitation that laws so made by him do not continue in force for a longer period than six months. These powers are, of course, for use on emergencies; and, as a matter of fact, the Governor-General has only on seven occasions made laws on his own authority. The prestige of the Governor-General ordinarily suffices to win the assent of his Executive Council in matters of importance. But he is under no positive obligation to summon the Council for joint deliberation, and under some Governor-Generals considerable intervals have elapsed between Council meetings. The Governor-General's official correspondence with the Home Government is known to his Council, the members of which append their signatures to his despatches. But he is in regular communication with the Secretary of State by private letters and telegrams, and of this correspondence the Council may remain in entire ignorance.

The Government of India—that is to say the Viceroy and his Executive Council—have their headquarters at Delhi and Simla. In theory they administer themselves the smaller provinces, which are in charge, not of a Governor or a Lieutenant-Governor but of a Chief Commissioner. In practice, however, except in matters of patronage, their interference in the affairs of these provinces is no more detailed than in the case of the larger ones.

The Indian Provincial Governments

The oldest provinces are those of Bombay and Madras, the Governments of which are, indeed, of as long standing as the Government of India, and represent "presidencies" which originally ranked with the "presidency" of Bengal. The legislation which established the Governor-General in Council endowed each of these two provinces with a Governor and an Executive Council of three members. The authority of the Governor in respect of his Executive Council, and the procedure adopted

SIMLA

for the disposal of business, are generally as in the case of the Government of India. The Governor may overrule a majority of Council that is against him, observing, however, more elaborate formalities than are required of the Governor-General. The Council of three originally included the Commander-in-Chief of the provincial or "presidency" army. In 1895, on the abolition of the Bombay and Madras armies as separate organisations, the military membership fell vacant. But on both Councils the vacancies have recently been filled by the appointment of Indian gentlemen. The other two memberships can be held only by persons who have had at least ten years' Indian experience, and their tenure has, in fact, been limited to senior officers of the Indian Civil Service.

Up to 1833 the whole of British India outside the presidencies of Bombay and Madras was administered by the Governor-General in Council at Calcutta. In that year, and subsequently, Parliamentary sanction was given to the creation of two new provinces,—in Upper India and in Bengal,—which were to be committed, like Bombay and Madras, to Governors, each with an Executive Council of three. But when the establishment of the provinces now known as the United Provinces and Bengal came actually to be undertaken, an alternative scheme was approved, and they were placed, not under Governors with Executive Councils, but under Lieutenant-Governors, who being members of the Indian Civil Service, with long Indian experience, would not need the advice of a Council and might be trusted to exercise an undivided authority. Subsequently similar Lieutenant-Governorships were created for the administration of the Punjab, of Burma, and of Eastern Bengal and Assam—a new province which was formed in 1905 by the union of Assam with the eastern districts of Bengal. There is, of course, no reason in the nature of things why a Lieutenant-Governor should not be assisted by an Executive Council, and in 1908 Parliament authorised the creation of a Council of three for the province of Bengal, one of the three members appointed to it being an Indian gentleman. Three years later, on the reunion of Eastern and Western Bengal, a completer reversion was made to the policy originally approved by Parliament, and the Lieutenant-Governor in Council of Bengal gave way to a Governor in Council. To the new province of Bihar, Chota Nagpur and Orissa, which was then established, a Lieutenant-Governor was appointed, but an Executive Council of three was associated with him; and it has recently been announced that such a Council is to be appointed for the assistance of the Lieutenant-Governor of the United Provinces.

A Lieutenant-Governor differs from a Governor in that, being selected from the Indian Civil Service, he is well acquainted with the people and the country, whereas a Governor is almost invariably a British statesman of rank, who has had no Indian experience. He brings an open mind to his duties, untrammelled either by knowledge or prejudice. He needs, then, the assistance of an advisory council. But the duties that are discharged by the Members of his Council have in the main also to be discharged under the rule of a Lieutenant-Governor, and are discharged less formally and by officials of lower status. The mass of business that presses on the government of a large province is beyond the unassisted capacity of a Lieutenant-Governor, and a very large proportion of the references that are made to him are disposed of by his secretaries, or by officers who exercise delegated powers. The establishment of an Executive Council in a Lieutenant-Governorship merely then regularises the disposal of business. But it owes much of the favour with which it is now regarded, to the occasion that it offers for the association of Indians in the government of their country.

The Government of India retain in their own hands the administration of certain "Imperial" departments—the Army, the Political Service, the Post Office, Telegraphs, and Railways, and all questions connected with general taxation, customs, tariff, currency, and State borrowings. With these matters provincial governments have no concern. Over other branches of administration provincial governments exercise full authority, subject to the general control of the Government of India, who, as a rule, content themselves with laying down from time to time general principles and watching the effect that is given to them, but keep a very strict hand upon the creation of new appointments or the augmentation of salaries. To meet their responsibilities, provincial governments retain a definite share of the revenue they collect, and accordingly benefit directly from all increases in income or economies in expenditure which careful administration may bring about.

The Executive Authority of Legislative Councils

During the past twenty years an entirely new force has come into the Indian political system, which is gaining increasingly upon the initiating and controlling authority of the official executive. We refer to the Legislative Councils, upon which non-official educated Indian opinion is effectively represented. In a succeeding chapter the history and constitution of these councils will be sketched, and an account will be given of their legislative functions. They must be sharply distinguished from the Executive Councils of the Governor-General and of Governors and Lieutenant-Governors, with which they have now only this much in common that they include the members of these Executive Councils on their benches, in right of office. They are much larger bodies, consisting of from 30 to 70 persons: their constitution is in great measure representative,—indeed, on all of them, except that of the Governor-General, non-official members are actually in a majority. Of the non-official members over four-fifths are Indians; and three-fourths are elected by bodies,—such as local and municipal boards, chambers of commerce, landholders' associations, and the universities,—upon which the non-official element has a preponderating influence. In one Provincial Council—that of Bengal—the elected members are actually in a majority. On other Provincial Councils they can secure a majority against the Government only by enlisting the assistance of the other non-official members, who are appointed, like the official members, by Government nomination. Even so, however, the elected members are sufficiently numerous to offer a strong resistance to measures of which they disapprove, and to render it irksome to the Government either to force unpopular measures through Council, or to withstand earnest recommendations. Although termed "Legislative Councils," they exercise, like the British Parliament, much executive power. Their members can guide or obstruct official proceedings by asking questions, and supplementary questions: they can in this manner place in the pillory any government official of whose conduct they disapprove. They can move resolutions affecting the policy of the State. And they are consulted in preparing the annual budgets, and are offered liberal opportunities for criticising the budgets when framed and submitted. Their deliberations are presided over by the Head of the Executive,—the Governor-General in the case of the Imperial Legislative Council, and the Governor (or Lieutenant-Governor) in the case of the Provincial Councils,—who has the right of refusing to answer interpellations which he may consider to be merely obstructive or injurious to public interests, and of vetoing resolutions or declining to put them to the vote. But so drastic an authority will not be lightly exercised in the face of an attentive and outspoken public press; and beyond all doubt these Councils have been endowed with powers which will, for good or evil, weaken the autocratic temper of British authority.

The Executive Officials

The Government officials in various departments who are actually in contact with affairs on the spot, generally work under the guidance and control of departmental authorities of their own—judges and magistrates, for instance, under the High Court, police officers under an Inspector-General of Police, engineers under a Chief Engineer, medical officers under an Inspector-General of Civil Hospitals, forest officers under a Conservator. The jurisdiction of these local officers is generally limited to a part or the whole of one of the "districts" into which British India is subdivided. There are 266 of these districts, with areas ranging from 2,000 to 10,000 square miles, and populations varying from half a million to four millions. In each district the collection of Government revenue of all kinds is supervised by a "Collector," who, following a custom that the East India Company inherited from the Moghal empire, is also appointed chief or "District" Magistrate of his district, with authority to hear appeals from magistrates exercising less than full magisterial powers, and to distribute criminal case work amongst the magistrates of his district. Appeals from his decisions, and from those of all full-powered magistrates of the district, lie to a Sessions Judge, who is, of course, entirely independent of the District Magistrate's authority. Magistrates exercising full powers are vested with some special authority for the prevention of crime; they can, for instance, call upon persons of criminal habits or pursuits to furnish security, and can commit them to jail in default: they can prohibit acts which may lead to a breach of the peace, and they exercise these preventive powers under the general control of the Magistrate of the District. Not only is the District Magistrate and Collector (variously styled "District Officer," and in some provinces "Deputy Commissioner") responsible for the fiscal and magisterial administration of his district, but in other matters he exercises general powers of supervision which enhance his authority up to something approaching that of a district governor. He sees all communications of importance that are received from their own chiefs by departmental officers, such as engineering, medical and forest officers, who are serving in his district, and he can intervene with advice when intervention seems required in the interests of the people. With police officers he is in still closer connection. It is their duty to consult him in all cases of difficulty, and he may then be said to control both the police and the magistracy—to be in a position to arrange at once for the arrest of an offender and for his punishment. He may try the offender himself, although he is generally too much occupied with other business to take many original criminal cases on to his own file. His authority over the other magistrates in his district does not extend, it need hardly be said, to instructing them to condemn or acquit. But his position tends, unavoidably, to influence them in forming their judgments, and they would generally not be disposed lightly to acquit a man whose arrest he had ordered. *Primâ facie* it may seem dangerous to trust a single officer with police and with magisterial influence. But it must be remembered that British rule is an exotic, and that a strong executive is needed to preserve it: this is recognised by the conferral of autocratic powers upon the Viceroy; and it is also recognised by making the threads of local administration converge to pass through the hands of the District Officer. Indian law is very generous in its provisions for appeal, and for the revision of sentences in criminal cases; and the working of the magistracy is in fact under the close control of authorities—the Sessions Judges and High Courts—which are free from all bias in favour of the District Magistrate. And the authority which the District Magistrate exercises over the police is a useful check upon police oppression,—the abuse of their authority by subordinates which, unless strictly repressed, will render the best intentioned of governments a curse to the people. The withdrawal from the District Magistrate of all control over either the magistracy or the police is the prime object of those who advocate the "separation of the judicial from the executive,"—a proposal which has exercised the consideration of Indian authorities for many years past. It is strongly supported by the Indian Nationalist party, which, naturally enough, would be pleased to diminish the effective authority of an alien government.

District officers are by no means free from all check or supervision other than that of the head of the province: between them and the secretariat are interposed inspecting and controlling officers, styled "Commissioners," who in Madras form a board, but in other provinces exercise localized authority, one being appointed to supervise a group, or "division," of five or six districts.

Institutions for Self-Government

According to Oriental ideas the State is sharply differentiated from the people: these represent two distinct and often antagonistic forces; and the notion, familiar to the West, that the State is in fact the people and is invested with its authority by the people, is in India an exotic which is as yet very imperfectly acclimatized. But the British Government has spared no pains to implant this idea and to nourish it,—to encourage the people to join hands with the State and assist it in the performance of its duties. For many years past private individuals have been commissioned as Honorary Magistrates for the repression of crime and the punishment of offenders, exercising powers which may be compared with those enjoyed in England by Justices of the Peace. At present there are no less than 3,000 Indian gentlemen who render voluntary and unpaid services in this capacity. As a general rule they sit in benches, and exercise powers which are less than those entrusted to stipendiary magistrates. But a considerable proportion are empowered to try cases alone, and are invested with the highest powers which a magistrate exercises under the law. In some provinces individuals have been entrusted with judicial powers as honorary civil judges, and some success has been attained in empowering village headmen, and committees of villagers, to settle petty civil disputes. But the assistance which the State derives from unpaid effort in the transaction of judicial business—criminal or civil—is of small account compared with the functions that have been committed to private citizens by its schemes of local government. Not only has every town in British India, down to places of 5,000 inhabitants, been endowed with a municipal board or committee: the village population has been distributed amongst rural boards whose jurisdiction, like a network, overspreads the country. There are 742 municipal (or urban) and 1,073 rural boards in British India. The revenues which they administer amount respectively to £1,700,000 and £2,100,000. These sums may appear inconsiderable to be shared by so large a number of authorities; and undoubtedly the resources that are at the disposal of very many of the committees are too small to encourage much active interest in their expenditure. But India is a poor country, and local taxation is not productive. The function of these bodies is to relieve the State, within their jurisdiction, of the conduct of such branches of the public service as in England are committed to town or county councils. It is in regard to *urban* areas (as might be expected) that official authority has gone furthest in its withdrawal. In some provinces as high a proportion as three-fourths of the town councillors hold office by election, and on an average the proportion is one-half, the remaining seats being filled by Government nomination. The chairman is sometimes appointed by nomination, but is more generally elected by the board, and is, as a rule, a non-official. Self-government of this description is new to India, and cannot be expected to win its way without some official guidance. But it is the policy of the State to provide this guidance from without rather than from within—not by insisting upon the preponderance of an official element upon the board, but by subjecting the board's proceedings to periodical inspection by the District Officer or the Commissioner of the division. Through these officers the State may veto unlawful or injurious orders; may provide that expenditure is not diverted from legitimate purposes; and may intervene in cases of serious neglect of duty, in extreme cases setting aside the board's authority and dealing itself with matters in respect to which the board has failed. In *rural* areas, where private effort is less adequately equipped with education and intelligence, the constitution of the board is on a somewhat less popular basis. Taking all rural boards together, one-third of their members hold office by election; but the chairman is usually an official, or, where he may be elected, his election is conditional upon the approval of the Government. In the administration of the local affairs of British India, popular aspirations for self-government are represented by 4,898 elected members on urban and by 5,216 elected members on rural boards.

If a general survey be attempted of the achievements of these boards, one is confronted with very conflicting opinions in praise or in blame. The ordinary affairs of very many towns, particularly in Western India, are efficiently administered by their leading citizens, and official authority is rarely compelled to intervene. On the other hand, instances are lamentably numerous, noticeably in Bengal, of the failure of town councils to provide for the most elementary measures of sanitation, or even to collect their revenues. Generally the authority of the committees is weakened very greatly by the nervousness of the elected committee-men. Representatives of the people naturally fear popular disfavour : but in India they are apprehensive of the enmity of however few of their fellow-citizens, and will scarcely face the risk of it even in the clearest interests of the public good. They can then hardly be trusted to effect public improvements. If the rates must be raised, they will hope that peremptory orders from the Government will provide them with an excuse ; and they will allow taxes to fall into arrears rather than press defaulters for payment. Little interest is displayed by the voters in election proceedings. But this is also the case in many English towns ; and it may be suspected that some of those who criticise the work of Indian town councils would be more sparing in comment had they some practical experience of municipal administration at home. It must be confessed, however, that local self-government in India has, hitherto, leant very heavily upon the directing influence of the State, or upon the readiness of the State to interfere, and that its vitality is rather that of a parasite upon the State than of an independent organism. It can hardly be conceived as outliving the downfall of the central authority.

The Indian Civil Service.

The executive Government of India is then, as it were, a nerve system of bureaux, actuated chiefly—so far—

by impulses of its own, but affected by popular ideas and aspirations which impinge upon it from the British Parliament, from the Indian Legislative Councils and the local boards in Indian towns and districts. This nerve system has for the most part been represented by the Indian Civil Service, which for over a century has practically held a monopoly of the administration of the country. With the technical departments of Government—such as engineering, medicine, police, and education—the Civil Service has, of course, little to do, although in the case of the two last it has sometimes assumed official leadership. But, until comparatively recent years, it has held, and for many years was secured by English law in holding, all posts of superior control in judicial or executive administration—from the top to the bottom of the scale,—excepting those of Viceroy, of some Members of the Viceroy's Executive Council, of the Governorships of Bombay and Madras and of most of the Judgeships on the High Court benches. It has thus the character rather of a government service trust than of a government service. Originally constituted from the East India Company's staff of commercial agents, it was for more than half a century recruited by the patronage of the Board of Directors: in 1853 its doors were thrown open to public competition in an examination which is at least a test of industry and determination. Indians—even when they come from homes in the Native States—can claim admission to the examination: but they compete, of course, under difficulties, and no more than fifty-four have been successful, fully half of whom belong to one community—the Bengali—the members of which are not amongst Indians the best qualified for posts of executive control. The posts reserved for members of the Indian Civil Service number 687, and to provide for the training of junior officers and for leave vacancies, the strength of the service is about 1,050—no very large staff for leading and controlling 244 millions of people. Nor does it appear large if compared with the number of posts, held almost wholly by Indians, to which authority is attached, whether executive or judicial, that is similar in kind to that exercised by members of the Indian Civil Service. These posts (classed as "provincial" as opposed to the "imperial" posts reserved for the Indian Civil Service) include the vast majority of the magistracies and civil judgeships, and number about 3,800: and if the incumbents receive much lower salaries than are enjoyed by members of the Indian Civil Service, they are more liberally remunerated than officers of corresponding functions in any country of continental Europe. With the advancing intelligence and probity of the educated classes it has been possible to relax the monopoly of the Indian Civil Service to the highest posts of control, and during the past generation, under authority given by Parliament, 93 of these posts have been thrown open to Indians who had proved their capacity by meritorious service in the "provincial" branch. Having regard, however, to the fact that an Indian living in his own country is untroubled by a number of expenses that are incidental to the life of a European in India, the salary enjoyed by Indians holding these posts is limited to two-thirds of that to which a European would be entitled. Europeans are, indeed, heavily burdened by charges connected with sick leave, furlough and the maintenance of separate establishments, in Europe or in the hill stations, for their wives and families.

For over a century India has been practically under the tutelage of the Indian Civil Service, which has superintended her conduct and her education as in nursery and schoolroom. The members of this service have generally shown the capacity which is awakened by responsibility in men of British race: with ample salaries they have hardly been tempted by dishonesty, and their detached impartiality has not been disturbed by the importunity of relations or friends. To the credit of their nation they have established and maintained a government, which, for its resources, is exceedingly efficient, and, in one honourable respect—its solicitude for the poor—has probably been the most painstaking the world has ever known. The chief defect of the service has been a jealousy of its privileges which has made it hesitate to believe that any of its members was unfit for responsible office, and should, in the public interests, be denied promotion. Its power must decline with India's growing intelligence: but this prospect has not affected the temper of its officers, and they have generally taken pride in their charge's intellectual development, and have not limited their sympathies to their business of control. Their rôle is becoming less prominent though hardly less important. Non-official voices in the Legislative Councils will put authority on its defence with explanations and arguments, and will claim an increasing influence upon lines of policy. And a growing self-respect will resent with bitterness any assumption of essential superiority—any tendency to treat the educated or influential as still under tutelage. Yet we may probably assume that, for many years to come, India's hands will remain less efficient than her brains—especially for tasks on exotic models—that she will be conscious of this fact when undisturbed by passion, and that she will require—and respect—the agency of a European service in the government of her people upon European lines.

CHAPTER XV

LEGISLATION AND LAW COURTS

A NATION that is developing political freedom holds it to be essential for good government that the function of law-making should be divorced from the executive authority of the State ; and its efforts are directed towards the transfer of legislation from the governing body to a popular assembly. But a popular assembly that has secured full legislative powers is not content with them but presses to annex executive powers also. Such has been the history of the British Parliament. And this history has been reflected in the development of the Indian Legislative Councils.

THE LEGISLATIVE COUNCILS

Up to the year 1833 law-making in India was frankly regarded as an executive process, and laws, or "regulations," were made by the Governor-General, or by the Governors of Madras and Bombay, in consultation with their Executive Councils. In that year a separate authority was created for legislative business : but it was entirely official, consisting of the Governor-General and his Executive Council, supplemented by some nominated officials. In 1861 provision was made for the nomination of some non-official members, and in this capacity some Indians found their way on to the legislative bodies of Calcutta, Madras and Bombay. But by the method of their appointment they were tied to official interests, and it was not until the Legislative Councils were reorganised in 1892—during the viceroyalty of Lord Lansdowne—that Indians, having views of their own, could obtain seats upon the Councils, and that anything approaching an opposition could be organised to the policy of Government. The Councils were enlarged, the number of non-official members was increased, and, while the majority of them continued to be appointed by the Government, a few might be elected by non-official bodies, such as the urban and rural self-government boards, chambers of commerce, associations of land-holders and the universities,—or, in the case of the Governor-General's Legislative Council, by the non-official members of the Provincial Legislative Councils. But the elections had the effect merely of submitting names for the approval of the Government, and did not of themselves give a seat in Council. In 1909 popular aspirations received a further concession. The size of the Legislative Councils was very greatly increased, the number of members being in fact trebled: the number of non-official members was increased in a still larger proportion, and much more scope was afforded to election as a means of securing capable, or representative, non-official members. Moreover, elected members were permitted to take office in virtue of their election, and not in virtue of its approval by the Government, although the State reserved to itself the power of excluding any person of such reputation and antecedents that his election would, in the opinion of the Governor-General in Council be contrary to the public interests.

The Imperial Legislative Council—that is to say, the Legislative Council of the Governor-General—now ordinarily consists of 68 members of whom 36 are officials (including the Governor-General and his Executive Council) and 4[1] are non-officials who are nominated by the Governor-General at his pleasure, and will presumably be supporters of his policy. The remaining 28 members

[1] Reduced to two at every other election, when the members for Mohammedan constituencies are increased from six to eight.

are all non-officials, and may be classed as follows according to the interests which they represent :—

Two elected by the Chambers of Commerce at Calcutta and Bombay :

One representing the Indian trading community—at present nominated :

Seven representing the landholders of seven provinces : 6 elected and 1 (for the Punjab), nominated :

Six representing Mohammedan constituencies : 5 elected and 1 (for the Punjab), nominated :

Twelve elected by the *non-official* members of the seven Provincial Councils, and (one of the twelve only) by rural and urban boards in the Central Provinces, which have not as yet been endowed with a Council of their own.

Twenty-five of these twenty-eight members are, then, elected : and it is probable that before long the privilege of election will be conceded to the three constituencies, representatives for which are at present nominated.

The franchise for landholders and for Mohammedans has been fixed high enough to exclude all but men of some means, position or repute ; and their representatives will not ordinarily hold extreme views in politics. The concession of separate representatives to the Mohammedan community needs explanation, since it establishes constituencies which are united by a religious, as opposed to a territorial or social, *nexus*. The justification is that, otherwise, the Mohammedans would not be at all adequately represented, since in five out of seven provinces they are in a minority, and in the present state of feeling, their candidates could hardly expect to be supported by the Hindus. The arrangement secures, then, the representation of a minority, which, of however great importance in the aggregate, would almost everywhere be outvoted in detail. It is not, of course, from the landholding or the Mohammedan communities that the ideas have sprung which of recent years have given advanced, or "nationalist," aspirations to Indian popular politicians,—aspirations which the enlargement of the Legislative Councils was in some measure intended to appease. These ideas have had their birth amongst the educated professional classes,—a society which is almost wholly Hindu, practically indeed consisting of the educated Hindus who have not secured service under the Government. No special representation has been conceded to these classes because the twelve members who are elected by the non-official members of the Provincial Legislative Councils can generally be trusted to express their views. The most strenuous of the non-official members of the Provincial Legislative Councils are those who are returned by rural and urban boards ; and, since the control of these boards has passed very largely indeed into the hands of the professional classes, men of these classes will ordinarily be elected by the boards to the Provincial Legislative Councils, and will certainly do their utmost to secure the return of men of their own type to the Imperial Legislative Council. On no Provincial Council, however, do the representatives of these boards hold a clear majority amongst the non-official members ; and, should they be outvoted in electing representatives for the Imperial Legislative Council, the educated Hindus of a province might find themselves without a spokesman. This is an annoying contingency, since it is very largely to their efforts that the Imperial Legislative Council owes the reform of its constitution.

It may not improbably happen that the Government may find arrayed against it all the "popular" representatives. But their votes only number 12 out of 68. In the unlikely contingency of the capture of all the landholding and the Mohammedan votes by the popular party the Government would still command a majority of 16,—no trifling margin in so small a parliament. But it must be realised, on the other hand, that non-official opinion is represented far too strongly to be lightly overruled, and that the Indian members can influence very materially indeed the government of the country.

The composition of the seven [1] Provincial Legislative Councils is modelled upon that of the Imperial Legislative Councils. But they are of a more popular complexion. In the first place, the proportion of non-official members is larger,—is indeed so large that should these members all combine they can outvote the Government. In the second place, the members who will endeavour to stand forth as champions of the people are elected solely and directly by rural and urban boards,—and not, as in the case of the Imperial Council, by a mixed electorate (namely, the non-official members of the Provincial Legislative Councils) which rural and urban boards may influence, but cannot command. It is likely, then, that popular leaders will be more stringent in animadversion and criticism in the Provincial Councils than in the Imperial Council. And in one Provincial Council—that of Bengal [2]—the elected members actually outnumber the nominated members, both official and non-official, so that they can place the Government in a minority even although it calls up the support of all its non-official nominees. But of the elected representatives three will ordinarily be Europeans, and their defection from the ranks of the opposition would just secure to the Government a bare majority. It is clear, however, that in these conditions, the Government will find it exceedingly difficult to hold a course that is out of accord with popular feeling.

Representatives of rural and urban boards constitute

[1] Shortly to be increased to nine by the grant of Legislative Councils to the Central Provinces and Assam.

[2] The boundaries of Bengal have recently been readjusted, and some changes will be made in the constitution of its Legislative Council.

about a third of the non-official members of the Bombay and Madras Legislative Councils,—less than this proportion in the Bengal Council and more in the Council of the United Provinces. They are generally nearly balanced by the representatives who are directly elected by landholders and Mohammedans. Upon the Provincial Legislative Councils some special interests are represented,—Universities, Chambers of Commerce, and, in the case of the Bengal Council, the Calcutta Trades Association and the European communities engaged in tea planting and in the jute trade. The members who represent landholders and Mohammedans are elected by much larger constituencies than those which send members to the Imperial Legislative Council: the property qualification for a vote is lower, and the franchise has (in the case of Mohammedans) been extended to all who hold titles, to graduates of a certain standing and to some classes of school teachers. Hindu graduates, as such, do not vote on elections to the Legislative Councils. But their degree generally enfranchises them for elections to rural and urban boards.

The upper and middle classes of Indian society,—be it understood, a very small fraction of the total,—will find occasion in the reformed Councils to promote or obstruct legislation according as it serves or conflicts with their interests. And their influence will not be confined to legislation. Their representatives have been granted a right of interference with the executive Government which will inevitably affect the tone of its orders. The reforms of 1892 included a concession in this direction, members of Legislative Councils being permitted to interpellate the Government on matters of executive administration, and to criticise the annual provincial and imperial budgets. In 1909 their privileges were widened. They may now cross-examine the Government by supplementary questions: they may move resolutions;

and the non-official members are consulted in the preparation of each year's budget, and can exert their influence constructively as well as critically. Non-official members of Council have thus been invested with very considerable powers which those of them who are elected will not hesitate to use. Official members are expected to vote unquestioningly with the Government, and to speak only when they are desired to give the Government argumentative support.

For the educated and the well-to-do the State is then no longer to be regarded as an esoteric institution, with whose behests their only concern is to obey. Encouraging results can already be observed, although, so far, they are mainly indirect fruits of the concession. At the Council board Indians meet British officials upon equal terms: this equality is advantageous to both parties: the one gains an invigorating self-esteem, the other loses an aggravating air of superiority. Non-official opinion is bridled by responsibility, and elected members, who make their entry in declamation, soon settle down to dispassionate discussion. The offer of an authorised opportunity to public criticism lessens its inclination for tempestuous attacks, whether in the press or in such informal gatherings as the National Congress,—a convention in which representatives of the educated classes have annually met to discuss and ventilate their grievances. These gains are indirect: but they are very substantial. In the direct exercise of their legislative functions non-official members have not as yet made any great mark upon State policy; they generally find that their earnestness is discharged by their eloquence; having spoken with credit they feel relieved of concern with practical issues. But in this they do not differ from many Western orators. There is, however, a real danger that, under the new régime, the State will find it so troublesome to interfere on behalf of the working classes (who have in Council no spokesman of their own) that it will treat their interests with the indifference which they have suffered under the middle-class Cabinets of the West. Indian legislation has been honourably distinguished by its solicitude for the tenant class,—by the enactments which have protected the cultivators from the aggression of their landlords. Councils upon which landlords can command an audience, but the tenants are unrepresented, will not readily agree to agrarian legislation; and of recent years there have been some notable cases in which the Government could carry through such legislation only by forcing it past the non-official members. This was when the non-official members were much less numerous than they have now become. As regards social reform, judging from past experience, the Government might expect to meet from the elected members the bitterest opposition to measures that ran counter to long-standing prejudice. The Age of Consent Act, which penalises the consummation of marriage with a child under twelve, was pressed through an opposition which agitated Indian society so deeply that the State has never cared actively to enforce its provisions. It may perhaps, however, be argued that in matters of this sort it is useless to legislate until the majority are prepared to welcome a reform. But, if such a policy had always been accepted, Hindu widows would still be burning themselves upon funeral pyres. It is, however, by no means clear that, under the revised constitution of the Councils, past experience will be a guide to the future; and we may indeed conclude from the subject and tone of recent debates that the elected members, finding themselves no longer a neglected, but an influential minority—able not only to oppose but to initiate—will themselves take up social questions and press them upon the Government. Many of them are convinced that only by social reform can India win the esteem of other nations. And changes that would be resisted if they suggested British interference, may be accepted when tendered by Indian hands.

By the inclusion in the Councils of a large number of official members who are bound to support official policy, the Supreme Government has marshalled round itself a force which, if pressed into service, can carry non-official opposition before it. But a direct clash between official and non-official judgments will provoke awkward consequences, which will ordinarily be avoided. And the government of the country suffers, of course, from the employment of a number of public servants as a legislative make-weight instead of in the discharge of their administrative duties. Nor must we overlook a serious contingency. The British are aliens in India, and alien influence, however beneficial, must always be disliked, and is liable to be vilified and spurned in sudden fits of national passion. On such an occasion elected members of Council will find it difficult to support the authority of the State. The Governor-General has power to overrule opposition in Council. But in so defying his councillors he may aggravate hostility of a kind which cannot be conciliated and must be repressed.

The President of the Council—that is to say, the Governor-General in the Imperial Legislative Council, and the Governor or Lieutenant-Governor in a Provincial Council —may refuse to reply to a question which is injurious to public interests, and may, for a similar reason, decline to permit a resolution to be put to Council. The legislation of a Provincial Legislative Council may be vetoed by the Governor-General, and that of the Imperial Council by the Secretary of State,—indeed no law passed in either the Imperial or a provincial Council can take effect until it has formally been approved by the Secretary of State : that is to say, the Indian Legislative Councils are subject to the ultimate authority of the British Parliament. The questions upon which the Councils may legislate are expressly limited by an Act of Parliament. The Imperial Council may not enact any law touching the authority of the British Parliament, or "any part of the unwritten laws or constitution of the United Kingdom whereon may depend the allegiance of any person to the Crown, or the sovereignty or dominion of the Crown." Provincial Councils are debarred from interference with religion, the customs duties, imperial taxation, the currency, the transmission of postal or telegraphic messages, the penal code, patents, copyright, the army, or foreign relations.

The reforms of 1909 have not trespassed upon the emergent powers of the Governor-General to launch, upon his own authority, ordinances which run with the force of law for a period of six months: nor have they affected the authority of the Governor-General in Council to legislate by executive order, or "regulation," for certain backward tracts which have not yet been admitted to representation upon the Imperial Council.

Laws

In Europe and America immigrating races have merged themselves with the peoples upon whom they trespassed, and the peculiar prejudices of the invaders and the invaded have gradually been absorbed by a sympathy for their common country. Laws are consequently general and territorial, and the courts make no distinction of persons in deciding cases. But in Asia there has been a different tendency: the conquerors have been segregated from the conquered by a jealous pride or by religious differences, and countries are inhabited not by nations but by collections of nations, each of which has endeavoured to preserve its individuality. In these circumstances laws have developed not territorially, with reference to the needs of the country as a whole, but sectarially, with reference to the ideas and customs of different classes of the population. So in Turkey the Armenian, Greek, and Jewish communities have each preserved laws and tribunals of its own: and when the British arrived in India they found not only that different laws were in force for the Mohammedans and the Hindus, but that the laws of various classes of the Hindus differed considerably. Mohammedan law is based upon the Korán: Hindu law upon ancient Sanskrit treatises. But, in application, both were profoundly modified by peculiar tribal or sectarian custom. The long predominance of Mohammedan rule, and the importance of criminal law as a protection for the State, had tended to concentrate in Mohammedan hands the exercise of magisterial functions, and Mohammedan criminal law was not limited in its application to Mohammedans. But no Mohammedan lawyer in dealing with Hindus would lightly have disregarded such a tenet of Hindu law as that which gave "benefits of clergy" to Brahmins. The line upon which legislation has developed under the British Government has been the gradual substitution of territorial for personal or sectarian law,—the evolution of provisions which would apply to everyone instead of provisions which applied to a class. In matters affecting religious and domestic life, progress in this direction has been difficult to win. But as regards civic life,—the practical relations of men in the market-place, as opposed to the temple or the house,—the British maxim has generally been established, that before the law all men are equal. In respect of criminal procedure and punishments, of civil court procedure, of evidence, of claims for performance of contract or for damages, the law takes no account of the status of individuals, and deals with the low caste man as with the most exclusive of Brahmins. One of the few compliments that it still pays to social susceptibilities is that it exempts men of rank and position from personal appearance in civil court proceedings. But with peculiarities of religious ceremony and domestic life the State has been chary of interference. It has, indeed, prohibited some religious observances which horrify the Western conscience: it has penalised human sacrifices, certain barbarous manifestations of religious asceticism, and the sacrificial suicide of widows, known as *suttee.* It has stopped these practices, but, so far, has not taught the public conscience to condemn them; and quite recent occurrences have shown that, if British rule were withdrawn, *suttee* might very possibly regain its popularity. The Indian Government has hardly ventured to envisage the degraded position of the Indian woman. According to the theory of Orientals, of whatever creed, the function of woman is limited to those processes that are concerned, directly or indirectly, with the reproduction of the species: she is concerned with her husband and with the bearing and rearing of children, and no occasion is afforded her for the exercise of faculties which are not connected, more or less closely, with these ends. She exercises no environal, as opposed to reproductive activities: indeed in the seclusion of the harem she is isolated from her environment. Her life is then exclusively one-sided: she is concerned with the race not with herself. Save in some minor particulars the British Government has not ventured to interfere with the workings of this theory, however degrading. It has given Hindu widows permission to remarry without the forfeiture of all civil privileges. Fifty years have passed since a law was so enacted: but at the present day an orthodox high caste Bengali would be ostracised if he arranged a second marriage for a daughter who had been left a widow in early childhood. It has offered immature girls the protection of the law against the violence of their husbands. For the rest, it has prohibited slavery: it has penalised the infanticide which to a struggling peasantry appeared a measure of relief; and it has declared that by his conversion to Christianity, or by loss of caste, a man does not forfeit his civil status and privileges. Here it has rested content: and it may be noted that its most venturesome trespasses upon the Hindu system —the abolition of domestic slavery and of *suttee*, and the legalisation of widow remarriage and of conversion—took place in days before the Mutiny. Inheritance and succession are still guided by the customary or religious rules of Hindus and Mohammedans. These rules are quite out of accord with modern industrial life: the minute subdivision of property under Mohammedan law, and the maintenance of communal ownership by Hindu law both impede the accumulation and disposal of capital. There are signs that this incongruity between custom and environment is becoming realized; and it is probable that, before long, Indians of intelligence will endeavour to lead an exodus from antiquated usages.

In matters which do not affect religious convictions, or the home, legislation in India has been quite sufficiently active; and a long list of statutes testifies to the fecundity of its proceedings during the past fifty years. A large proportion of them are, of course, directed to assist the State in the discharge of its functions, in maintaining order and repressing crime, in collecting its taxes and in managing the large concerns,—forests, railways and canals, the post office and the telegraph,—which are in the nature of business enterprises. Of late years the appearance of political disaffection has compelled the Government to add to its armoury measures for the suppression of seditious utterances on the platform and in the press, although it has, so far, made no great use of them. There has been much legislation of a benevolent character. Mention has already been made of efforts to mitigate the harshness of the Hindu religious and domestic systems. A Factory Act limits the hours during which factory hands may be asked to labour, and protects the interests of women and children. There are laws securing tenants,—

or certain classes of tenants,—against oppressive enhancement of rent or capricious ejectment from their holdings: also providing for the assistance of agriculturists by the grant of State loans, by the equitable composition of debt, and by the establishment of co-operative credit societies. In some provinces an attempt has been made to check the growing tendency of cultivators to mortgage their holdings, in order to provide themselves with funds for wasteful expenditure, by limiting their rights of transfer and making their land less easily negotiable. But perhaps the most interesting feature of the Indian Statute Book is the illustration it affords of the successful codification of law. The Indian Penal Code is a striking instance. It brings within the compass of 512 sections a criminal law which in England must be pursued through a multitude of disconnected Acts and decisions. The procedure of the police, of criminal and civil processes and trials has similarly been codified: so also the law of evidence, and the law that is concerned with contracts, and with easements. It has been objected that by the intelligible description of legal contingencies the State has enhanced their attractiveness as subjects of legal proceedings, and has encouraged litigation amongst a people that is naturally over-inclined to it. There may be some truth in this. But, on the other hand, it may be urged that the legal training of Indian magistrates and judges cannot be very elaborate, and that their deficiencies in this respect are supplied by a clear and comprehensive statement of the law.

Law Courts.

The Indian law courts have sprung from two very diverse origins,—from the tribunals which were set up by the East India Company as its territorial responsibilities extended, and from the judicial appointments which were made by the Crown, in complete independence of the Company's authority. The former were generally modelled upon the native tribunals which they superseded, and the law which they administered was, in civil matters, Hindu or Mohammedan, according to the religion of the parties; and, in criminal matters, the Mohammedan law corrected and softened where glaringly opposed to Western standards of humanity. The latter were represented by the High Courts of Calcutta, Bombay and Madras: they were fashioned upon English lines and the law which they dispensed was English. A clash of jurisdictions ensued, provoking jealousies which have lingered to this day in Calcutta. The two systems were finally combined in 1861 when the High, or Chartered, Courts were definitely set at the head of the Indian judicial system, with authority, on appeal or petition or of their own motion, to revise the decisions of all subordinate courts, criminal and civil. In exercising these functions they administer of course, the law of the Indian Statute Book, supplemented in domestic and personal matters, such as marriage and inheritance, by Hindu, Mohammedan and customary law.

For the administration of the criminal law the principal tribunals (apart from the High Courts) are the Courts of Session: there is one such tribunal for each district or group of districts, presided over by a single judge who is generally a member of the Indian Civil Service. Sentances of death passed by a sessions judge are not final unless confirmed by the High Court: in other respects (save when European British subjects are concerned) his authority is as extensive as that exercised by English judges of assize. Below the court of session are magisterial courts which are graded as of the first, the second, or of the third class, according as their powers of punishment are limited to the infliction of two years' imprisonment and a fine of Rs. 1,000, of six months' imprisonment and a fine of Rs. 200, or of one month's imprisonment and a fine of Rs. 100. First-class magistrates are, further, charged with the preliminary investigation of serious cases that can only be dealt with by courts of session, and with the commitment of offenders for trial by courts of session. At the head of the magisterial staff of each district stands the District Magistrate. In the infliction of sentences he exercises no higher powers than other first-class magistrates: but he has authority to distribute work amongst the other magistrates of his district, and to hear appeals from magistrates of the second and third classes. He also guides the district magistracy in the exercise of some special powers with which Indian law invests first-class magistrates for the prevention of crime—as, for example, power to require security for good behaviour or for keeping the peace, power to deal with unlawful assemblies, or power to abate or remove public nuisances. All decisions of sessions judges or first-class magistrates are appealable to the High Court, unless they affect cases of minor importance that are tried summarily. And the law has placed no limit upon the authority of the High Court to send for records, upon its own motion, and pass any order which may seem to it fitting.

European British subjects that are accused of a criminal offence do not forfeit by their residence in India the privilege of being tried by courts that are superior in status to those which the Indian Government can afford generally to maintain. If their cases are dealt with magisterially, they can be taken up only by a magistrate who is himself a European British subject or by the District Magistrate: the former can inflict no severer sentence than one of three months' imprisonment: the latter can inflict six months' imprisonment but must sit with a jury at least half of whose members must be European British subjects or Americans. If their cases are committed for trial at sessions, the judge—also assisted by such a jury—cannot inflict a sentence of more than one year's imprisonment. Before the High Court they are also entitled to trial by jury; but they are liable to the full sentences that are prescribed by the Indian Penal Code.

The people of India are generally law-abiding, and the criminal courts affect but little the lives of those who are not criminals by profession, except in so far as they are misused (and they are misused somewhat extensively) as a convenient and inexpensive means of securing redress or revenge for private injuries. Resort to the civil courts is much more costly, since the charges for civil court fees are considerable. The civil courts are, nevertheless, exceedingly popular as a means of obtaining, not merely justice, but excitement. Success in litigation gives social distinction, and copies of judicial decisions are exhibited with pride. In some provinces an experiment has been made in empowering village headmen or committees to deal with petty civil cases. Excluding these rural tribunals, there are no less than 1,563 civil courts in British India. The judges are generally Indians, and receive liberal salaries. The civil court fees paid by litigants yield a large income to the State, which, over British India as a whole, covers the cost of civil court establishments, and in some provinces leaves a considerable profit. Compared with the total population the volume of litigation does not appear excessive: in no province are there annually more than three contested cases per 1,000 of population. But, if the comparison is limited to the better classes, who actively support the law courts, its results are much more striking. It is noticeable that civil litigation increases very markedly in years of good harvest: so does also the consumption of spirituous liquor. Each gratifies a taste which affords, respectively, to the well-to-do and the poor a congenial means of spending a surplus. The Indian law offers disappointed suitors liberal facilities for appeal; and in Bengal, where the fullest advantage of them is taken, there are no less than thirty appeals to every hundred contested cases. Litigation absorbs so high a proportion of the surplus funds of the community that the legal profession is by far the most lucrative of callings. To it resorts practically all the intelligence of the middle classes which is not provided with an opening in the public services. In Bengal, even in country districts, the local bar is so strong and influential as to be a material factor for good or for evil in the sentiments with which the State is regarded by the people.

Juries are never employed in civil suits. They are, as already stated, empanelled for the trial of European British subjects, whether by magistrates, sessions judges or the High Courts; and the Criminal Procedure Code provides for their association with sessions judges in any areas which the Government considers to be sufficiently advanced to supply satisfactory jury lists. The Government has formed such a conclusion in the case of all the districts of the Madras presidency: but elsewhere only in the case of certain districts of Bengal, and certain towns in the United Provinces and Bombay. And in these areas juries are only empanelled for certain classes of cases. The verdict of a jury is determined by a majority and need not be unanimous; and, if the judge considers a verdict to be perverse he may withhold judgment, and submit the case to the High Court for orders. In areas where sessions judges are not assisted by juries, they sit with two Indian "assessors," as advisors, whose counsel, guided by their knowledge of Indian life and manners, may be exceedingly useful, but may be disregarded for reasons which must be placed upon the record.

The *personnel* of the Indian courts, criminal and civil, is for the most part Indian. Of the High Court judges, only a third may be appointed from the ranks of the

Indian Civil Service: the others are selected from the English or the Indian bar. Many of these judgeships are held by Indians, who have generally become a credit and, in some cases, an adornment to the bench. At least two-thirds of the superior criminal magistrates are Indians, and, if all criminal magistrates are taken into account, the proportion of British officers falls to a sixth. The civil tribunals are almost exclusively Indian. The chief civil judge of a district is more generally British than Indian, but this post is gradually falling into Indian hands, and the multitudinous civil judges of inferior status are practically all Indians. There are few such conspicuous illustrations of the progress of India as is afforded by the increasing efficiency and honesty of Indian magistrates and judges. This may in part be due to the effects of English education. It may also plausibly be ascribed in some measure to the growing acuteness and influence of the Indian bar.

CHAPTER XVI

THE ARMY AND THE POLICE

FOR the protection of the people—and of itself—the Indian Government maintains a force of over 450,000 men, of whom (in round numbers) 75,000 are British soldiers, 156,000 are Indian soldiers, 38,000 are British or Anglo-Indian[1] volunteers and 187,000 are Indian police. Save for the volunteers, this force is always on an active footing : there are reserves, but they are not included in these figures. The cost of this establishment falls heavily upon the resources of a poor country. It absorbs, indeed, 42 per cent. of its *net* income ; and it is to be observed that of this large expenditure but a small share goes to the police—about £4 millions of the total of £23 millions.

THE ARMY

The British and the Native troops which together compose the Indian Army are linked by the fact that both are commanded by British officers. The British force has grown from very small origins. Guards of European soldiery were employed by the East India Company from the time that its activities excited the jealous hostility of neighbouring powers : they were maintained partly by small drafts from England, partly by the enlistment of deserters of various nationalities, who drifted from the service of rival companies and Native princes ; and, in later years, they were augmented by the transfer of men from regiments of the British Army, which had been sent out on Indian service. It was not until 1754—three years before the battle of Plassey—that the Home Government assisted the Company

[1] Hitherto generally known as " Eurasians."

by the despatch of reinforcements from the Home Army: previously, it was to the successes of the British fleet in Indian waters that the Company owed the preservation of its factories on the Madras seaboard from French aggression. On land it commanded forces which appear absurdly inadequate. In 1748, when the French under Lally were at the height of their power, the Company's European troops only sufficed to form three battalions. Clive won the battle of Plassey with only 900 Europeans. In later years the Company's British forces were strengthened by the transfer of several regiments from the service of the Crown. But until the days of the Mutiny the British troops employed in India were sharply distinguished according as they belonged to the Company or were lent by the Crown,—on payment by the Company of all their expenses.

By the beginning of the nineteenth century the wars with the Mohammedan dynasty of Mysore, and with the Mahratta Confederacy had necessitated a large increase in the number of British troops. In 1803 it had risen to 24,500. Further increases were required by the Afghan campaign of 1842, and by the Sikh war of 1848, and at the time of the Mutiny the number stood at 39,500. After the Mutiny the British strength was raised to 65,000, and all the Company's white regiments were amalgamated with the forces of the Crown.

If was, of course, more easy to recruit Native soldiers than British. But there were obvious dangers in the employment of Indian mercenaries in their home country, and it was not until the French set the example, at the end of the eighteenth century, that the Company's officers committed themselves to the assistance of Native auxiliaries. The country at that time swarmed with condottieri, who were willing to serve those who offered them regular pay and prospects of plunder. Bands of such men appear to have been engaged. These bands were subsequently formed into companies, commanded by countrymen of their own, under the supervision of a few of the Company's British officers. The genius of Clive organised these companies into battalions, drilled, disciplined, and clothed on the European model. But at the time of the battle of Plassey there was only one such battalion in Bengal. After Plassey a second battalion was formed for Bengal: the Native troops in Madras were formed into six battalions, and reforms followed in Bombay which grouped the Native auxiliaries first into companies, and then into battalions. Further reforms were undertaken in 1796, marked in particular by an increase of the British *personnel* in command. To each cavalry regiment were allotted fifteen British officers: to each infantry regiment twenty-four, and the British element in their control became approximately as strong as in the British Army. But at this time the strength of the Native Army was only 57,000. Under stress of continuous war it rose very rapidly. In 1803 it was 130,000, and by the time of the Mutiny (after the Sikh war) it was no less than 311,038, including 11,256 artillerymen. There were eight Native soldiers to one British.

The material of which these Native levies were composed differed very greatly in the three presidencies. In Madras and Bombay Mohammedans from Upper India and the peninsula, Arabs, and even Abyssinians were mingled with Hindus of the locality. The Bengal authorities found their best recruiting ground in Oudh,—then under Native rule,—and formed their regiments very largely of Brahmins and Rajputs—high-caste men who were united by the traditions of a common homeland. To Brahmins of certain classes military service is not forbidden: there are two Brahmin battalions at the present day. Our adversaries of one time became our allies at another, and each successful war extended our recruiting grounds. Some Gurkhas were drawn from Nepal, but in no such numbers as now render them so important a constituent of the Indian Army. In the Punjab Sikhs were enlisted, attracted by the power that had defeated their armies : but they were for the most part enrolled in a local force on the Afghan frontier. We drew comparatively few men from the Mahrattas : these hardy guerillas retired to village life when British arms repressed their energies. The dense population of the Bengal rice plain had no taste for soldiering, and hardly furnished to to the army a single recruit.

In the Mutiny it was the Bengal army that revolted. This was not the first experience of its kind. There had been three serious mutinies during the preceding half century,—with lesser outbreaks of insubordination, which were not always repressed with sufficient firmness. It hardly detracts from the loyalty of Indian troops to observe that the fidelity of alien mercenaries,—regular pay once assured,—depends very greatly upon the degree of self-esteem which they obtain from their service. This again depends upon the reputation for success which is enjoyed by the power that employs them ; and there can be little doubt that British credit suffered from accounts of the Crimean war which reached India during the two years which preceded the Mutiny. A similar doubt of British prowess resulted from the events of the South African war, and probably contributed to the unrest which disturbed India during the years 1906 to 1911. The annexation of Oudh in 1856 was also injurious to the pride of the troops which were drawn from this province : for one thing, soldiers at home on leave lost certain privileges which the Native court had conceded to them. And Oudh, as already mentioned, had been the favourite recruiting ground for the Bengal army. The Madras and Bombay armies had little in common with the mutineers :

they had been organised from distinct centres and were under Commanders-in-Chief of their own. The spirit of revolt hardly touched them ; and it left the Sikhs of the Punjab Frontier Force quite unaffected. In the darkest days of the Mutiny the Indian Government could view Southern India without great anxiety, and could rely upon the active loyalty of the Punjab.

The immediate result of the Mutiny was the withdrawal of almost all artillery from the Native army, and a great increase in the proportion of British to Native troops. This was fixed at 1 to 2, and in 1864 there were 65,000 British and 140,000 Indian soldiers. The organisation of Native regiments was changed. The Bengal army had vanished ; and in creating a new one, the model of British regulars was discarded, and the number of British officers in each infantry battalion was limited to seven. This reform was extended to the infantry of the Madras and Bombay armies. With the exception of some regiments in Madras, the whole of the cavalry was reorganised on the irregular system known as the "silladari," under which the troopers provide their own horses and receive inclusive pay for horse and man. Seven officers are, of course, quite inadequate for the control of a regiment : below them was a large staff of Native officers, but these men were sharply distinguished from the British officers in pay, status and title. They were all appointed by promotion from the ranks. In their staffs for direction and command Native regiments were, then, weaker than the British regiments which served alongside them. They were also armed with an inferior weapon. Another safeguard which at that time seemed of importance, in order to check the combination of soldiers against their officers, was that army organisation should run across the lines which group Indians into social compartments, the men of each regiment being recruited from different classes and castes, so as to be united only by the ties of discipline and loyalty.

In 1885 the violation of the Afghan frontier by Russian troops opened a new and formidable prospect to the Indian Army. During the century that had elapsed since the defeat of the French, it had been regarded as an instrument for Asiatic warfare; and its operations, if India be considered as a whole, had been comparable to those of an armed police force. Indeed, the Madras regiments had been permitted to make their homes in their barracks, and had settled down into a condition of domestic immobility. The horizon was now darkened by shadows from Europe. Indian troops might find themselves opposed to Russians, and their military efficiency became of first importance. The strength of the army was raised to 73,600 British and 153,092 Native troops. But this 153,092 was exclusive of a reserve that was instituted,—a small monthly pay being granted to men who, having served at least three years with the colours, would hold themselves ready for active service, and would come up for two months' training every other year. In the Punjab these conditions have proved attractive and the reserve can now supply 35,000 men. The material of the Indian regiments was improved by the elimination of men to whom the barrack yard was the most congenial field of service; and in particular the greater portion of the Madras army was recast by the substitution of up-countrymen for those locally enlisted. Gurkhas were recruited in larger numbers from Nepal, and men of fighting castes—the Sikh, the Jat and the Pathan—from the Punjab: these became the principal recruiting areas. The encouragement of *esprit de corps* has outweighed in importance the warnings of the Mutiny, and regiments have been formed of men of the same caste or tribe, who would act in sympathy, and would feel that danger was less appalling

GURKHA SOLDIER

than the contempt of their kinsmen. Out of the 153 infantry battalions of the Native army 49 are now "class" battalions: and most of the others are composed of "class" companies, each of which is homogeneous in the caste or religion of its men. The fidelity of the Native troops is no longer safeguarded by a sacrifice of efficiency: they are armed with the same rifle as that with which the British soldiers are equipped, and their staff of British officers has gradually been augmented until it now stands at 15. The status of the Native officers has been left unchanged: but a quarter of them are now appointed direct from military families instead of rising from the ranks. That the troops should not be withdrawn from field exercises by distant outpost duty, the immediate charge of the north-western and north-eastern frontiers has been committed to strong forces of military police, assisted on the Afghan border by a militia and irregular levies which are raised from the tribes of the border-land. Troops have been concentrated as far as possible in large garrisons where the different arms can receive training in combined tactics. Finally, these garrisons have been linked up into nine divisional commands, each capable of contributing a complete division for war service, without trenching upon the minimum reserve that is judged to be sufficient for the repression of internal disorder. These war divisions would together form a field force of some 140,000 men. The commands all face the Afghan frontier, curved, or echeloned, one behind the other, so as to be ready to dispatch their field forces as in a succession of waves. The nearer the frontier the closer they lie together: one-third of the army is concentrated within 100 miles of the north-western border line.

Such an organisation would have been impossible had the Madras and Bombay armies maintained their separate identity. In 1895 they were amalgamated with the Bengal army, and the whole military force of the Indian

Empire was brought under the authority of a single Commander-in-Chief.

The north-western frontier line has been strengthened by fortresses and strategic railways. The mobility of the troops has been increased by the organisation of transport corps in which the pack mule, the pony cart, or the camel is substituted for the bullock cart, that, slowly crawling at the tail of a column, has in the past been a drag upon its activity. The British cavalry are mounted for the most part on Australian horses: but a Remount Department is developing a local supply by selecting young stock and rearing it on horse runs. Horse-breeding, stimulated by the Government, has greatly improved the quality of the mounts with which the Native cavalry regiments supply themselves. By its ordnance factories the Indian Army supplies itself with stores and munitions of war.

The British troops have also gained immensely in efficiency. The maintenance of this large body of Europeans—mostly, of course, unmarried—in the climate and surroundings of southern Asia is beset with difficulties for which history affords no parallel. There has been a surprising improvement in the health of the force. Only ten years ago death and invaliding annually cost the army 5 per cent. of its numbers: the loss has been reduced to 1½ per cent. This improvement relieves the drafts from England of about 2,500 men a year. Nor is this all. Ten years ago the hospital wards never contained less than 6½ per cent. of the men: they now contain 4 per cent. only, and this difference represents an addition of 1,800 men to the army's active strength. The admissions to hospital for venereal disease have fallen from 28 per cent. to 7 per cent. In regimental recreation rooms, and on the football ground, the men are provided with interests which were formerly localised in the canteen, and nearly half of them have become total abstainers.

Bourne and Shepherd, Calcutta

BENGAL CAVALRYMEN

Volunteering is not so general as it should be amongst the European and Anglo-Indian communities. Judging from the Census statistics the Volunteer regiments—38,000 strong—hardly include two-thirds of the numbers that are capable of joining them. The indigo and tea-planting districts maintain three regiments of light horse which may be counted upon for dash and activity. The capitals of the various provincial Governments are the headquarters of regiments, mostly of foot, which are largely composed of men in the clerical service of Government, but bear on their rolls the names of officials in superior service throughout the province. In the commercial cities they include a considerable number of business men. But the most practical element in the Volunteer force is contributed by the railways: almost the whole of their large European and Anglo-Indian staff is enrolled, providing a force which in time of trouble would render invaluable service in keeping communications open.

The cost of the army has been enhanced of recent years by special expenditure entailed by schemes of reorganisation, but it has now settled down to about £19·5 millions a year, of which £12 millions are spent on the pay and food of the troops, £3·6 millions on army services (transport, ordnance, etc.) and £3 millions on the provision of pensions. The British troops are, of course, proportionately very much more costly than the Native troops. The pay of the Indian soldier has recently been increased, and now stands (in infantry regiments) at 14s. 8d. a month. He provides himself with food, but, should prices rise above the average, he is granted a supplement, calculated on the assumption that he should be able, at normal prices, to feed himself on 4s. 8d. a month. This may seem a very small sum: but as a matter of fact in some regiments it takes trouble to ensure that the men, in their anxiety to remit money to their families, spare this much to keep themselves in healthfulness. More attractive than the pay is the pension of 5s. 4d. a month which is earned by 18 years' service; and the hardships of foreign service are mitigated by the knowledge that a special allowance will be granted to the widow, son, daughter, father or mother of a soldier who is killed or dies when enduring them. A Native commissioned officer of senior rank draws £80 a year, and a pension of half this amount; and there are two classes of decorations to which extra allowances are attached.

The loyalty of the Indian troops is so vital a matter that its foundations, however anxiously considered, are seldom discussed. It gathers, of course, no strength from religious sentiment. The East is more sentimental than the West and is moved very deeply by such feelings as fidelity to the salt, and allegiance to the King. The expectation of a pension touches other strings, and touches them strongly. It must, however, always be realised that, with soldiers as with others, self-esteem is the greatest treasure of adult life, that they cling to a service of which they are proud, but that they are proud of a service only when it stands high in the estimation of their fellows. The prestige of Britain is for them her great attraction, and any blot on this prestige is reflected in their minds and disturbs their feelings. They are not offended by the thought that their British officers are, in rank, a class apart: British supremacy is obvious, and, when accepted by all, creates no jealousy. The admission of Indians to an equal status with the British might be pleasing to politicians: in the army it would create a distasteful surprise, and the supersessions that it would involve would certainly cause discontent to the Native officers in present employ. The general loyalty of the Indian troops is beyond question: but it would undoubtedly be affected by any changes in organisation or discipline which would lower their position in the eyes of their kinsfolk; and for this reason it is desirable that they should be assured that a final appeal lies to one who knows them. They had such an assurance under the dual supremacy of the Commander-in-Chief and a Military Member of the Viceroy's Council, since one of two authorities was always an officer of the Indian Army; and, from this point of view, it is to be regretted that the Military Membership of Council has been abolished. The Commander-in-Chief may be an officer without any special Indian experience.

The Police

When a Government and its subjects are convinced of the obligations of the same religion, an established priesthood is an efficient instrument of police; and in early Hindu times Brahmins not only advised the prince, but controlled the people. Each village maintained, however, a village watchman whose nightly vigilance permitted the inhabitants to sleep in peace. Such watchmen are still in office: there are no less than 700,000 of them, and it is through them that the police keep touch with village life, and are informed of the occurrence of offences, and of births and deaths. With the advent of the Mohammedans, force became needed for the ordering of a population who differed in faith from their rulers: part of the standing army was employed on police duties, and in large towns a police force was established which was accepted by the British as a starting-point for their reforms. The organised crime which racked the country during the early days of British rule could be suppressed more effectively by military than by police. But a network of police stations was gradually extended. The owners or lessees of large estates were by ancient custom held responsible for the repression of minor crime in their villages; and to this day in Bengal, where landlords are particularly influential, the action of the police is surreptitiously coloured by their wishes. But in theory the whole of British India is safeguarded by State police, about 187,000 strong, acting under the direction of a hierarchy of controlling officers. Part of this police force is charged with the repression of overt crime of a violent character, such as is of the nature of an insurrection against State authority. At the head-quarters of each district a small force is kept at hand for this purpose, armed and drilled in military fashion ; and in the larger districts this force may attain the dimensions of half a battalion or even more. Of recent years this armed police has been increased and developed so as to set free military garrisons for eventualities on the Afghan frontier. On the north-western and north-eastern frontiers police battalions are maintained which in character and efficiency approach a military standard, each battalion being generally commanded by two British military officers. But the main and characteristic duty of the police force lies with the preservation and detection of surreptitious, not of insurrectionary, crime,—with the business of detecting offenders and bringing them to justice. Certain classes of minor crime,—technically known as "non-cognisable,"—lie outside their direct interference : illustrations are intimidation, assault, and simple trespass : in these cases it is left to the aggrieved person to bring his complaint before the magistrate, and, if the police assist him by an enquiry, they only do so under the magistrate's order. Into "cognisable" cases the police enquire forthwith, upon the receipt of information : they arrest the offender, if detected, and forward him to the magistrate together with the recorded results of their investigation. All persons who suffer by the commission of a cognisable offence are bound to report it ; so also are village headmen, and village watchmen. These reports are made to the police station of the circle : they may in certain cases be made to the magistrate having jurisdiction, but will ordinarily be remitted to the police for preliminary investigation. Thefts, burglaries and attempts at these offences constitute fully three-quarters of the cognisable crime : loss which involves no personal humiliation is in the East suffered more patiently than the harassments that attend police enquiries and criminal trials, and hence a very large number of offences would not be reported were it not for the pressure of a legal obligation and for the supervision of the police through the village watchmen. There is some excuse for the apathy of the public, for in fully half the number of reported offences against property the police are unable to detect the offender; and, of the men whom they actually send up for trial, about half are acquitted by the magistrate. In truth, the Indian police are confronted by singular difficulties. They can expect little voluntary co-operation from the public, for in India the State is regarded as self-dependent,—as overshadowing the people, not as embracing them, and as wielding an authority, which, however beneficial, no private individuals can be expected to assist at any cost to themselves. And it is no small hardship to attend police enquiries, to proceed for several days to a distant tribunal, with the risk of being rough-handled in cross-examination by the defendants' pleader. Thus it comes that an investigating police officer, on arriving at the spot, finds in many cases that those who are acquainted with the facts deny all knowledge of them unless they realise that their pretended ignorance will subject them to as much annoyance as their attendance in court. The investigating officer is expected by the State to elicit the truth : this is indeed the object of his calling. He is accordingly tempted to extort it, by subjecting unwilling witnesses—or the accused person—to annoyances and hardships which sometimes approach torture, and in rare cases actually amount to it. In cases of sedition the police are still less likely to meet with willing witnesses; and recourse to spies and secret agents is as tempting, and has proved to be as dangerous, as it is in Russia. A peculiarity of public opinion lends another danger. In the East, as was the case in mediæval Europe, immense importance is attached to a confession, which according to popular ideas fixes guilt far more satisfactorily than any evidence. Moreover it relieves the police and the people from the trouble of discovering and furnishing witnesses. Naturally, then, the first question which presents itself to both parties is the possibility of endorsing their suspicions by securing a confession from the person they suspect. Confessions made to a police officer are not admissible in evidence: but they become admissible if repeated to a magistrate and formally recorded by him. Confessions are not often extracted by simple persuasion: nor, as has been seen, are the testimonies of witnesses; and accordingly the police in their enquiries have not infrequently resorted to expedients which are sometimes scandalous and occasionally cruel. Again and again, since the commencement of British rule, the improvement of police procedure has received detailed and sustained attention. Of recent years not only has the pay of all ranks been increased, but the making of enquiries has been limited to police officers of superior standing—speaking generally, to police officers who have enjoyed some English education, and may be presumed to have realised English standards of conduct. For it must be understood that, in the processes they employ, the police offer no shock to the morality of the country: when villagers, exasperated by an offence, deal with it themselves, they follow the mediæval method of beating a confession out of the man whom they suspect. It is probable that the Indian Government has gone too far in its interference with crime, and would have done better to have left it to the people to protect themselves against such offences as petty theft. Suspected offenders would have fared equally badly:

but the Government would have escaped responsibility for their treatment. Nor must it be believed that the police are unpopular: a proposal to close or transfer a police station-house is nearly always opposed by the people of its vicinity.

For the prevention of crime the Indian law is equipped with some special provisions. No one may possess arms without a licence, and, save in cases where firearms are required to protect crops from wild animals, licences for them are generally only granted to men of respectable position. Men who, having no ostensible means of honest livelihood, are suspected of living by crime may be called upon to furnish security, and, in default, may be committed to jail for a year,—and in some cases for two years. A similar provision has been applied to those who can be shown to have stimulated sedition. When a breach of the peace is apprehended the parties to the quarrel may be bound over to control themselves; and a magistrate has power to prohibit any act which is likely to goad ill-feeling into violence.

The Indian people are generally law-abiding. The number of cognisable offences under the Penal Code is less in proportion to population than in any European country; and in towns and in villages a European traveller will mark with surprise that little children wearing silver ornaments are trusted, unattended, to play about the streets. Such crime as occurs is very largely professional: a high proportion of the prisoners in jail are repeating an experience, and indeed there are certain well-known gipsy tribes to whom theft is the only means of livelihood. In the complicated subdivision of social activities crime has in fact become a caste occupation. In the early days of British rule the villagers were harried by *dacoits* (armed burglars); and travellers who fraternised with strangers were not uncommonly poisoned, or strangled, and robbed by members of a secret semi-religious association known as *thugs*, whose operations extended far and wide throughout the country. The dacoits might be professional brigands. These have been rooted out,—as also have been the *thugs*,—by a special department of police which had authority to carry its operations into the Native States, and so to deprive these criminals of their final refuge. Dacoities still occur : but they are generally committed by bands of enterprising men, organised for the occasion, who not infrequently are found to belong to respectable families. Violent crime of this description commonly breaks out in times of stress or hardship : it is a not infrequent accompaniment of famine ; and of recent years, in Bengal, it has accompanied manifestations of anti-British feeling. The pacification of Upper Burma was delayed for some time by dacoities in which discontented spirits showed their dislike of annexation by robbing and mutilating their own fellow-countrymen. In Bengal dacoities have been serving a more practical purpose : they have been used as a means of procuring funds for a seditious campaign.

The police administration of Indian has generally been regarded as the department upon which British rule has had least reason to pride itself. It may be doubted whether those who have criticised it most severely have realised the character of the environment which the police have been expected to resist. But during the past ten years strenuous efforts have been made to procure greater efficiency, and the expenditure on the department has been increased by no less than 68 per cent. Indian police officers must have been gratified by the course of a recent debate in the Viceroy's Legislative Council, which arose out of a motion for a special enquiry into police administration. It was noticeable that even the elected members of Council who pressed for such an investigation, frankly admitted that the *morale* of the force had immensely improved.

CHAPTER XVII

TECHNICAL DEPARTMENTS OF GOVERNMENT

To an alien Government the maintenance of the law must always appear of paramount importance, and the Indian Civil Service, to whose hands this function has specially been committed, has accordingly figured very conspicuously on the Indian stage. But, having assured the public peace, British authority in India has interested itself directly in the welfare of the people, and has developed activities which some years ago might have been ridiculed as paternal but are now quite in accord with the socialistic fashion of the day. These activities are generally exercised through separate technical services, the European staffs of which, taken together, vastly outnumber the Indian Civil Service.

PUBLIC WORKS

So far, Britain's deepest marks upon India have been made by her engineers. It is not only that their railway, canal, and road enbankments could stand when all else had slipped away,—that, should British rule be withdrawn, and the exotic ideas and institutions that it has introduced vanish in a welter of obliterating strife, these would remain, the only memorials of such a passing tutelage as Britain herself once experienced at Roman hands,—but that, through these public works, the life of the common people has been changed as by nothing else that Britain has accomplished, the produce of their land augmented, their wages raised and the comfort of the poorest families increased by some simple novelties. Touched by railway communication, the very appearance of the fields is changing. Villages need no longer be self-supporting, growing in varied patches the different crops they require. Cotton is sown in large stretches for Europe and Japan, and sugar-cane is disappearing before the tempting cheapness of sugar from Java and Mauritius. These are material changes. To railways are also owed moral changes which are of still greater moment, since they may lead the way to social reform. Such relaxations as have become permitted in the rules of caste have proceeded in great measure from the novel exigencies and experiences of railway travel.

There are now 32,398 miles of railway in India,—a larger network than in any country of Europe except Germany and Russia. In proportion to population the mileage falls very short of European standards—even that of Russia. But it is as large as that of Japan. The railways carry annually over 330 millions of passengers and 80 million tons of goods. They represent a capital outlay of £292 millions. Their rates are exceedingly low: for a penny a passenger may travel, third-class, five miles, and a ton of goods will be carried 2½ miles. Yet the railways not only pay their way, but ordinarily yield a surplus profit which in four of the last ten years has touched two millions sterling. Three-fourths of the railway system is the property of the State. But State ownership was not the policy on which railway construction was initiated. In accordance with the ideas of those days it was left to private enterprise to pioneer the ground; and, when it was ascertained that private companies could not borrow money at moderate interest, for outlay in India, the State engaged to add so much to the railway traffic receipts as was required to give a return of 5 per cent. to the shareholders, subject to the conditions that should the receipts yield more than 5 per cent. it should be entitled to a moiety of the excess, and should further have a claim to purchase the railway on the expiry of 30 years. On these terms the three principal trunk lines were constructed. As the paying prospects of Indian railways became more and more evident these concessions appeared unnecessarily liberal: the rate of guaranteed interest for new companies was reduced to 4 per cent., and subsequently attempts were made to attract private capital by offering concessions which fell short of a firm guarantee. At the same time the Government decided to enter upon railway construction itself; and a railway department was formed which took a very active part in extending the network. Most of the lines made by guaranteed companies have now been purchased. But the State has not attempted the task of managing this large system, and has leased the greater portion of it, for purposes of management and upkeep, to private companies which are generally assisted by a guarantee of interest on their working capital and divide surplus profits with the Government in settled proportions.

The original trunk lines were built not on the English 4 ft. 8 in. gauge, but on a special Indian gauge of 5 ft. 6 in., and this has been adopted for the greater portion of the lines that have since been constructed by private enterprise. But when, some 40 years ago, the Indian Government determined itself to take a hand in equipping the country with railroads, it decided in favour of the metre gauge (3 ft. 3⅜ in.) for its own lines, and its choice in this matter was accepted by some of the companies to whom, later on, concessions for railway construction were granted. The earnings of Indian railways have always suffered from the sharp seasonal fluctuations to which their business has been subject. At certain seasons of the year traffic offers itself in greater quantity than it can be carried, while at other seasons it hardly suffices to keep the line in working employ. This fluctuation, primarily due, of course, to the fact that the consignments mainly consist of agricultural produce, was formerly aggravated by the absence of feeder lines and by deficiencies in road communication which left only the dry months of the year available for the transport of produce across country. In these circumstances it seemed desirable, by reducing the cost of construction, to minimise the loss that was sustained during the slack months : a considerable saving in capital outlay is effected by the adoption of the smaller gauge. The Indian main lines of railway form, then, two distinct networks—one on the 5 ft. 6 in., and the other on the 3 ft. 3⅜ in. gauge—there being 16,758 miles of the former and 13,633 miles of the latter. Transfers of goods from one system to another involve break of bulk, and, could the increasing amount and regularity of the traffic have been foreseen, it is improbable that the saving of capital outlay would have seemed so great an object. But in truth until recent years it has been necessary to economise very carefully in railway construction, since experience had shown that the Indian Government, while unable to attract Indian investors, could only borrow at low interest in the London market if it carefully moderated its demands. Fifteen years ago the capital expenditure upon railways rarely exceeded £2 millions a year. At that time the railways, taken together, did not pay their way, and it fell upon the general revenues to supply a deficit on their account. By 1896–97 it had, however, become evident that the Indian railways were financially promising, and a more venturesome policy was adopted in borrowing on their behalf. Assisted by grants from surplus revenue, the annual capital expenditure has since risen in some years to as much as £9 millions. But some two-thirds of this has been absorbed in the improvement and equipment of existing lines ; and the construction of new lines, although very greatly accelerated, is still too slow to satisfy the interests of British manufacturers, merchants and engineers.

In the past some critics have nourished suspicions that railways exploit the country for the benefit of capitalists, but are of little permanent advantage to it; and the Indian Government has at times been urged to spend less upon railways and more upon irrigation works. Canals increase the produce of the land and enrich the people. So also do railways. Their construction has led to wide extensions of cultivation: by raising prices they have largely increased the profits of cultivation: they save the poor from starvation in times of famine, and they have increased the wages of labour by widening the market within which labourers can sell their services. It would be possible, of course, to overload the country with railway communications. But so long as the railway system, as a whole, yields a substantial surplus to the State, it does not appear that extension has reached its profitable limits.

There are some railways which are administered by provincial governments; but, generally, they are upon an imperial footing, and their affairs are supervised by a Railway Board acting directly under the Government of India.

By the engineers of all countries the Indian canals are accepted as models for the diversion of large masses of water to irrigate the fields of a thirsty country. Some account of their marvellous achievements has been given in Chapter IV. In their case also an idea was formerly entertained that their construction might suitably be entrusted to private enterprise: but it very soon became apparent that this was really a task with which the State should charge itself, since the distribution of water and the collection of water rate involved very close and authoritative relations with the people. Practically all the existing canals have been made by officers of the Public Works Department, working, however, not under the Government of India, but under the provincial governments. The canal system, as it stands at present, includes 58,000 miles of canals and main distributaries, and irrigates the enormous extent of 17 million acres, which will be increased by about a fourth if we reckon twice over the area which bears two irrigated crops within the year. The cost of these canals has amounted to over £35 millions, and the rates paid by landholders and cultivators for the use of the water yield to the State interest at about 7 per cent. on this outlay. The profits naturally increase with the shortness or uncertainty of the rainfall: the canals in Bengal hardly pay 2 per cent., those in the Punjab return 9 per cent., and there are in the latter province particular canal systems which actually return over 25 per cent. on their capital cost. But quite apart from the interest that they return to the State, irrigation works increase very greatly the produce of the country,—indeed, it is estimated that each year the value of the crops raised by canal irrigation is equal to four-fifths of the total capital expenditure that has been incurred upon the canals. They also protect against famine the areas they command. It would then be shortsighted to reject irrigation schemes simply on the ground that they are not a profitable commercial investment. The projects so far carried into execution have generally been profitable to the State as well as to the country. But very large sums have been spent upon canals that are merely protective; and the extensive irrigation programme which has been elaborated for the future,—aiming at the extension of irrigation to 10 million acres at a capital cost of about £37 millions,—provides very liberally for the needs of areas in the peninsula in which irrigation, although very beneficial to the people, may not be commercially profitable to the State.

The Public Works Department has provided the country with a network of main roads, 37,000 miles of which are metalled. It has constructed most of the government buildings throughout the country, and if it is often charged with indifference to architectural pretensions,—and indeed

Hoffmann, Calcutta

THE GREAT HINDU TEMPLE AT MADURA (MADRAS)

its buildings not infrequently add to the dreariness of their surroundings,—it can plead in some excuse the rasping economy of straitened finance. Until comparatively recent years it was charged with no definite responsibility for the care of the architectural monuments of the past,—of temples which in all Asia are the most notable and enduring expressions of Oriental polytheism and theosophy, and of memorials of Mohammedan piety and devotion which are famous for their beauty throughout the world. Such repairs as were effected were carried out spasmodically, and with insufficient attention to artistic requirements; and edifices which were no longer in religious use were frequently turned to unworthy purposes in order to save expenditure upon new public buildings. In pursuance of a policy which will always be associated with the name of Lord Curzon the conservation of these monuments has been definitely undertaken as a function of State, having been committed to the Public Works Department under the advice of a staff of archæological experts.

The superior officials of the Public Works Department were originally recruited from the commissioned ranks of the British army: but the need of appointing civil engineers soon became apparent and for many years they were trained at a special college in England. This has now been closed and the superior staff is now for the most part maintained by the appointment of qualified engineers by the Secretary of State. But admission can also be won by men, whether Indians, Anglo-Indians or domiciled Europeans, who have specially distinguished themselves at the college of engineering which has for many years been maintained by the Public Works authorities at Rurki,—a privilege which will no doubt be extended to other Indian colleges when they arrive at the high standard upon which this college justly prides itself.

Postal and Telegraph Department

Judged by a European standard, and compared with the total population of the country, the operations of the Postal and Telegraph Department may not appear very considerable. But when we realise that only 6 per cent. of the population—or less than 19 million persons—can read and write, the use that is made of letters and telegrams is surprisingly large. The letters and post cards annually despatched exceed 920 millions in number, and the inland telegrams exceed 10 millions. Both have nearly doubled within the last ten years, and there has been a noticeable increase in the number of newspapers despatched by post—from 32 to 51 millions. During this period the number of post offices and letter boxes has increased by nearly 70 per cent. But they still leave multitudes at a distance. There are more than half a million towns and villages, but less than 65,000 places where letters can be posted.

In many parts of the country you will hardly find in a village two or three persons who can write. But the use made of the post office depends more upon the character than upon the literacy of the people, since the services of professional letter-writers are available almost everywhere. Taking the country as a whole there are about three letters annually posted per head of population. In the Bombay presidency, where 7 per cent. of the population is literate, the number rises to 9. In Madras, with a similar degree of literacy, only 4 letters are issued per head. On the other hand, in the Punjab 5 letters are posted per head, although only 4 per cent. of the population can read and write. In the use of the post office the provinces of Bombay and the Punjab are in advance of the rest of India, and this is not the only sign that they are leading in the development of new social activities.

THE TÂJ MAHAL WITH ITS FLANKING MOSQUES: VIEWED FROM THE JUMNA

The use made of the Post Office Savings Bank has been rapidly increasing and there are now a million and a quarter Indian depositors. Their deposits maintain in the Bank a balance of £8·5 millions. A third of this balance is annually renewed by withdrawals and deposits, and it appears, then, that the Bank is largely used for purposes of temporary safe custody. But its popularity is a satisfactory proof of growing confidence in the stability of the Government.

Medical and Sanitary Departments

In nothing do Indian habits need change more urgently than in matters that affect the preservation of health. Apart from famine, plague, and cholera, the death rate is exceedingly high: allowing for some understatement by the registration offices, it may be put, one year with another, at 32 per thousand. Annually between eight and nine million deaths occur, and even a small reduction in the death rate represents a great saving of human wastage. During the last ten years plague has exacted over six million victims. Cholera in some years carries off 200,000, in others nearly a million persons. But far more destructive than these diseases is fever, which in no year causes less than four million deaths, and at its worst has caused 5½ millions. In a large proportion of these cases fever merely sets a term to old age: but, when full allowance is made for this, it remains by far the most destructive force for human vitality. Over many parts of the country the inhabitants are saturated with malaria, and its prevalence accounts no doubt for much of the apathy and listlessness which deaden the spirit and the industry of the people.

The majority of Indians see no connection between precautions and health, and do not think that precautions are worth the trouble. Sanitary regulations are viewed with hostile suspicion and are angrily resented if they cross the path of domestic custom: they will, indeed, excite riots where the injustice of officials would be suffered quietly. In regard to drinking water there are fanciful prejudices, but no such suspicions of pollution as one finds amongst the Japanese: in cholera time people will not boil it except under official pressure. The poorest classes all sleep on the ground, and would not purchase a bedstead at the cost of a little extra labour. Mosquito curtains are not generally used, even by the well-to-do, as they are in parts of China. Until recently vaccination was opposed as disrespectful to the providence of the goddess Káli. The remedies generally used by villagers are of the nature of magic; and those prescribed by either of the two schools of Indian physicians are purely empirical, and are unguided by any knowledge of nursing or sanitation. It is a very striking fact that amongst the Christian population—nine-tenths of which is of Indian race—the death rate is less than two-thirds of that to which Hindus and Mohammedans are subject. However humble be their circumstances, Indian Christians endeavour to live like the Christians of Europe.

By secular means to change the habits of a conservative and unlettered population may seem almost beyond the powers of a government. But there is something to show that ideas are being awakened at last to the danger of a polluted water supply, and to the advantages of vaccination. And, with or without the support of public opinion, much has been accomplished in medical and sanitary measures that can be directly taken by the State. Most of the large towns have been provided with a good water supply, and are gradually being cleansed by drainage works. Over 8 million children are annually vaccinated, and one rarely sees them disfigured by small-pox. The State maintains or assists 2,652 hospitals and dispensaries, at which 28 million persons are annually treated, nearly half a million of them as in-patients.

Particularly appreciated is the surgical work of these institutions: it has completely won the confidence of the people. A Pasteur Institute at Kasauli, in the Himalayas, has during the last ten years earned the gratitude of 3,296 Europeans and 8,099 Indians who have been in danger of hydrophobia. Other similar Institutes are to be established, and indeed in India, where the abundance of jackals preserves hydrophobia from extirpation, wide facilities are needed for the cure of this disease. As a prophylactic against fever quinine is offered for sale at all post offices at less than its cost price. But, although the spread of malaria by mosquitos was discovered by an officer of the Indian Medical Service, India is one of the most backward of countries in putting this discovery to practical purposes. To limit the reproduction of an insect that can breed in any roadside puddle, throughout a country which is water-logged during four months of the year, may seem so gigantic a task as to be hopeless. Here and there attempts have been made: but it may be regretted that they have not been pushed more determinedly. Fever denies India a chance of being industrious, and its extirpation would be amongst the greatest benefits that could be hoped for by the country.

The charge of hospitals and dispensaries and of urgent measures to combat plague and cholera, the control of vaccination, and the general direction of sanitary improvements are the business of the Indian Medical Department. This was originally the medical branch of the Indian Army: its officers are still liable to transfer from civil to military duties or *vice versâ*, and those in civil employ still bear military titles. From military duty medical officers were at first detailed for the charge of important civil hospitals, or the medical care of Government officials at district headquarter stations, and gradually these practical duties have been expanded by the addition of administrative functions until at present the civil surgeon of a district is generally more occupied by the control of hospitals, dispensaries and vaccination for the benefit of the Indian public than by his purely medical duties. The general control of the medical and sanitary administration of a province is vested in senior officers of the department. But it is unfortunate that, in order to distribute the promotion that falls due in a graded service, these officers are very frequently transferred, whereas their efficiency depends very greatly upon their local knowledge and influence ; and it seems probable that the interests of the people would be better served by the institution of a separate civil medical department. Admission to the superior (or commissioned) ranks of the Indian Medical Service is won through competitive examination in England, in which 40 Indians have, so far, been successful. For the subordinate ranks Indian medical schools and colleges provide an ample supply of candidates.

Veterinary Departments

There is a Veterinary Service for the prevention and cure of disease amongst horses and cattle, and for the improvement of cattle and horse-breeding. The latter is of much importance in the Punjab for the supply of remounts to Indian Cavalry regiments, and its immediate supervision is in the hands of military officers, through whom landholders are encouraged by various concessions to keep brood mares of approved quality. The Veterinary Department maintains throughout the country numerous veterinary dispensaries ; but its most notable success has been won in the control of rinderpest by inoculation,—one of the most marked achievements for the benefit of the farming classes that has been accomplished of recent years. Rinderpest is endemic in India, and, since the cattle have become partially immune to it, the losses that it causes are by no means so formidable as they have been, for instance, in South Africa. But they are still sufficient to throw back the cultivation of a district, and to ruin large numbers of cultivators, and inoculation has proved so indisputably successful that it has overcome all the objections that at first were urged against it. The number of cattle that are annually inoculated has risen to a quarter of a million.

Agricultural Departments

The simplest and directest means of lessening the poverty of the Indian people is undoubtedly to improve their methods of farming. The cultivators have much to learn and to reform. Certain of them, generally low-caste men, work their fields with the industry and skill of the best market-gardeners. But, on the whole, the land produces much less than should be expected of it, subdivided as it is into very small holdings. Under a similar pressure in Japan the plough has given way to the spade : the fields are hand-tilled : wheat and barley, when irrigated, are carefully dibbled on the ridge and furrow system which permits the water to reach the roots without caking the earth that overlies them : the utmost use is made of sewage. The Indian cultivator turns the smallness of his holding to no such practical advantage, and farms three or four acres in the methods that he would follow with a holding of tenfold this area. His implements are of the lightest : but he works them with cattle power. Good cultivators recognise the advantage of selecting their seed, and reserve for this purpose the finest heads of maize, and the first pickings of cotton. But the generality sow the seed that first comes to hand, often obtaining it on loan from their landlord, or the village money-lender, or, in the case of cotton, from the ginning factory, where good and bad pass together through the mill. Manure is not preserved, and sewage will not be handled. That some Indian cultivators will move outside the ring of their traditions, if tempted by a clear advantage, is proved by the widespread adoption of such exotics as tobacco and potatoes, and by the popularity that has been gained by iron roller sugar mills. But there are only a few castes that will adopt improvements that cost labour; and the most disheartening fact to those who look for progress is the failure of the many to learn from the skill and industry that are daily displayed by a few of their neighbours.

For a generation and more the State has held the improvement of agriculture to be one of its functions, and, through provincial agricultural departments, has maintained experimental farms and published their results. But it is only within the last ten years that these departments have been equipped with an effective staff of European technical advisers, have been provided with funds that are in any way adequate, and have been able to look to agricultural colleges for the training of the subordinate staff they require. So far no extensive practical results have been obtained,—indeed, alongside of the government farms, you may see cultivators pursuing their ancient methods, changed in no respect by the example. But it must be admitted that the results of experiments have not always been trustworthy : research must precede efforts at conversion, and Indian conditions offer much that is strange to the agricultural science and practice of the West. Iron ploughs of European patterns have in some localities been purchased in hundreds : so also have simple water-lifts : in the Madras presidency there are some 300 irrigating pumps worked by oil engines. The wooden roller and pestle mills used from time immemorial for the crushing of sugar-cane are being driven out of use by a light iron mill. But these improvements only touch the surface of what is possible, and widespread reform cannot be expected until an idea gains currency that to raise better crops is meritorious, and may even be considered fashionable. Such an opinion appears to be arising in Western India—the Bombay presidency and the Central Provinces—and perhaps also in the Punjab. The experiments of the Agricultural Departments are watched with interest : visits by their European experts are welcomed : pure seed is in rapidly increasing demand, and seed farms and nurseries are being established by private enterprise. At the Poona Agricultural College in the Bombay presidency there are students who have come to learn farming for use on land of their own. But elsewhere, it must be confessed, young men are only attracted to study agriculture by the hope of obtaining service under the Government.

A movement that is closely connected with the Agricultural Departments, and has spread with quite unexpected rapidity, is the organisation of co-operative loan societies on the lines of those which have benefited so greatly the peasant farmers of Germany, Italy, and France. Such societies, first initiated and legalised eight years ago, now number 3,500, with a membership of 225,000, and a capital of £800,000. These figures may appear trifling when compared with the multitudes of those who need financing and the amount of their requirements. But the movement is spreading rapidly. During a single year (1909–10) the number of societies increased by 74 per cent., and the number of their members by 24 per cent. There are societies of artisans and of clerks ; but the vast majority are associations of cultivators, organised on the basis of unlimited liability, and with no claim to distribute profits. They are then careful to admit no person to membership—with its privilege of borrowing from the funds of the society—who cannot be depended upon for honesty ; and, since each society deals with a limited area, its members are well acquainted with one another and with those who apply for admission.

Of the capital of these societies only 6 per cent. has been borrowed from the Government : more than half consists of loans which the societies have been enabled to contract —at moderate rates of interest—by the security that is provided by their organisation. In some cases the societies borrow direct ; in others they are financed through a central association which, constituted by some men of position, can borrow from commercial banks for distribution to the village societies,—which serve, in fact, as a means of communication between the banks and the cultivators. There are now 31 of these central associations: their number doubled during the year 1909-10. In Bombay the Government has assisted a central bank to borrow cheaply for this purpose by guaranteeing interest upon its debentures. The rate of interest at which the societies lend to their members ranges between 9 and 12½ per cent. : in one province it is as high as 18 per cent. These demands may seem excessive : but they are very moderate when compared with the rates charged by money-lenders, which generally range from 24 to 37½ per cent., and not infrequently exceed 100 per cent. Curiously enough, the money-lenders have not generally manifested the hostility which was expected. In some localities, it is true, they are refusing assistance to men who have joined a co-operative society : but in others they actually assist the societies by depositing money with them. We may probably assume that the high rates which they ordinarily charge hardly compensate them for the bad debts which, when dealing with organised credit, are not expected to occur. For, so far, loans have been repaid with great punctuality. But a reduction in the rate of interest by no means exhausts the value of these societies. Their members are actively concerning themselves with such social improvements as the reduction of wasteful expenditure on marriage ceremonies, and also with improvements in farming, the introduction of better seed and more efficient implements. Much diversity has wisely been permitted in the lines on which the societies may develop activity, and their members are displaying an enthusiasm which, a few years ago, would have seemed incredible. It must, however, be realised that the movement has, so far, been under close official supervision : the societies are watched and their accounts scrutinised by registrars who are all government officials, specially selected for their sympathy with the people and organising powers. Indeed it is to the registrars and to the district officers that the movement owes its initiation ; it is the outcome of official intervention, and, although a spirit of self-help is undoubtedly arising, it would at present be rash to believe that, if left to itself, this new form of co-operation would grow or even maintain its vitality.

The Forest Department

The bare hill-sides of Turkey, or of China, testify to the callousness of man in destroying forests which in no way impede the extension of his cultivation. Hardly less barren are the hills of Western India : the villages lie sufficiently near them to have exploited their produce, and a scanty and uncertain rainfall gives vegetation no strength to reassert itself even if herds of browsing goats would leave it an opportunity. The Himalayas—at least the central and eastern portions of the chain—are separated from the inhabited plains by a belt of jungle of such extreme unhealthiness that they have remained comparatively unscathed. But, indeed, elsewhere, hill-side forests have not escaped destruction because they have been remote from settled villages : they have in many cases suffered very greatly from hill-tribes, who cut down the trees and burn them in order to plant crops in the ashes, passing every two or three years to a fresh patch. Where the rainfall is plentiful the jungle springs up again, but generally with a changed character, a thick growth of bamboos taking the place of forest trees. The Indian Government has fortunately enjoyed a wide scope for introducing a system of forest conservation. When it recognised, or granted, proprietary rights in village lands, it reserved to itself extensive stretches of forest, and it is at present the sole proprietor of an enormous estate covering 241,774 square miles. More than two-thirds of this lies in the distant provinces of Assam and Burma ; but, if we exclude these provinces from consideration, the Government's forest estate covers a tenth of the total area of the country. It is most extensive in the peninsula : in the provinces of the Indo-Gangetic plain —apart from the distant Himalayas—very little forest has been spared by advancing cultivation.

Of this vast State property 94,561 square miles have been brought under regular forest management, and are systematically conserved and worked by the Forest Department. Boundary lines have been cut, destructive grazing has been prohibited, tree felling is only permitted upon licence and under supervision, and efforts have successfully been made to prevent the occurrence of the forest fires, which, during the hot season, sweep up the Indian hill-sides, destroying all young growth, and charring the trunks of such trees as can keep their heads above the flames. Fire protection has unfortunately produced an evil of its own in a growth of rank grass which effectively prevents seeds from germinating ; and it may be a question whether, when brought under strict control, firing is not advantageous so long as it is effected before the undergrowth is so dry as to kindle into hot flame. But, generally, conservation has improved the forest growth very strikingly, and the thicker covering of vegetation, by checking the surface drainage, will at once render floods less destructive, and give longer vitality to hill-side springs.

Forest conservation has cost something in popular discontent. Villagers who live near the forests, and have been accustomed to exploit them at pleasure, are naturally disturbed by restrictive regulations, which, moreover, have not always been framed with due consideration for their urgent necessities. But with the passing of time they are accustoming themselves to economise in forest produce, and are less disposed to see oppressiveness in measures which are taken by the Forest Department to preserve the resources that contribute to their livelihood.

Commercially the forests are of profit to the State, yielding a net revenue of about three-quarters of a million sterling. In Burma a large income is derived from teak timber, and here and there in India proper, forests occur which can supply heavy logs to the timber market. But the greatest utility of the forests is in the production of small poles, bamboos, and fuel, and in the grazing which is permitted on hill-sides that are not under strict conservation. This, during the hot weather months, preserves large herds of cattle which would starve on the herbless pasturages of their villages. Generally, of course, the utility of the forests to the people depends greatly upon their proximity ; and a very large proportion of their produce is taken by the villages that lie close to their borders. But these villages, which in the peninsula are very numerous indeed, are as a rule of poor soil and depend upon forest produce to eke out the profits of their cultivation. Did the forests fail them their fields would hardly yield a livelihood, and in preserving the forests from wasteful exploitation the Forest Department is preserving the existence of a large area of cultivation.

The superior staff of the Forest Department is appointed in England by the Secretary of State, and the selected officers have hitherto undergone a special training at the University of Oxford. For the training of an Indian subordinate staff the Department maintains a Forest school of its own.

Other Departments

We have by no means completed the list of technical departments. A strong Finance Department is maintained for the compilation of the accounts of income and expenditure, and also for the more practical purpose of watching expenditure, and detecting any that is incurred without due authority. The Opium, Salt, and Customs Departments are concerned with the administration of these sources of revenue. The Survey Department has triangulated and mapped the whole of India, and is responsible for the periodic revision of the maps: but its activities have not been limited to the theodolite and plane-tables, and to its officers science owes many elaborate investigations and valuable discoveries in matters connected with the physical conditions of the earth. The Departments of Meteorology and of Geology are for purely scientific enquiry: they also have established for themselves a wide reputation for the advancement of knowledge, and of recent years the Geological Department has rendered material service in the development of the mineral resources of the country. The functions of these departments, however important, do not directly affect the life of the people. This cannot be said of the Departments of Education and of Police. But their achievements have been separately described in Chapters X and XVI.

CHAPTER XVIII

TAXATION (INCLUDING LAND REVENUE), FINANCE, AND CURRENCY

EXTREMES may meet: the Brahmins of old time, in maintaining that the land of a community should be the principal source of its public revenue, are supported by the ideas of modern socialism. This feature of Hindu policy commended itself to the Mohammedan conquerors of India; it was also adopted by the British Government, and at the present day the Land Revenue constitutes 37 per cent. of the true[1] income of the State. It is a contribution levied from the *surplus* profits of agriculture, —upon the profits which are not won by the efforts of the land-holder, but are presented to him by the increase in demand and the rise in value that accompany the growth of the community. It has been argued that, since no land is specifically freed from payment on the score that it lies on the margin of cultivation, the Indian land revenue must affect prices, and is, therefore, a tax on the people as a whole. This conclusion is fallacious. The land revenue is carefully graduated according to land values, and the poorest land in cultivation may nominally be assessed, but certainly does not pay more than a few pence per acre. It may safely be stated that this,—the largest of the streams which flow into the Indian exchequer,—is drawn from sources that are filled, but not shared in, by the community as a whole. The need of imposing taxation of a general character is further reduced by the profits which the Indian Government makes upon its quasi-commercial undertakings,

[1] Taking into account, that is to say, not the *gross* income of such commercial undertakings of the State as the management of its railways and forests, but the *net* income which they yield after deducting the expenditure incurred upon them.

the principal of which are the construction and management of railways and canals, the export trade in opium, and the management of State forests. We may also exclude from the category of taxation the income that is derived from court fee stamps, and from the registration of documents: it represents in both cases payments received for particular services rendered. The tributes or contributions that are rendered by some Native States also go to lighten the taxation of British India. Taxation, pure and simple, is represented by the salt monopoly, customs and excise, an income tax, the rates levied for local purposes by provincial governments, and a stamp duty on documents. The revenue of the Indian Government from these sources during the year 1910–11 was :—

Apart from Taxation.	£	From Taxation.	£
Land Revenue	20,877,521	Salt	3,175,950
Profits :		Excise..	7,030,314
On Forests	796,296	Customs	6,619,009
On Railways	2,017,496	Income Tax	1,593,301
On Canals	1,322,000	Provincial Rates ..	554,378
On Opium	6,271,531	Document Stamps ..	1,499,132
For services ;			
Judicial Stamps ..	3,312,557		
Registration Fees ..	425,855		
Tributes & Contributions	607,447		
		Total from taxation..	20,472,084
Total apart from taxation	35,630,703	Grand Total ..	56,102,787

To arrive at the actual pressure of taxation, we should add municipal rates and taxes. These yielded £3·1 millions, and the total amount realised by taxation amounted then to £23·5 millions, falling at the rate of 1s. 11d. per head of population.

Land Revenue

According to early Sanskrit treatises, the Hindu rája was entitled to receive a proportion of the gross produce of the land, which appears generally to have been a sixth, but might in some cases amount to as much as a fourth. This may seem a heavy exaction; but Indian landlords of the present day not uncommonly take from their tenants one-half of the produce of such crops as are produced without expenditure upon irrigation or manure. The actual amount of the rája's share depended no doubt upon the necessities of the State: the revenue was generally levied in kind, and large stores of grain could only be utilised when multitudes were employed in military enterprises or on public works. And in those days the State commonly exacted the services which it required by the systematic levy of forced labour. The more varied—and more costly—activities of Mohammedan rulers needed cash for their indulgence: payments in kind were converted into payments in money, and, under the pressure of ever-increasing expenditure, their amounts were enhanced until they left but the barest pittance to the cultivators. The demands of the State were no longer limited by the idea that they should conform to a certain proportion of the produce; and the agricultural classes lost touch with a safeguard which might serve to restrain the caprice of their rulers. Under a popular government, the amount of the taxes may be regulated by the annual necessities of the State; but the wishes of a despot commonly outrun the exigencies of his administration, and it is well for the people if custom can interpose to protect them in possession of a definite share of their earnings. When heavy exactions spared no profit, land retained no exchangeable value: relinquished fields were left deserted, and the attention of some Mohammedan governments was greatly occupied with the wholesale abandonment of land and with expedients to retain the cultivators at their labours. The Mohammedans introduced another innovation of far-reaching effect. The collection of land revenue in detail was beyond the powers of an alien tyranny. It was, then, farmed for a term of years to publicans or contractors, whose engagements bore the name of "settlements." The British Government took over this system; and at the present day the land revenue is still periodically "settled" for a definite term of years, during which the State is pledged not to enhance it. This arrangement has the effect of blocking legislation for the raising of revenue: however great be the needs of the State, the unearned increment of the land is secured against contributing to them until the time comes round for revising the settlements. The inconvenience of this result is illustrated very forcibly in tracts, such as Bengal, which at the end of the eighteenth century were settled, somewhat hastily, on a permanent basis. They are secure for all time against additional levies; and it is estimated that at the present day their permanent settlement deprives the Indian exchequer—and the Indian people—of £4 millions a year. The period for which settlements are made is generally thirty years; in some less advanced provinces a shorter period—of twenty years—has been adopted. The revision of a settlement is a laborious and complicated process. Under the supervision of a specially selected "Settlement Officer," the fields are mapped, classed according to their productiveness, and catalogued with full particulars of their occupancy. The amount of enhancement which the Government may impose is calculated, in some provinces, by working from aggregate to detail, and in others by the contrary process. The Settlement Officer who employs the former method estimates this amount for a tract of country, taken as a whole, by reviewing such considerations as improvements in communication, increase in population, rises in the prices of produce or in the selling value of land; and he distributes the enhancement over the estates in detail, in proportion to their area and their estimated relative productiveness. Where his calculations are from detail to aggregate, he directs his attention to ascertain the net produce, or profit, of each class of land: in this difficult proceeding he is generally assisted by the rental that is received by those who have leased their holdings; he finally settles the amount of his enhancement by taking such a share of the net produce, or profit, as is authorised by the standing orders of the Government. The procedure of settlement is further differentiated from province to province by the size and character of the tenures that are taken as the limits of assessment,—on which, that is to say, separate sums are assessed for payment to the State. Where the Government found no persons occupying the position of middlemen between itself and the cultivators, it took the field as the unit: the cultivators (*ryots*) pay direct to the State, and this system is accordingly known as "ryotwari." It prevails throughout the greater part of the Bombay and Madras presidencies, in Burma and in Assam. Where, on the other hand, between the Government and the cultivators there intervened middlemen through whom the Government dues were collected, the limit of assessment was the area for which the middlemen collected, whether consisting of a portion of a village, or a whole village, or a group of villages. These middlemen might be, in origin, mere farmers of the revenue who had obtained contracts under the Mohammedans, or ancient landed families that held manorial rights on a semi-feudal tenure, or colonising brotherhoods who in troublous times had seized villages and expelled the original cultivators. A general term for land-holders of position superior to that of cultivator is "zamindar," and settlements on this system are known as "zamindari." They prevail in Bengal, the United Provinces, the Punjab, and the Central Provinces. These two forms of settlement are sharply distinguished in official literature. But, in substance, they tend to approach one another. Under a *zamindari* settlement the units of assessment—the revenue-paying estates—are generally very much larger than under a *ryotwari* settlement. But by the subdivision of inheritances, their size is constantly diminishing. On the other hand, the free transfer of land which is generally permitted leads to the amalgamation by purchase of ryotwari holdings. Again, as a general rule, zamindari revenue-payers are rent-receivers, not cultivators, while ryotwari revenue-payers are cultivators, not rent-receivers. But zamindars commonly farm a part of their estates, and sometimes the whole of them ; and ryotwari holdings are sub-let on an increasingly extensive scale. From the fiscal point of view, an important point of difference is that zamindari holdings include much unassessed waste land that lies in and about their cultivated areas, whereas ryotwari holdings include little or none. Waste land that is included in zamindari villages pays thus no revenue to the State (although it may pay rent to the zamindar when taken up for reclamation) until the time comes round for revision of settlement. In a ryotwari village, a cultivator who takes up waste land pays upon it forthwith.

In revising the *ryotwari* settlements of the Bombay presidency and of Assam, the Settlement Officer works from aggregate to detail on the lines sketched above. In similar proceedings in the Madras presidency and in Burma, the contrary process is followed. The Settlement Officer ascertains the value of the "net produce" of each class of land, and takes, nominally, half of this value as the land revenue. If by "net produce" were understood the balance that remained after providing for the cost of cultivation and the subsistence of the cultivator and his family, it would be approximately equivalent to one-sixth of the *gross* produce—the share which appears to have been generally demanded by the

Hindu rája. But, as a matter of fact, the appraisement of the gross produce is lowered very freely indeed to ensure that it is no more than an average; and the cost of cultivation is raised very generously to provide against exceptional expenses and for a rise in the ryot's standard of living, so that the share of the *gross* produce that is taken approximates more nearly to an eighth than to a sixth. Indeed, in Burma the share falls to an even lower proportion: the resources of the country have increased very rapidly, and the Government has abated something of its full dues in order to avoid imposing very large enhancements.

In the *zamindari* province of Bengal the land revenue is, as already stated, settled in perpetuity. In the United Provinces, the Central Provinces, and the Punjab, the Settlement Officer works from detail to aggregate—the detail which he investigates being the "net profit" or "rental value" of each zamindari holding. This ascertained, he takes a share of it as the land revenue. The amount of this share, which, under the Moghals, was at least 85 per cent., has been lowered at succeeding settlements, until it now stands at about a half. Compared with the *gross* produce, the land revenue payable under a zamindari settlement rarely exceeds one-tenth of the out-turn of the land. Over large tracts of country it is very much less than this.

Care is taken not to include in the assessable produce of the land any increase which has resulted from the expenditure of money on improvements, until the improver has had ample time to recover his outlay. Indeed, under the ryotwari settlements of Bombay and Madras improvements are exempted for all time from assessment,—the land being, for purposes of settlement, classed as if unimproved.

Leaving intact, as it does, the additional profits that accrue to the revenue-payers during the period—generally thirty years—that elapses between a revision of settlement and the revision that succeeds it, the State has the stronger claim to take its share in full when the time for revision comes round. But it does not insist upon its claim. Very large enhancements are mitigated, either by reducing the share, or by foregoing for several years the full levy of the enhanced demand; and in fixing the share payable by individual zamindars, their circumstances are carefully considered, an abatement being granted when they would be hard pressed by a full assessment. Nor are the revenue-payers forced to comply with their contracts when their crops are destroyed by seasonal calamities. In such cases, collection of the revenue is held over for a period, or revenue may be remitted altogether. After the famines of 1896–97 and 1900–01, arrears amounting to nearly a million and a half sterling were written off.

The effect of these concessions has naturally been to enhance very greatly the selling value of landed property. At the commencement of British rule, land was hardly saleable. It now passes from hand to hand at prices from which it may be inferred that, in the aggregate, it is worth at least £300 millions. Rights of transfer have been granted to practically all revenue-payers, whether ryotwari or zamindari, including the large body of men who, under Mohammedan rule, were employed, on contract terms, for the collection of the revenue. This departure offered, no doubt, some substantial political advantages. But it had the effect of degrading the actual cultivators of the soil from a position of independence to the status of tenants. The grant of proprietary rights has not generally had the anticipated effect of stimulating expenditure upon the improvement of the land: proprietary profits are, as a rule, expended unproductively. But the landlords have, nevertheless, striven to enhance the rents of the tenants,

—in which they have been assisted by the growing pressure of population,—and during the last thirty years the land policy of the Government has been characterised by legislation for the relief of tenants. In Upper India a large proportion of the tenants are now protected against enhancement during the currency of the revenue settlement; and in the Central Provinces the Government has undertaken, with great success, to fix the rents of all tenants concurrently with the settlement of its land revenue.

During the last twenty years the land revenue settlements have mostly come under revision, and the amount of the land revenue has risen by 30 per cent., or—if Burma be excluded—by 25 per cent. Within this period there has been an increase of 14 per cent. in the cultivated area, so that the actual increase in the *rate of assessment* has not exceeded 14 per cent.

Forests

The Crown lands, which are classed as Government forests, cover 241,774 square miles and the profit,—of about three-quarters of a million sterling,—which they annually yield to the State, may appear to be a very small return from so large an extent of country. Taken in the gross, the income derived from them is more considerable; but 60 per cent. of it is spent by the Forest Department in conservation and management. Beyond doubt, the forests would yield a larger income were they managed on commercial principles as a source of revenue. The operations of the Forest Department must not, however, be judged narrowly from this point of view: they are, indeed, concerned rather with the protection of forest growth than with its exploitation; and careful conservation is needed in order to remedy the wasteful misuse which in accessible localities has well-nigh stripped the hill-sides.

It has, moreover, been recognised that villages which lie near forests have grown up in dependence upon them, and must be permitted to use them, within proper limits, on much more lenient terms than could be justified by purely commercial considerations.

Railways and Canals

Mercantile opinion not uncommonly denies that a State which owns railways is entitled to make such profits upon them as might reasonably be enjoyed by a private railway company; should the railways yield more than suffices to defray their working expenses and provide the interest that is payable on the capital outlay, the surplus, it is urged, should be devoted to a reduction of rates or to improvements in transport. Accordingly, the profits which the Indian Government makes on its railways are, from time to time, severely criticised by the commercial members of the Legislative Council, or by deputations which wait upon the Secretary of State. But, as a matter of fact, the Indian railway rates are exceedingly low; and a country of low taxable capacity may not unreasonably lighten the taxes by accepting from traders and the travelling public what they would render without question to a private company. Within the last seven years the Indian railways have increased their usefulness to the country by providing a substantial contribution to the public exchequer. During the five years 1903–4 to 1907–8 they yielded, on the average, over a million and a half sterling a year; in 1908–09, owing to deficient harvests, there was a *net* loss of over a million sterling on their working, but their receipts rapidly recovered themselves, and in 1910-11 provided a surplus of over £2 millions. In the succeeding year it rose to £3 millions. Irrigation works have been less profitable to the State, although of immense productive value to the people.

But of recent years they have been subscribing materially to the general resources of the exchequer. In 1910–11 they yielded a surplus of £1·3 million. But this is reduced to £584,389 if Minor Irrigation Works are brought into the account. These include a multitude of tanks and small canals, the management of which is, from the purely financial point of view, much less remunerative than that of the great canals which are classed as Major Works.

Opium

Opium is grown in British India both for consumption in the country and for export. The dues which are levied upon the portion that is consumed in India are classed in the financial accounts under Excise, and we are concerned here only with the portion which is exported. In either case, its production is a State monopoly, no one being permitted to sow the poppy except under a licence which binds the cultivator to render up the whole of his produce at a fixed price. It is prepared for consumption in a government factory, about seven-eighths of it being consigned to Calcutta for export. There is poppy cultivation in some of the Native States of Central India, and a portion of the produce is exported from Bombay. But this Central Indian—or, as it is called, " Malwa "—opium does not constitute more than 30 per cent. of the total export. It is taxed, on its way to Bombay, by the British Government at £40 per chest, equivalent to 5s. 8d. per lb. The profits that the State derives from British Indian produce depend upon the price that is paid by the exporting merchants who purchase the drug from the Government. This formerly amounted to about £100 per chest (or 14s. 3d. per lb.) ; but since the supply of opium has been limited under an agreement with the Chinese Government, the price has advanced to double this amount, and even more. The profits which the

Government has derived from the taxation of "Malwa" opium and from its own business in opium have, until recently, ranged between £3 millions and £4·5 millions a year. During the last two years, owing to speculative demands which have forced prices up enormously, the profits have considerably exceeded the highest of these figures; but they are not estimated to exceed £3 millions during the current year.

Opium is exported to Persia, the Straits Settlements, and Java; but five-sixths of the total is consigned to China. The business with China is now under sentence of death: in deference to expostulations from the Chinese and from British philanthropists, the Indian Government has agreed gradually to reduce the stock annually offered for sale, so that five years hence none will be placed in the market. Already the area under poppy cultivation has been reduced from 565,000 acres to 200,000 acres; and the Indian exchequer must prepare to meet a loss which, calculated on the receipts of normal years, will reduce its revenue by over £3 millions.

The importation of Indian opium appears always to have been distasteful to Chinese officials. It is true that in the course of negotiations which took place in 1861, and again in 1886, official anxiety was apparently confined to the rate at which it should be taxed on entry; but this may be explained by the fact that, owing to its superior quality, Indian opium was so eagerly desired by the masses of the people that, once landed at the treaty ports, it found its way inland, in spite of every obstacle that the officials could interpose. In these circumstances, by refusing to recognise the trade, the Chinese authorities were merely losing customs revenue. The reasons for their opposition are open to speculation. The effect of opium smoking is a controversial question. Persons that are intimately acquainted with Chinese life, and in sympathy with the Chinese people, assert that it is ruinous to health and character ; others of not less experience deny that, in moderation, it is more harmful than the drinking of spirits. But, however this may be, it is difficult to believe that the Mandarins' opposition to the import trade was moved by philanthropy, when we remember that the quantities offered for importation have always been inconsiderable if contrasted with the amount which the Chinese have themselves been producing. It has, indeed, been computed that the imports from India have not exceeded one-fifth of the production of the single province of Szechuan. From the Chinese point of view, the opium trade would doubtless appear exceedingly injurious in draining large quantities of silver from the country ; and it is further tainted by its association with a disastrous war and national humiliation. Moreover, the idea has taken hold that the habit of opium-smoking is responsible for China's decadence and her inability to withstand foreign aggression. Accordingly, when it was ascertained that, by ceasing herself to produce opium, China could induce the British Government to stop the opium trade, the Mandarins, by an effort which appears almost incomprehensible in a moribund government, succeeded in entirely suppressing the cultivation of the poppy, and so confirming agreements that the supplies of Indian opium for export to China should annually be reduced so as to be altogether extinguished in the year 1917 ; and that, in the meantime, its import into any of the Chinese seaports (except Canton and Shanghai) should be stopped, if it is proved that, in the area served by the port, the people have ceased to produce opium or to import it from other parts of China. With the establishment of the revolutionary government, poppy cultivation has revived, apparently on a very large scale. But Indian opium is boycotted ; and the importers, who have stocks on their hands to the value of many millions sterling, find themselves in a very difficult position. Should the new

Chinese authorities be unable to drive out the poppy, the Indian Government will be free from its engagement. But the trade can clearly no longer be relied upon as an assured source of income. And, indeed, according to modern notions, it is hardly respectable for a government to make money by the manufacture and sale of an intoxicant.

Salt

Salt is, of course, a necessity of life, and there are those who would object to its taxation. But the cheapening of transport by railway communication has, throughout the greater part of the country, lowered its price more than the salt duty has ever raised it,—and this, too, when the duty stood at its maximum rate. During the past decade the tax has been reduced by 60 per cent., and now falls at one-fifth of a penny per lb., constituting about one-half of the retail sale price. In England the price of tea is raised by the customs duty in quite as large a proportion. The large reduction in the rate of taxation has not increased the consumption of salt so materially as was expected. Deducting such increase in consumption as may be accounted for by the increase in population, the rise in demand has not exceeded 12 per cent.; and it seems evident that the higher rate of duty had no great effect in restricting the purchase of salt by the poorer classes. The reduction of duty has involved a loss to the exchequer of nearly £3 millions a year. But the taxation of salt provides a fiscal reserve which may be of great value in emergencies, and it is desirable that in ordinary times it should be kept as low as possible.

Excise

About a sixth of the Excise revenue is derived from the taxation of opium that is consumed in India. Its production and refinement—effected in a Government factory—costs about 5s. 8d. per lb. The rates at which excise is levied vary in different provinces, but are exceedingly heavy: the maximum (levied in Assam) is 19s. per lb. An additional revenue is secured from those who are licensed to sell opium: they pay large sums for this privilege. As already remarked, opium is eaten—not smoked—in India, and is commonly taken by the respectable classes. Indeed, in Assam,—where the consumption per head is at its maximum,—there is some reason to believe that it serves a medicinal purpose, since its popularity varies in different localities according to their unhealthiness.

But the bulk of the Excise revenue is contributed by those who drink fermented and spirituous liquors. Their consumption is forbidden by the religious scruples of both Hindus and Mohammedans; but India abounds with materials for alcoholic fermentation, and the common people have always turned them to account. The Tibeto-Burman tribes of the north-eastern frontier ferment rice water, and devote to the brewing of drink a large proportion of their rice crop; the hill men of Central India make a similar use of a small millet: where palms occur their juice is tapped, in one species from the trunk, in another from the flower-spathe, and is fermented into a drink, the name of which—"toddy"—has entered into the English vocabulary. In all of these drinks, the alcohol is too weak to be distilled. But over a great part of the country the *mahua* tree abounds, bearing flowers that are charged with sugar, and yield, on fermentation, a spirit that can be distilled, and has been distilled from time immemorial. Where the *mahua* tree is scarce, a coarse rum is distilled from fermented sugar-cane molasses. Mohammedan rulers obtained a revenue from distilled spirit by farming out the monopoly of manufacture and sale, and the British

Government for many years continued this practice. But the contractors could not be trusted to state the amount of spirit they sold, and it was their interest actively to encourage habits of drinking. Radical changes have accordingly been introduced, the manufacture of spirit being concentrated in large distilleries, whence it can only be issued on payment of a still-head duty, and then only to persons who have paid competitive prices for the right of selling it retail. The number of licensed vendors is limited according to the circumstances of the locality. The Government has striven to obtain the maximum of revenue from the minimum of consumption, and its Excise duties have enhanced the price of spirits out of all relation to the cost of their production. But its efforts cannot check the growth of the revenue, which has nearly doubled itself during the last ten years. Judged by English standards, however, the amount spent on liquor is not considerable. It does not appear that the Indian "drink bill" reaches £10 millions a year, or a sixteenth of the amount that is spent in England on the purchase of liquor.

Customs

Over the Customs tariff, British interests clash with those of India, and future events may not improbably accentuate the disagreement. To Oriental ideas, taxes upon trade appear the least objectionable means of raising revenue: when such taxes stimulate local manufacture, interests are benefited which can make light of the advantages of low prices to the poor. Britain, on the other hand, desires that her manufactures should sell as widely as possible: they should be cheap, and customs duties raise their prices. Especially do these considerations apply to cotton goods and metals—her principal exports to India. The history of the Indian customs tariff has been swayed irregularly by these contrary influences. After the Mutiny, a general customs rate was raised from 5 to 10 per cent. Within the succeeding twenty years it was gradually reduced to 5 per cent., and in 1882 it was abandoned altogether. Twelve years later it was re-imposed; but, after much negotiation, it was settled that cotton yarns should be admitted free, and that the duty on cotton cloth should be limited to 3½ per cent., an excise tax of like amount being levied upon the products of the Indian mills. Indian mill-owners resent this tax keenly, and are not mollified by appeals to the principles of free trade. Very wide exceptions are also made in the case of metal goods: machinery worked by power and the more important kinds of railway material are admitted free; semi-manufactured materials pay at 1 per cent. only; similarly privileged are the metal vessels known in trade as "rice-bowls." There are special rates for the taxation of imported arms, liquors, petroleum, tobacco, and silver. Salt is, of course, taxed at the rate levied by the Excise on the Indian product. Countervailing duties are levied upon bounty-fed sugar imported from Argentina and Denmark. The only export duty that is charged is imposed upon rice—exported in the main from Rangoon: it falls at less than 4d. per cwt.

Income Tax

From the payment of income tax agricultural incomes are exempted; and the tax serves the purpose of enabling the Government to levy contributions from the professional classes, from those engaged in industry and commerce, and from its own employés. In 1903–04 the minimum income liable to taxation was raised from £33 to £66. Since that year the collections have risen by no less than 29 per cent.; but the ascertainment of incomes is exceedingly difficult, and it is probable that Government officials—from whom 18 per cent. of the total is realised—provide considerably more than their legitimate proportion. It is through the income tax that the European residents in India contribute most largely towards the upkeep of the State.

Basis of Taxation

The customs tariff, the stamp duties, and the income tax are fixed by law: they are charges which were initiated under British rule. The precise share of agricultural profits which is taken as land revenue, the rates at which excise is levied on country-made spirits and opium, and the salt[1] tax are determined by executive orders, the Government following in this respect the practice of the Native governments, from which it inherited these sources of revenue.

Finance

It will have been gathered from the foregoing abstract that, notwithstanding the reductions that have been made in the salt and the income taxes, the revenue has been growing with satisfactory rapidity; indeed, setting aside the receipts from the opium traffic, the *net* receipts of the Government are larger by a fifth than they were ten years ago. Expenditure has been mounting with equal steps. There has been a considerable increase in the military charges; but, proportionately, they have risen less than those of many civil departments. Police expenditure has increased by 70 per cent.; educational expenditure by 160 per cent.; the cost of judicial and revenue establishments by 30 per cent. Yet this liberality of expenditure has, of recent years, generally left the Government with handsome annual surpluses.

[1] The *maximum* duty that may be levied upon salt is fixed by law: but this is three times the amount of the duty that is now levied.

In five[1] out of the last ten years the surplus has exceeded £2 millions, and has enabled the Government of India not only to make special grants to provincial governments, but materially to reduce the unproductive debt by spending upon railways and canals sums which, provided out of revenue, are debited in the capital accounts by a transfer from the unproductive to the productive side. In one year (1908–09) there was a deficit of over £3 millions. The harvests were poor, and the exports shrank so greatly as to leave a balance of trade against the country—a condition which in India is quite abnormal. This illustrates the danger to which Indian finance is exposed by uncertainty of the rainfall. During the last decade the harvests have been generally good, and there have been surpluses to encourage the relinquishment of the opium revenue. But a run of such ill-fortune may be approaching as afflicted the country —it must be remembered—in the course of two of the three preceding decades.

The finances of the whole of British India are exhibited as administered by the Government of India. But for collecting most of the revenue, and for spending a large proportion of it, the provincial governments are immediately responsible. They make over to the Government of India the whole of their collections under certain heads, as, for instance, the proceeds of the customs duties; under other heads the collections are divided between the Government of India and the provincial governments in a settled proportion. The expenditure that is incurred directly by the Government of India is about three-fifths of the total. Its principal items are the military charges; the cost of the political and the survey departments; and the remittances that are

[1] In 1911-12 the surplus amounted to £6,000,000. But this proceeded very largely indeed from the abnormal prices which opium commanded.

made to the Secretary of State to cover the expenditure which is incurred in England on military accounts, in the purchase of stores, in the payment of pensions, and in the upkeep of the India Office in London. Expenditure upon railways, and upon the postal and telegraph department, is also imperial; but in these cases outgoings are covered by receipts which are credited directly to the Government of India. The provincial governments provide out of their share of the revenue for the whole of the ordinary functions of the State,—the collection of the taxes, the maintenance of judicial and executive establishments, the construction and care of public works, and the operations of the police, the educational, the medical, and the forest departments. But, in discharging these responsibilities, they do not enjoy a free hand: they are controlled by the Government of India in matters of principle, and to some extent in details also, especially in regard to the creation of new appointments and expenditure upon salaries. They have a right to retain any surpluses which accrue to them. But they can assert no financial independence, since they are not empowered to raise money either by imposing taxes of a general character, or by borrowing.

The Indian National Debt amounts to £267 millions; but of this, £221·5 millions represent State investments in railways and canals, which not only fully pay the interest that is due upon them, but yield a generous profit. The ordinary unproductive debt is thus only £45·5 millions. If we set against the interest that is due upon this amount the surplus profits which accrue from railways and canals,—that is to say, if we calculate the amount of the unproductive debt from the payments of interest that must be provided by taxation,—we may conclude that the actual indebtedness of the Government of India hardly exceeds £30 millions. After the Mutiny it stood at £98 millions. This large reduction has resulted in great measure from the transfer to the productive debt—that is to say, to the railway and canal account—of the large sums which have been spent upon these undertakings out of revenue. India does not contribute to the cost of the British fleet; and it is, in the main, to this fleet that she owes a financial position which is, perhaps, stronger than that of any other country in the world.

Currency

The Indian rupee is a token coin. The actual market value of the silver it contains is less than 10d., but its circulating value is one-fifteenth of a sovereign—that is to say, it is equivalent to 1s. 4d. in English money. It maintains this artificial value by its scarcity: the mintage of rupees is carefully regulated by the Government in a quantity sufficient to preserve the ratio of fifteen to the sovereign. The sovereign is legal tender in discharge of a debt of fifteen rupees; and, since the Government will give rupees in exchange for sovereigns at this ratio, there can be no material rise in the exchange value of the rupee. A fall in its exchange value is generally obviated, so far as India is concerned, by the readiness of the Government *ordinarily* to give sovereigns in exchange for rupees. But a peculiar risk besets the value of the rupee, in that the Government, out of its rupee resources, has to meet heavy charges in London (amounting to some £18 millions annually), which must be defrayed in gold. Pressed to purchase gold, it might find gold raised in value against it. Fortunately, however, merchants in London are generally compelled to purchase rupees in order to satisfy their Indian obligations, since India generally exports (in value) far more than she imports. Moreover, English capital that is invested in India, and sterling loans that are contracted by the State, also seek conversion from gold into rupees. The Government can then, as a rule, count upon finding a demand for rupees in London sufficient to balance its demand for gold, and is able to procure the gold that it requires by the sale (in London) of bills for rupees drawn upon its Indian treasuries. But a safeguard is needed in order to provide against such a sudden drop in the export trade as actually occurred in 1908–09; and this is provided by a gold standard reserve, that is to say, by money invested in gold securities that are easily realisable. This reserve now stands at £18 millions.[1] It has been provided out of the large profits that are made on the coinage of rupees.

Sovereigns have not as yet found their way into general circulation, although they are annually imported to the value of about £8 millions. The unit of value which they represent is too high for the ordinary transactions of a poor country. The stock of rupees in circulation is estimated to be equivalent to £100 millions. In addition, there is a rupee-note circulation of about £33 millions, supported by a reserve consisting partly of the gold and silver received at Government treasuries in exchange for notes, and partly of an amount (now £8 millions) that is invested at interest.

[1] At the present time, £3 millions of this reserve are represented by gold coin held in England, and £2·5 millions by silver coin held in India.

PART IV
FUTURE PROSPECTS

CHAPTER XIX

SOCIAL AND ECONOMIC PROGRESS

To many it will appear that the future of India can be discerned as accurately by gazing into a crystal as by the most anxious consideration of her present and her past. Yet there are few who are not interested in theorising about human society,—in attempting to trace its various phases to influences which can be perceived to be acting upon it. And up to a certain point our theories will guide us: moist heat generally enervates those who live in it: a commercial race is generally progressive: a flesh-eating people is generally more energetic than one which subsists upon vegetable diet. But the development of nations abounds in eccentricities which discredit our generalisations, and can only be referred to peculiarities of race, or of locality, which are so subtle as to elude our observation. We are driven from the definite to the vague, as when we conclude that a foxhound hunts by scent and a greyhound by sight, not because they have been taught, but because it is their nature to do so. But, although we may not then forecast the future of a nation as though it were to be entirely the resultant of known causes, we may set in array such causes as we perceive and endeavour to estimate their effective value.

The hopes that may be entertained of Indian progress may conveniently be discussed under two separate headings, according as they concern the social and economic condition of the people or the political status of their leaders. Advances on these two lines may, it is true, interact and assist one another ; but they present two very different sets of problems.

In reflecting upon this subject, we can hardly avoid the difficult question whether there is any essential permanent difference of character between Eastern and Western peoples. Reason is inclined to be sceptical of such a distinction, reminding us that mediæval Europe abounded in conditions which we now regard as characteristically Oriental. On the other hand, when brought into touch with Eastern peoples, we appear intuitively to discern that they are actuated by motives and ideals which are radically different from our own ; and we may find that this conclusion is admitted by Indians of intelligence and candour. The view with which Asia regards life may be comprehensively, if somewhat indefinitely, contrasted with that of Europe by stating that Asiatics accept their environment as inevitable, and are content to act on the defensive towards it ; whereas Europeans are at constant strife with their surroundings in attempts to modify them. By modifying them they provide a continuous stimulus for changes in their own aspirations, whereas the ideas of Orientals, amidst unvarying impressions, crystallize into invariability. The optimistic energy of the West may be seen in a wish for neatness, cleanliness, and prettiness ; in a desire to surround oneself with manufactured possessions ; and, generally, in endeavours to extract from Nature all the comforts and conveniences she is capable of yielding. These, it may be objected, are artificial characteristics : some of them, at all events, are shared by such races as the Chinese ; they represent ideals which were not conceived by mediæval Europe. It is by no means clear, however, that their origin cannot be traced very far back in Western history. Speculation may, indeed, suggest that woman has owed her freedom in Europe to man's restless distrust of the natural relations which physical strength has imposed upon the sexes. Less disputable illustrations may be found in the attitudes of the East and the West towards religion and politics. Religion in the East has mainly concerned itself with faith or ceremonial; in the West it has been materialised by a more practical regard for social and moral government, for religious edifices, and for philanthropic endeavours,—in fact, for external purposes, as opposed to the inner life of the individual. Politics in the East have hardly ventured to question an authority which is endorsed by religion or supported by force: Western history has been disturbed by denials of this authority,—indeed, of any authority,—by attempts to modify the forces of government that are amongst the most influential elements of our environment. These contrasts postulate no difference in intellectual ability. But, taking refuge within itself, the Oriental mind has directed its attention to its individual personality; whereas Europeans, actively contending with their surroundings, find a thousand interests in the material world. This contrast must, however, on both sides, be limited by exceptions: Japan must be regarded as a country apart; and Southern Europe must not be credited with the initiative energy which has characterised the North, and especially the nations of Teutonic descent. Southern Europe may have assimilated Northern ideas, but it has acquired them by imitation. So, also, may Asia assimilate them if she can bring herself to the view that she may copy the West without treason to herself.

Climate

The acceptance of one's environment is, however, quite compatible with industry in making the most of it. The people of India cannot claim to be very industrious. It is easy to assert that, since the Indian climate is responsible for the prevailing listlessness, no radical improvement can possibly be expected. But the world abounds in facts to show that a hot climate is not destructive of industry. The Cantonese, in the latitude of Calcutta, are the most hard-working, as well as the most intelligent, people in China. The energy of the Japanese is not damped by a summer of oppressive heat; nor do Indian cultivators tend their fields less assiduously in the continuous heat of Madras than when refreshed each year by the cold weather of the Punjab. But it seems conclusive against the connection of heat with idleness that there are certain castes in India which cultivate their land with a skill and thoroughness which not even the Japanese could surpass.

Malaria

But whatever be the effect of the Indian climate, there can be no doubt of the enervating, exhausting influence of the malaria by which the country is pervaded. It is not only that it causes great mortality: this might, perhaps, be suffered by a dense population without much industrial injury. From the economic point of view its most harmful effect is the demoralisation of the people by ill-health,—a general loss of stamina, showing itself in a listlessness of demeanour which an observant visitor will notice everywhere. The villages on a mountain side, rising from the plains, illustrate very strikingly the debilitating effect of the disease. You will remark, on ascending, a gradual improvement in the physique of the inhabitants until, on passing—about 5,000 ft.—above the fever zone, you are amidst a sturdy, cheery people, with some traces of the ruddiness of a European complexion,—infinitely more industrious and courageous than the people of the malarious foot-hills, although they may be of the same tribe and speak the same language. Malaria occurs in China ; but it makes no such mark as in India, where, on occasions, almost everyone is invalided, the crops remain uncut, and the government offices are deserted. Investigations made in some districts of Northern India have shown that malaria is in the blood of four-fifths of the children. Some of the circumstances which are accompanied by epidemics have, so far, not been squared with the conclusion that man only receives malaria by infection from another man through the bite of an *anopheles* mosquito : fever, for instance, will almost certainly prevail during the rains that follow a year of short rainfall, and will decimate settlers who are attempting to reclaim land from forest. But it has been demonstrated that malaria can be controlled, if not eradicated, by checking the breeding of the mosquito ; and in this campaign sanitary science has gained very signal triumphs, although on no such scale as is presented by the malaria-stricken population of India. The Indian Government has made some isolated experiments, but has not set itself as yet to combat the mosquito pest on the lines that have elsewhere proved successful ; and its expenditure in this direction has, so far, been trifling. Some hesitation may easily be understood in undertaking to extirpate an insect throughout so vast a country. But there are few benefits which the British Government could confer upon the Indian people which could compare with their emancipation from the scourge of this disease, and expenditure towards such an object could hardly be wasteful. It is true, of course, that the people must co-operate with the Government. The more intelligent have learned to fear the mosquito ; but the masses will need energetic persuasion to believe that a connection between an insect and fever is not merely fanciful.

Child Marriage

Indians of intelligence have begun to suspect that

child-marriage, and the encouragement of sexual precocity, are responsible for moral and physical harm. A girl is given in marriage during early childhood; her father is, indeed, disgraced should she be unmarried when Nature—with what strange inconsistency!—pronounces her sexually mature, although physically she is quite unready for the functions of motherhood. She may be given to a boy or to a middle-aged man, but by the age of twelve she has become in fact, as in title, a married woman. Sometimes, it is feared, at an earlier age,—for many years have not passed since legislation, which made it criminal for a husband to cohabit with his wife before she was twelve years old, excited passionate resentment even amongst the educated classes of Bengal. With both boys and girls, sexual precocity is allowed to compete with physical and mental growth; it would be considered harsh—at least, in Bengal—to punish a schoolboy for visiting a prostitute's quarters. There are castes that defer marrying their children until physical maturity actually approaches: they are generally industrious cultivators, in little esteem; and, should they rise in the world, they adopt child marriage in order to gain the respect of fashion. But there are also castes of high social repute who have always repudiated this sacrifice of the immature. Such are the Brahmins of Western India, who do not marry their daughters until they are fifteen or sixteen. To raise the marriage age to this limit is the object of an active propaganda now on foot in the Punjab. Once married, a Hindu girl cannot attend school, and female education has no chance of reality unless marriage is postponed till schooling is finished. Patriotic Indians have also realised the wholesome effect of celibacy during student life; and in Bombay and in the Punjab there are educational institutions, on Oriental lines, from which the influence of women is as rigidly excluded as it is from an English boarding-school.

Marriage within the Caste

A suspicion is also gaining ground that the limitation of marriage within the caste,—within, indeed, even a narrower limit, the sub-caste,—may be causing the degeneracy which results from in-and-in breeding; and amongst the educated classes a movement is growing in favour of widening the area of marriage choice. Within recent years the spiritual leader of the Brahmins of Western India has pronounced in favour of marriages between the sub-castes of this community; and one or two leaders of advanced opinion have actually married out of caste,—an experiment which, a few years ago, would have been almost unthinkable. But such men are at present remote from public sympathy: their daring excites more wonder than admiration. Yet it is a notable fact that lately in the Viceroy's Legislative Council several of the elected Indian members should have advocated a change in the law which would legalise inter-caste marriages,—or even marriages between Mohammedans and Hindus,—and that one of their number should have pushed home his arguments with reflections upon the marriage customs of the Hindus that one would have expected to excite the bitterest feeling. They were repudiated by members of the orthodox school, but without show of passion. Words do not always disclose the heart of the speaker; and the masses would no doubt suspect any move which could be misrepresented as an attack upon religion. But to one who listened to the debate it seemed clear that the Government would receive strong support from the ranks of the intelligent if it permitted mixed marriages to be contracted without the formal abjuration of creed which the law now exacts from a Mohammedan or a Hindu. That the prejudices of caste should be publicly attacked seems to indicate that they are losing vitality. They have been attacked, it is true, many times during the past five centuries by reformers whose disciples have gradually fallen away to the old faith. But at that time social reform was not urged by the spur of political or patriotic motives.

Custom

The prejudice of custom which opposes itself to any change of habit is not, of course, peculiar to the people of India. It grows up in communities whose intercourse is limited within a narrow circle, and whose minds have not been excited by the stimuli of novel experiences. In villages of Europe that are remote from communication you will find as rigid a conservatism as that which fetters the inhabitants of India. The vast land-locked populations of India and China have become compacted in an unchanging environment: for centuries the only changes they have known are in the nationality of their oppressors, and in the methods of oppression, and, against these, custom has been the only protector to whom they could appeal. In the islands of Japan, where travelling has been invited by an inland sea, there has been no such crystallization of habit, and the people were curious from the first to learn ideas from Europe, however carefully their rulers might endeavour to seclude them from foreign influences. In speaking of the "progress of society," we are apt to be misled by our own phraseology. Society does not progress with the simultaneous regularity of a regiment on parade. It owes its advance to the appearance of men of special talent or energy, and to the disposition of a certain number to accept them as leaders,—in fact, to the birth of inventors and to a more or less general inclination to make use of inventions. Why men of genius should be born at some time and not at others is beyond our understanding; but they may be likened to "sports" that appear amongst flowers, and the occurrence of these is known to be stimulated by a changing[1] environment. In India, railways have been the strongest solvent of ancient prejudices, and the relaxations that are permitted in food *taboos* have resulted, in the first instance, from railway travel. At present, neither they nor changes in costume have gone very far; and the general abandonment of caste prejudices is still hardly conceivable to one who has lived amongst the people. But they are being rapidly abandoned by those who, on visits to Europe and America, have come directly under the influence of novel surroundings; and, although the country is little affected by the experiences of the thousands of coolies who return from labour in foreign countries, the people of the Punjab must certainly be learning from the hundreds of Sikhs who serve as police officers and watchmen in Hong-kong and the Chinese treaty ports. These men occupy places of some dignity and importance, and the impressions they bring home with them will be listened to with interest.

In one notable respect the custom of village life is showing signs of a radical and far-reaching change,—in the use of co-operation as a means of procuring temporary loans, in place of borrowing from money-lenders. Some account of this movement has been given in Chapter XVII. It is gaining a popularity which surprises the most sanguine of its supporters. The success so far obtained is due in great measure to the efforts of the officials who have been deputed by the Government to initiate the scheme, and it is uncertain whether co-operative credit societies would retain their attractions if they became too numerous to be closely supervised by the State authority. But the idea of co-operation undoubtedly appeals to a very general liking for protective association; and, if it takes root, may in time affect the national outlook

[1] It has often been remarked that a period of war appears to favour the up-springing of exceptional genius.

by popularising voluntary and selective brotherhood at the expense of hereditary relationship or caste. From the material point of view, it will ameliorate the peasant's life, and stimulate his industry, by reducing very materially the rate of interest. Some societies are, moreover, using the influence of their solidarity to induce their members to take up improvements in farming. The moral effect of co-operation may be still more valuable: men who are shiftless, or are suspected of dishonesty, will not be elected to the societies; and the members are combining to give prudence an excuse by fixing definite limits to ceremonial expenditure.

Religion

Religion has strengthened and dignified the conservatism of the people by investing it with a halo of sentiment. The desire to proselytise which is of the life of Christianity, sets it in violent antagonism to other creeds, and the votaries of these creeds have displayed their resentful disbelief of Christian doctrines by rejecting the customs and habits of Christian society. You will accordingly find that Indians, whether Hindus or Mohammedans, who have adopted European dress and manners of life, have generally lost exactitude of belief, and that those who are orthodox in their faith show their orthodoxy by being old-fashioned in their habits. It is probable that the spread of Christianity would hasten very greatly the economic development of the country. The poorest families who embrace Christianity—and, in particular, Christianity of the Reformed churches—raise their standard of comfort, and endeavour, however humbly, to adopt the mode of life which has become associated with Christianity. It is surprising that Christianity has not spread more rapidly. For a century it has not only been preached in the streets, but has been taught in numerous schools and colleges: it has behind it the prestige of the ruling race; yet there are probably less than two and a half million Native Christians in India, if we deduct those who owe their conversion to Nestorian missions or to the Portuguese. The seclusion of women has deprived the missionary of sympathies which are more easily enlisted than those of men, and contributed very greatly to conversion in the early and mediæval days of the Christian churches. Of the many personal messages which St. Paul sent to the Romans, more than a third were addressed to women. Proselytising in India owes little or nothing to woman's influence. Opposition to Christianity is becoming less acute; indeed, one learns from time to time of surprising indications of genuine sympathy. But Christianity can hardly be expected to take perennial root so long as its seed remains an unacclimatised exotic, sown and watered by foreign hands,—so long, that is to say, as its doctrines are uninfluenced by Oriental ideas and its organisation is in the control of European ministers.

Position of Women

If the men of India would set free their women they would liberate a force which would act in some measure as a change of environment. On one point Hindus and Mohammedans are agreed,—that the aspirations of woman are fully satisfied if she ministers to her husband and propagates his family. Severely secluded from her environment, she neither influences it nor is influenced by it, so that the nation loses the developing force of half its population. She does not affect the tone of society, nor help manufacturing industry by her fashions. Take out the women that pass up and down a street in Europe: nine-tenths of the shops would be closed; the omnibuses and tram-cars would run half empty; the scene would lose all colour and gaiety. Unenlivened by woman's flattery or ridicule, or by the desire of attracting woman's regard, such of man's life as is not occupied by business or sensuality is overclouded by thoughts of his own dignity and importance. Life is brightened by women in Japan and Burma; and in Cairo, Constantinople, and the cities of China the ladies are demanding social freedom, as their husbands aspire to political rights. A similar movement may be discerned in India, and it is producing more than a surface effect. Indian ladies of rank have for some time past been entering European society, and Anglicised Indians in high Government employ are generally anxious that their wives should take part in their social duties, and assist them in entertaining their guests. Not infrequently the ladies need much persuasion before they will show their faces to a company of men. The Parsi ladies are almost wholly emancipated, and so, also, are Bengali ladies who belong to the small Brahmo Samáj community. In Western India and the Punjab there are signs of a still deeper current. Here, in parks and similar places of public resort, one is struck by the large number of Indian ladies who are accompanying their husbands and brothers unveiled,—a defiance of custom which a few years ago would have aroused much scandalised comment. The emancipation of woman is proceeding slowly,—and it should proceed slowly, for its path is strewn with pitfalls. Captives who are liberated from long confinement are apt, in their transports, to forget that there remain any rules to bind them. But it is advancing beyond doubt, and to well-wishers of the country this is the most hopeful sign that its conditions display.

Education

Current ideas would place education in the van of the forces that are stimulating social and economic reform; and it would naturally be supposed that the Indian youths who, during the last half century, have been passing by hundreds of thousands through schools and colleges, must have acquired from English literature and science something more than facility in the English language. They have learnt to respect official honesty and the morality which is enjoined by Christian writers; they have also learnt to suspect the authority of their religious dogmas. But the new knowledge has hardly frayed the extremest edge of their social prejudices. School-life and home-life are as two separate circles, the circumferences of which are nowhere in contact. Lessons are for the student useful exercises; but they are so remote from his actual surroundings that they lack a convincing sense of reality. He reads, and may dream, of romantic love; but at home a little girl—in wifely adoration—holds the key of his future, and has locked it fast against sentimental experiences. The liberty of conscience which the English classics extol is wholly inconsistent with the rules of his caste; and his mother would suffer agonies of shame were he traitorously to desert her cherished traditions. Nor have we found in Europe that knowledge of itself releases mankind from narrowing prejudices: a stay-at-home scholar is apt to be intolerant in judging opinions which differ from his own. An impression is abroad that education has been the strongest of disturbing forces in India; but in fact it has been much less effective as a social ferment than ideas that have come from novel experiences. It facilitates progress,—provides it, so to speak, with wheels for it's advance. For the direction of reforms and the administration of justice, for medical relief, and engineering achievements it is required in a high degree of efficiency. Nor can the State afford to risk a waste of talent by failing to provide an educational career for youths of promise. And elementary schooling is needed by the masses, since without its assistance they are unable to guard the fruits of their labours. But we may be convinced that education is necessary for development while doubting whether it is itself a developing force.

Political Aspiration

How far is it true that political aspirations have been conducive to social and economic reform? It does not appear from the experience of Europe that the development of social or industrial activities is intimately connected with forms of government. It is necessary, no doubt, that the spirit of reform should be free to express itself to the world in exhortation or criticism. But, granting this much, we cannot conclude that its fire only touches self-governing nations. When, however, as in India, a people has lain a-dream for centuries in its social habits and political ideas, and at last awakens to compare itself with others and seek the causes of its arrest in growth, it can hardly distinguish between domestic and political conditions, and, desiring changes in the one, demands them also in the other. It is towards political changes that Indian leaders have first addressed themselves, since official authority is more easily invaded than the sanctity of caste or the traditions of the home. But they know in their hearts that their political gains must be wholly fruitless unless they are accompanied by social reforms, and they hope, without doubt, that the feelings of patriotism, which they have freely excited in their political campaign, may be turned to arouse a social movement. It is futile to look to political passion as a means of stimulating industrial enterprise. A boycott may serve to annoy others, but it will not give strength to improve oneself. The Bengalis have learnt this by bitter experience: hardly one survives of the native enterprises that were started by hundreds during the recent unrest. But it may legitimately be hoped that the masses of the people will consent to change their methods of life if they are brought to believe that only by change can they lift a reproach from the name of their country.

Yet India may feel that she bears her reproach with the sympathy of many thoughtful observers. Judged by the standards of modern life, she has been far out-distanced by commercial nations. Her people do not appreciate the importance of riches, or, at least, do not see that the pursuit of riches is the most effective means of securing happiness. Given to philosophise, they are infected with pessimism, and are inclined to believe that, in the presence of an all-pervading injustice, man's safest refuge lies in himself. It is not everyone who will condemn their ideals, which at all events make for human dignity. A Sikh police-officer looks a gentleman amidst the hurrying Chinese crowds of Hong-kong.

CHAPTER XX

POLITICAL CONDITIONS

THERE are champions of the Indian Nationalist party who on occasions will loudly demand that the British should evacuate India entirely: this is at times of popular excitement, and it is hardly to be believed that in calmer moments any one of them would support this contention with his vote, if he thought that his vote would decide the question. For Indian politicians that command popular respect, are generally men of keen intelligence, who may be trusted to appreciate the insuperable difficulties with which India would be confronted if she endeavoured to stand alone. Across her northern borders her prosperity is watched by the Afghans and Nepalese,—warlike nations, who in their present disposition could not be peaceful neighbours of people they could raid. They possess well-equipped armies, recruited from races,—Pathans and Gurkhas,—that supply the Indian army with many of its best fighting regiments. The Nepalese would certainly be joined by the Indian Gurkha troops, which would bring them an accession of 20,000 well-trained soldiers, admirable for dash and spirit; while the Afghans have only to raise the war-cry of Islám to throw Hindus and Mohammedans into violent antagonism, to attract sympathy throughout the country, and to gain the assistance of Mohammedan regiments that are amongst the pillars of India's fighting strength. Not only would the country be invaded by forces which would have no respect for such conventions as in Europe protect women and private property in time of war, but it would at the same time be racked with internal dissensions,—with internal conflict, for into the turmoil the Indian feudatory princes would certainly fling themselves. United by loyalty to the British throne, they contribute to the stability of the Empire; but if this tie were withdrawn there is no reason to hope that the rivalries which are natural to their position could possibly be settled except by force. Many of them possess well-trained armies, and could hardly be expected dispassionately to watch the efforts of politicians to govern territory which they could easily overrun. Were the country not threatened with invasion, its condition would, then, still be perilous in the extreme, for it contains within its borders all the materials for destructive explosions. With invasion superadded, there would be a welter of confusion, in which all traces of civilisation might disappear. The country would, in fact, revert to the anarchy from which the British rescued it a century ago. Should no European power intervene to take up the mission that Britain had abandoned, rulers of capacity might in time emerge,—but only to govern ruined provinces. Nor have we exhausted the list of dangers which would beset the path of India if left at large. Excluding from our prospect foreign invasion, and the ambition and jealousies of the rival Indian princes, and assuming that the civil administration of the country could be carried on by an establishment of popular committees, the peril would remain of disaffection in the army. Soldiers may be induced by civilian influence to overturn a government; but, this accomplished, they are likely to find civilian ideals quite unsatisfying. So difficult is it to perceive a way through all these dangers, that the Nationalist party have never ventured to sketch the vaguest of programmes, or to consider in practical fashion how the government of the country would be carried on, if dropped from British hands. And, as a matter of fact, Indian Nationalist politicians, when elected to the responsibilities of a legislative council, are disposed rather to invoke British authority than to contemn it,

25—(2134)

and not infrequently turn to British officials to assist them in the details of their schemes of reform.

There are critics,—in Europe and America, as well as India,—who, refusing to draw an analogy from childhood, maintain that national growth, in order to be real, must be wholly spontaneous, and should owe nothing to direction from without. To them, British rule may appear as a cramping force, stifling India's development and lowering her vitality. But it may be likened with more justice to a protecting rampart, which assists evolution by excluding forces that would certainly cut back its earliest essays. Social reforms may be coming very slowly in India; but, to judge from the conditions of Turkey, Persia, and China, it is owing to British influence that they are coming at all. The corruption which poisons the life of those countries is no worse than India once endured: to exorcise it requires stronger determination than a corrupt society can develop of itself. Except in Japan, a country of peculiar aptitudes, nowhere in Asia does meritorious talent enjoy such opportunities as in India for exercising itself and winning distinction in the public service. The Indian party of political progress owes, indeed, its existence to the British Government. In Native States its activities would not have been tolerated; and, if some of them, following British example, have commenced to admit private citizens to their official councils, in none does independent criticism receive so much attention as in the Legislative Councils of British India.

The Indians greatly appreciate the education which British rule has fostered, and the many material benefits with which alien hands have endowed the country. Yet it is abundantly clear that British rule can count upon little active sympathy,—indeed, may, without exaggeration, be described as unpopular. To an Englishman this may appear inconceivable, if he is persuaded of his title to India's gratitude. Yet he will easily understand the Indian's prejudices if he will imagine himself in the Indian's position. An alien rule cannot but be disliked, however great the personal esteem that may be won by its officers. At ordinary times the dislike is masked by feelings of content—even of obligation—aroused by the blessings of peace, of justice, and by the appreciation of such evident benefits as railways, canals, and the relief of famine. But the dislike subsists beneath the surface, as a smouldering fire which a storm of passion can instantly fan into violent flame. Such storms occasionally pass across India, just as they at times excite the Chinese to frenzy, and blind the nations of Europe to the horrors of war. In India they may imperil the existence of the Government, for it is subject to a latent antipathy which they can excite. Indeed, they threaten not only the Government, but the interests of the nation's social progress. They generally arise from wounded sentiment,—from impressions of contemned religion or slighted feelings,—and, if not checked when first they are forming, they may envelop the country, sweeping before them the leaders as well as the masses of the people. The educated and intelligent cannot keep their feet ; they will not dare to assist the Government ; rebellion may be preached, assassination condoned, nay, even canonised ; and neglect to suppress the whirlwind, as it arises, may involve later resort to most drastic measures. Students are naturally the first victims of the storm, and are drawn into the net of criminal conspiracies. These dangerous possibilities can only be obviated by an unsleeping watch for approaching trouble and an unswerving firmness in enforcing the law. On the walls of Indian Council Chambers should be inscribed the dictum of Aristotle, that " revolutions arise out of trifles, albeit not concerning trifling issues."[1] Complaisance

[1] γίγνονται μὲν οὖν αἱ στάσεις ὀυ περὶ μικρῶν ἀλλ ἐκ μικρῶν.

does not soften antipathy, and concessions will surely prolong the excitement. The storm once passed, the people return to their ordinary tranquillity, and it is difficult to believe that their placid faces can ever have been clouded by the frowns of dislike.

But, it will be said, by repressing sedition you merely drive it underground. This hardly applies in the case of peoples who have a traditional respect for strength in their rulers. Indeed, Indian experience seems to show that seditious opposition, if firmly encountered, loses its bitterness in respect for the State. The Hindu classics insist very strongly upon loyalty to a rája who protects his subjects, but absolve the people from obedience to one who neglects to check crime and criminal associations. With those who are influenced by such an opinion, loyalty to the State depends upon its prestige : this has always been recognised by seditious agitators, who turn their most strenuous efforts to lessening the respect with which the masses regard the British Government. The prestige of the State is of immense importance in securing the loyalty of the Indian troops ; they naturally feel that their dignity suffers if they are associated with a power of waning authority. There are, it is true, other springs of loyalty ; and we may gratefully remember that during the anxious days of the Mutiny, fidelity to the salt, affection for individual officers in command, and the duty which is reverentially owed to the King kept Indian soldiers attached to hazardous fortunes. But tendencies have not changed since Warren Hastings wrote that " in no part of the world is the principle of supporting a rising interest, and of depressing a falling one, more prevalent than in India."

British authority must, then, be maintained not only in the interests of British manufacturers and officials, but in the interests of India's peace and progress. And it has been an accepted function of British rule to foster progress, to encourage the adoption of Western ideas, and to provide such opportunities as it can for their exercise. Rooted in these ideas are aspirations for power in politics, and these are naturally entertained by Indians who have sat at the feet of Western teachers. To meet them without risking the stability of the Government is a problem of ever-increasing complexity.

These aspirations are guided very largely by sentimental considerations, and British rule would have attracted more sympathy had it appreciated more vividly the influence of sentiment upon the Indian character. We are strangely neglectful of psychology in our thoughts upon politics, and search too exclusively in material considerations for explanations of the feelings with which other races and nations regard us. In India the most strenuous exertions for the public good may arouse the resentment of even those that they benefit, if by manner or method they should plainly declare that Indians are naturally and essentially inferior to Europeans. The Indian will admit that he is excelled by individual Englishmen in some of the qualities which a man of action requires; but he naturally resents an assumption that his race is generally not comparable with the European, and should be treated as on an essentially lower footing. The Englishman, representing as he does the ruling race, and condemning as archaic and unpractical much that he observes in Indian thoughts and habits, is apt to use a brusqueness of manner, a harshness of comment, which an Indian feels none the less keenly if he is conscious that he, in a manner, deserves them. Racial inferiority is, indeed, the sharpest of reproaches, since it forbids any hope of attaining equality; and an Indian dislikes to be termed a "native," because this term is associated with uncivilised races. Formal in his manners, he suspects a slight in an Englishman's freedom from punctilious constraint. And he may, it must be confessed, have bitter recollections of unmistakable discourtesy that he has suffered from individual Englishmen, who have not realised that they are making a blot upon the British race which all the good intentions of the Government will not serve to obliterate. He cannot ascribe his wounded feelings to the assertiveness of official dignity, for non-official Europeans are still further aloof from him: no Indian may enter the leading clubs in Calcutta and Bombay,—not even although he be a ruling prince or belong to the most exclusive of London clubs. It is, therefore, a high achievement of the recent political reforms,—the admission of Indians to the Legislative Councils in numbers sufficient to influence debate, and their appointment to still more responsible positions on the Executive Councils of the Viceroy and Governors,—that they should have brought Europeans and Indians closer together in relations which foster mutual esteem. Men meet at the Council table in social equality. The Indian members represent a new and important force,—official power in no subordination to official authority. But they are generally moderate in asserting their privileges, and are, indeed, the more inclined to defer to their British colleagues, as they can claim to meet them upon an equal footing. These official relations have produced an effect outside the Council Chamber, and have given a freer and more genial tone to social intercourse between Europeans and Indians. And we may safely assume that social constraint will be lessened by the experiences of the Delhi *durbar*, where the customs of the past were—very wisely—ignored, and Europeans and Indians were invited together to sit at the King-Emperor's dinner table. The announcement made on the same occasion that the Victoria Cross might in future be won by Indian soldiers was a welcome recognition of Indian sentiment.

The national sentiment of patriotism has been stifled by the course of Indian history. Under British rule it is coming to life; it is spreading beyond the educated classes, and may in time arouse the masses of the people. It may not unreasonably be suspected by the British Government, for it may inspire revolutionary attacks upon authority. But if those who invoke it pretend to understand the necessities of India's position, they will turn it towards gradual reform—not sudden upheaval. It might show itself with advantage in a narrower feeling, —such a patriotic regard for the province of one's home as would create a rivalry between province and province in the development of resources and in social progress. Unfortunately, provincial boundaries do not coincide with linguistic or racial limits; they subdivide the Mahrattas, the Uriyas, and the Kanarese, and group together very diverse sympathies. It was the apprehension of the Bengalis that their solidarity would be broken that so earnestly opposed them to the partition of Bengal.

Sentiment apart, the educated classes desire an increasing share in the government of the country. This involves two distinct ambitions,—to be an element of more importance in the machinery of the State, and to have a more compelling voice in the direction of policy. The first is concerned with appointments to the public service; the second with the constitution and functions of the Legislative Councils.

It has been shown in Chapter XIV how mistaken are those who imagine that the superior administration of the country has jealously been monopolised by British officials. As a matter of fact, Indians hold three-fourths of the superior judicial and executive posts, which, in total number, may be computed at 4,700. It is true that 627 of these posts, including those of largest authority and highest pay, have, in past years, been reserved for members of the Indian Civil Service, and to these should be added 265 of less degree which are committed to members of the service while under training. But some 140 of these "reserved" posts are held by Indians who have either passed by examination into the Indian Civil Service, or have been specially appointed or promoted.[1] The posts that are included in the "reserved" class carry much higher pay than those outside it. But the latter are remunerated on a more liberal scale than corresponding officers in any country of continental Europe, and very much more liberally than in any Indian Native State, or, indeed, in any other country of Asia. Indians who, not being members of the Indian Civil Service, are promoted to "reserved" appointments draw only two-thirds of the salary to which a member of the Indian Civil Service would be entitled, and one might suspect that Indians might draw from this an annoying contrast. But Indian opinion makes no strong appeal for increasing the salaries of these promoted officers; they are sufficiently remunerated for their position and requirements, and to enhance their pay would weaken the case for making these special promotions. The expenses of an Indian are very much less than those of a European employed in India. There has been an insistent demand for simultaneous examinations in India and in England for admission to the Indian Civil Service, since this arrangement would greatly improve Indian chances of winning appointments. But the demand has apparently weakened. If simultaneous examinations were established, Indians would be debarred from

[1] In 1870 Parliament authorised the appointment of Indians to posts that had previously been "reserved" for the Indian Civil Service. Accordingly, a certain number of young Indians were from time to time nominated by Government and introduced into the Civil Service as "statutory civilians." But this policy did not prove successful, and was abandoned in favour of the promotion to "reserved" posts of Indian officials who had proved their merits by service in responsible posts outside the "reserved" list.

competition in England, and this would place India upon a different footing from that enjoyed by the rest of the Empire. And it is no doubt becoming recognised that a training in England is a valuable preparation for high responsibility in the public service.

The capacity of Indians for business that requires intellectual aptitudes has been recognised by the freedom with which they have been appointed to the judicial service. They are an element of much importance on High Court benches: also on district courts of appeal: they preside over all the courts of lower grade, and, indeed, they have in their hands almost the whole of the original judicial work of the country. In other departments of State they are not so widely employed in responsible office. They are generally less suited for executive than for judicial duties,—for tasks which involve not the intellectual solution of difficulties, but the control of subordinates, or the effecting of practical changes in the men or conditions that surround them. It would, indeed, be unreasonable to expect an Indian official to be as efficient as a European in the control of Indians: he is not supported by the European's prestige. Yet in the circumstances of the country there is hardly a quality which is so urgently needed in an executive officer as the capacity of influencing others, and, in particular, of controlling his own subordinates. The officials are few in proportion to the population; they are employed at scattered centres; the subordinate staff has hardly yet emerged from a state of morality which permits any laxity of supervision, or the exigencies of the people, to be turned to the purpose of obtaining money. Moreover, Indians generally lack the zeal for practical improvement which is the highest qualification for posts of executive authority: they are too much inclined to accept their environment as inevitable, and seldom find, in the discovery of an abuse, an impulse to rectify it. By no means are all British officials inspired by an active desire to initiate changes; but Indians are moved by it very seldom indeed. They may condemn their surroundings; but they halt there: they do not take up arms against them unless they are encouraged by the influence of British authority. They may, however, claim with reason that as, under European example, they have advanced in judicial honesty, so they are also advancing in executive capacity, and that they should gradually be admitted to an increasing share of responsible posts. The abrupt transfer to Indian hands of a large proportion of posts of control would certainly lower the standard of administration; and, although it is possible that the Indian Government may have pitched its standard higher, in some ways, than the circumstances of the country warrant or require, a material retrogression would sacrifice the past and involve a serious danger in the future. For it must not be forgotten that the efficiency of British rule is the fundamental justification for its continuance in the country. The aspirations of the leaders of Indian thought would probably be satisfied were enquiries[1] instituted at stated intervals to review the question of promoting Indians to "reserved" appointments, to consider past results and present capacities, and to fix the proportion of posts which might reasonably be thrown open until the time comes round for a further revision.

In the Police, the Educational, and the "technical" departments of the Government, a line has similarly been drawn between the highest posts of control (together with such junior posts as are occupied by officers in preparatory training) and the other appointments in superior service; and the former are reserved for officers who are appointed

[1] The circumstances of the Indian public services are now to be enquired into by a Royal Commission, whose consideration will certainly embrace this question.

in England by the Secretary of State, either by exercise of patronage or on the results of competitive examination. In either case, the successful candidates have practically all been of British nationality until quite recently, when the Secretary of State has included some Indians in his appointments to the Public Works department. It is needless to emphasise the imperative need of effective control over the work of the police; and there are, of course, good reasons of policy for maintaining in British hands the ultimate command of the force which is concerned with peace and safety. But the position of Indian police officials has recently been much improved by their admission to a number of well-paid appointments, with responsibilities which fall only just short of those committed to the chief police officer of a district. In the Educational department, Indians hold the vast majority of professorships and many principalships. But in discharging an inspector's duties they lack initiative force, and suffer the difficulties that are experienced by one who is called upon to criticise and admonish his fellows. It certainly appears that for some time to come, education will only be reasonably efficient if it is tested by European standards of thoroughness and discipline. The ranks of the Indian Medical Service include forty Indians, who have entered by competitive examination in England: Indians take kindly to the medical profession; they make skilful physicians and deft-handed surgeons; and, if a separate civil medical branch is established, they may expect to occupy high positions on its staff. But, unless encouraged and directed by Europeans, it is unlikely that they will grapple with the tremendous practical problems which are involved in any efforts to improve the general health of the country. The profession of engineering is not so popular; Indians do admirable work as engineering subordinates when supported by European authority, but in responsible charges they can seldom cope with any serious difficulties of organisation or command. So, also, in the Forest department, experience has rarely justified the employment of an Indian in superior control. It does not, then, appear that the time has arrived extensively to displace European by Indian agency in the highest ranks of these public services. Nor to educated Indians do these departments offer so attractive a career as the judicial and executive services of the Government.

The commissioned ranks of the Native Indian Army are constituted upon a similar basis. There are two distinct regimental cadres: one is reserved for British officers, the other is staffed by Indian officers. These are entitled Subahdár-Major, Subahdár and Jamadár,[1] and obtain their posts, three-fourths by promotion from non-commissioned rank, and one-fourth by direct appointment. Conceding that insuperable difficulties are opposed to the association, on a single cadre, of the British and Indian officers of a regiment, the question may be asked why the Government should not follow the precedent that has been set in Egypt, and commit certain regiments wholly to Indians. Such a policy would, however, be open to a weighty objection: it would seriously offend the natural susceptibilities of the existing Indian regimental officers. They are a remarkably fine body of men, whose ambitions are not hurt by the distinctions between themselves and their British leaders. But they would, with reason, be mortified if their position were lowered by the creation of a superior Indian service.

It is a reasonable desire of intelligent men that they should not only be employed as the hands of the Government, but should also be associated with its thinking processes,—that they should have some concern with the policy of the State as well as with its routine business

[1] "Rissaldar" in cavalry regiments.

or the execution of its orders. Such an ambition has secured an acknowledgment in the recent reconstitution of the Legislative Councils. The elected members have now to prove their new powers, and will be wise to abstain for some time from pressing for wider privileges. The only point on which a change seems likely to be urged is a distinction which is made between Hindus and Mohammedans in the method of electing representatives: the Hindus elect through the medium of the local government boards, which are used for this purpose as electoral colleges; whereas the Mohammedans elect some of their representatives by directly voting for them. In this, Hindu electors feel a loss, not only of excitement, but of prestige. The elected members of Council are not in such strength as would enable them to enforce an opinion which the Government determinately opposes. But they are sufficiently numerous to influence the atmosphere of the Council Chamber, and to render it politic to defer to them; and the Government will certainly be indisposed to insist too narrowly upon its own judgment, and to reject resolutions simply because in its opinion they are in advance of absolute necessity. In promoting legislation that affects social reform the elected members are in a favoured position: their condemnation of existing usages will involve no invidious racial comparisons. On their initiative, questions may be considered which the Government could not itself prudently move for discussion. There is one subject on which the Government may not improbably find itself obliged strenuously to resist an attack towards which, in its heart, it will not be altogether unsympathetic, —the introduction of a protective customs tariff. Feeling in India is strongly protectionist: those who are acquainted with the circumstances of the country are generally impressed with the value of a tariff, at least in fostering nascent industries. There are certainly a large number of imports which might be taxed for the assistance of Indian industry without interference with the interests of British manufacturers. But in the Indian Legislative Councils the influence of local cotton spinners is considerable, and they would welcome assistance which might in some degree compensate them for their falling profits in the China trade. To add materially to the customs on British cotton goods—or metals—would threaten, not only the profits of British manufacturers, but the livelihood of thousands of working families, and would certainly be withstood by the British Parliament.

Everywhere the course of politics is set with rocks which may suddenly turn the current of events: in India there are unusual risks of unexpected deflections. The future would be less doubtful could we believe that the Indians would accept the Empire as encircling their ambitions, and their membership of the Empire as a source of pride. We may picture the gradual uprising of ideas which would look beyond the borders of India, and would glory in the possession of a larger citizenship,—in contributing to the amplitude and strength of a world-wide dominion. Such a sentiment might, indeed, be fostered by the estimation in which English literature is held, and by the rapid spread of the English language. It may be that India's share in warlike exploits beyond the seas, and in imperial gatherings on State occasions, have strengthened a conception of an English-speaking federation, in which India may with credit bear a part. But this conception is nipped by chilling experiences. How can we expect that Indians should feel pride in the solidarity of the Empire when their membership does not even privilege them to set foot in many of its lands? They might, it is true, introduce into the English-speaking dominions elements that would be in conflict with the ideals of a white population. But, differentiated as they are, they can hardly be moved by the feelings which made Roman citizenship so precious a possession. There remains the King-Emperor. He, indeed, represents a unifying force which can draw British and Indians together by ties of sentiment,—which brings home to the Indians that they stand equal with the British in subjection to the Head of the Empire. His authority is, to them, a more wonderful thing than are the limited powers of a constitutional monarch. Their loyalty is a devotion which is rendered only to institutions which manifest the actions of Unseen forces. Of such do they consider a hereditary kingship; and they reverence it with feelings more impulsive than those which gather the British round the throne of their Sovereign.

INDEX

INDEX

INDEX

INDEX

INDEX

INDEX

INDEX

INDEX

THE END